Growing Orchids in Your Garden

Growing Orchids in Your Garden

Robert G. M. Friend

TIMBER PRESS
Portland ▪ *Cambridge*

Portions of this book were previously published in *Orchids in Your Garden* (Halstead Press, 2000).

Published in 2004 by
Timber Press, Inc.
The Haseltine Building
133 S.W. Second Avenue, Suite 450
Portland, Oregon 97204-3527, U.S.A.

Timber Press
2 Station Road
Swavesey
Cambridge CB4 5QJ, U.K.

www.timberpress.com

Printed in China

Library of Congress Cataloging-in-Publication Data

Friend, Robert G. M.
    Growing orchids in your garden / Robert G.M. Friend.
      p. cm.
    Includes bibliographical references (p.   ).
    ISBN 0-88192-659-0 (hardcover)
  1. Orchid culture. 2. Orchids. I. Title.
    SB409.F738 2004
    635.9'344--dc22
                        2003028259

A catalog record for this book is also available from the British Library.

For Lilinoe,
the real love of my life

Contents

Preface

I wrote *Orchids in Your Garden* (Halstead Press, 2000) to share with readers my lifetime fascination with orchids, how they grow, and how they can adapt to cultivation in the garden. Some readers wrote back asking for information about growing orchids in their particular climates. In response to their requests and following subsequent travels, I have written this new work, *Growing Orchids in Your Garden.* It includes a section on growing temperate orchid genera in gardens subject to snow in winter and details for growing tropical and subtropical genera in Florida, California, and other Mediterranean climates. As readers will dis-

cover, adventurous gardeners were growing subtropical orchids successfully without winter protection in Nice in southern France and near Naples in Italy more than one hundred years ago.

Many regions around the world with similar climates will support the growth of some exotic subtropical orchid species with a modicum of care and ingenuity. This book will tell you how. For those whose climate is too extreme yet who would enjoy orchids growing naturally within their home, I have included a section on establishing orchids on container-grown host trees indoors.

Acknowledgments

I would like to acknowledge and thank specifically the late Hermon Slade, renowned worldwide as an orchid lover and the original Australian orchidscaper. I also thank the following individuals.

In Australia, Philip Altmann, the late Bert Bronson and Amy Bronson, Steve Clemesha, Bill and Joy Giust, Ilsa Hartmann, Brian and Gloria Pearce, Mary Pollard, Mary Rossiter, and the late Gordon Vallance for allowing me to photograph their orchid plants and gardens; Brian and Gloria Pearce, Mary Pollard, Grant Smith and Graham Gamble for use of their slides; and Murray Shergold of Easy Orchids at Woodburn for his assistance with various plant materials and exotic species. Special thanks to Les Nesbitt of Nesbitt's Orchids in South Australia for his help and advice with Australian deciduous terrestrials and for his slides. All the illustrations of Australian terrestrials are from Les and his hybrids show what can be done. My thanks to botanical artist Louise Saunders for her illustrations. I thank too Lyn Purss and Roslyn Pryor of Brisbane City Council library at Mount Cootha Botanic Gardens for tracking down so many obscure reference works for me.

In the United States, my thanks to all the wonderful orchid people my wife and I have met. You are such welcoming and generous hosts, too many to name. I especially thank Dick and Karen Cavender of Red's Hardy Orchids in Oregon who went out of their way to have us as their guests and then supplied me with the excellent slides of pleiones and other temperate orchids. I give particular thanks to my old friend Godfrey Levy who, despite an absence of more decades than either of us care to remember, had my wife and me to stay, took us round the sights of southwest Florida, and entertained us royally. Thanks too to Robert Fuchs of RF Orchids in Florida for having us visit his beautiful nursery and for the personal tour of his lovely orchid garden; to Milton and Nancy Carpenter of Everglades Orchids for their information and hospitality; and to Andy and Harry Phillips of Andy's Orchids in Encinitas for allowing us to photograph their fabulous species collection. By no means least though mentioned last, thanks to Andy Easton for his hospitality and advice and for showing us round the burgeoning garden at the American Orchid Society's International Orchid Center at Delray Beach, Florida.

9

In England, thanks to Richard Manuel of Orchis Nursery, Ross-on-Wye in Herefordshire, for his beautiful slides of European terrestrial orchids which he supplied so graciously and willingly. To Elizabeth Gilbert of the Royal Horticultural Society Lindley Library, my special thanks for allowing us access to the library in the throes of rebuilding, and for her cheerful fetching of old and large volumes in difficult circumstances. My thanks also to the staff at the Royal Botanic Gardens Kew library, especially librarian John Flanagan and archivist Kate Manners for looking after us and providing us with all that fascinating archival material, much more of which is included in another work.

Thank you to all at Timber Press and particularly to Neal Maillet, my editor, for your enthusiasm and support.

Thank you Xanthe and Nick, my daughter and son, and their families, for your continued encouragement and support. Noelani, my lovely daughter who died before I wrote this book, worked with the family in our nurserying days deflasking and potting thousands of species seedlings. The pleasure I get from seeing gardeners enjoying orchid species reminds me of her love and support. Saving the best until last, thank you my beloved Lilinoe. I've written this book in some strange parts of Australia and revised it in other parts of the world. I couldn't have done it without you, so thank you for your input, your research, your practical help and advice, your encouragement, patience, and company. Your belief in me and, above all, your love have never wavered.

Introduction

Many books about orchids outline how to grow them in artificial conditions, in containers, and in special structures. This book explains how to grow orchids naturally within the garden—without pots, without special houses—just as they grow in the wild.

The orchid family is the largest and most highly evolved of all the flowering plant families. Estimates put the number of distinct naturally occurring orchid species at between 20,000 and 30,000. The number of man-made hybrids is approaching 150,000. Orchids are found in almost every country in the world, from inside the Arctic Circle in the north to Macquarie Island off the coast of Tasmania in the south. They grow from sea level to above the snowline in the great mountain ranges of the tropics. The majority come from frost-free areas between the tropics of Capricorn and Cancer. More orchids grow at higher elevations, from about 3000 feet (915 meters) to about 6000 feet (1830 meters) above sea level, than in the hot steamy lowlands.

Where Orchids Grow

In nature orchids grow in three different situations. The members of one group, called epiphytes, grow on trees or shrubs, but are not parasites. Epiphytes use trees only for their physical support. Members of the second group, the lithophytes, grow on rocks. Members of the third group, the terrestrials, grow in the ground. Some orchids grow in full sun exposed to all the elements. Others grow in deep shade with little air movement. Most orchids grow in the range between these two extremes.

Growers in temperate countries must protect their warm-growing orchids from freezing weather. This usually involves building a special orchid house and heating it. However, fortunate

Cattleya warneri, at home in warm Brazilian forests.

11

Orchidae are, perhaps the largest natural order in the Khasia, where fully 250 kinds grow, chiefly on trees and rocks, but many are terrestrial, inhabiting damp woods and grassy slopes. I doubt whether in any other part of the globe the species of orchids outnumber those of any other natural order, or form so large a proportion of the flora.
— Sir Joseph D. Hooker,
Himalayan Journals, 1891

Hooker chronicled his travels in the Himalayas and northeastern India in the mid-nineteenth century. As a botanist and later the director of the Royal Botanic Gardens, Kew, he made copious notes on the botany, geology, and geography of the areas he visited including the orchid-rich Khasia Mountains.

Moist European meadows are home for *Dactylorhiza praetermissa* and *D. coccinea* at lower left. (Courtesy Richard Manuel)

growers in coastal and other frost-free areas of many countries can grow a wide range of tropical and subtropical orchids in their gardens without any orchid house whatsoever. Frost is the limiting factor to growing tropical and subtropical orchids successfully in the garden. Growing orchids from temperate regions, usually terrestrials or lithophytes, in gardens subject to frost and snow is another matter (see "The Temperate Garden" in chapter 3).

We have all seen landscaping which has intrigued us. In some gardens our interest is piqued by a winding path which draws us along to discover what is round the next bend. In other gardens our senses have been stirred by a delicate perfume from a hidden flower, our eye drawn to a contoured bank of massed planting, or our spirits lifted by the discovery of a tranquil pool perfectly placed for quiet contemplation. Growing orchids naturally in the garden landscape can heighten the sense of intrigue and mystery. Orchids add immensely to the pleasures of the garden.

One of the charms of growing orchids naturally in the garden is the plant shape many assume. Orchids in containers grow in a regular fashion, stems upright, the spreading types progressing horizontally across the surface of the container. When you attach epiphytic orchids to trees, they start to grow as they would in nature. Sometimes the types with stiff bulbs, like cattleyas, will march right along a branch, while the clumping types, like some maxillarias and oncidiums, will encircle a branch, looking for all the world like large green pincushions. Slender-stemmed types, like many dendrobiums and vandas, will hang with their growing tips curving upwards. Seeking the light. This natural growth habit im-

Sophronitis coccinea growing where moisture and humidity from the large bromeliad's leaf bases keep the ambient temperature cool.

I thought at the time I should never like to see orchids, and other rare exotics stewed up in a glass shed again, after seeing them thus luxuriant in the open air.
—Frederick W. Burbidge,
The Gardens of the Sun, 1880

An orchid personality of the nineteenth century, Burbidge was variously a gardener, writer, botanical artist, plant hunter, lecturer, and finally curator of the botanical garden at Trinity College, Dublin. From 1877 to 1878 he traveled to Borneo to collect *Nepenthes* (pitcher plant) and other orchids for the famous nursery of James Veitch and Sons.

Unknown species in Madagascan rainforest on a mossy branch.

parts a graceful line to the plants never achieved in containers.

The flowers of orchids grown in the natural way display themselves as nature intended. Many growers of orchids in containers stake flower stems erect, giving the flowering plant a stiff, unnatural look. The canes of spring–flowering soft-cane dendrobiums, for example, are usually staked upright, resembling soldiers at attention. Grown naturally on a tree at head height, the same plants produce graceful, slightly pendant

growths with a curving line like an ancient eastern scimitar. In bloom, the flowers seem to smile and nod at the gardener—a far cry from the regimented ranks of container-grown orchids. Naturally grown orchids in the garden look cheerful and independent, taking full advantage of their surroundings. Their free forms and lovely blooms are alluring. They are more robust, growing subject to all the seasonal changes in light, temperature, and humidity just as they would be in their wild homes.

Types of Growth

In broad botanical terms orchids fall into one of two types, differentiated by the way they grow. The first is monopodial, where growth takes the form of a single stem which elongates from a single point at its apex. Stems do sometimes branch and monopodial orchids sometimes grow as dense clusters, but the growth of each stem always proceeds from its apex. Roots are produced from the stem itself. Monopodial orchids that are useful in the garden landscape include *Aerides*,

Stauropsis giganteus. A very large species. Raceme drooping, one foot (30 centimeters) or more long consisting of large yellow flowers 3 inches (about 8 centimeters) across, marked irregularly with round spots of a reddish-brown color. It forms masses of incredible size. One plant I found on the Shan border was a great deal more than I could have packed on an elephant.

> —Reverend Charles Parish, quoted
> in Bartle Grant, *The Orchids of Burma,*
> 1895

When adjutant of the Rangoon Volunteer Rifles of the Border Regiment in Burma, Captain Grant wrote about orchids and quoted descriptions of plants discovered by Parish, the foremost orchid explorer of the region.

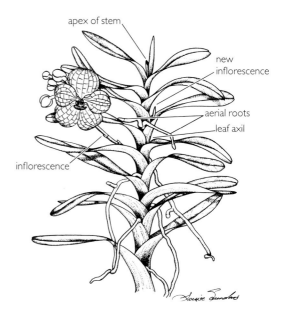

A monopodial orchid—*Vanda.*

Arachnis, Ascocentrum, Renanthera, Rhynchostylis, Vanda, and hybrids within and between these genera.

The second growth type is sympodial, where growth consists of stems, usually leafed, emerging from a rhizome that elongates and gives rise to successive new stems. Roots are produced from the base of the stems or from the rhizome itself. Sympodial orchids good for garden landscaping include *Cattleya, Dendrobium, Oncidium,* and *Stanhopea* together with their hybrids.

The glossary at the back of this book and the two line drawings here illustrate the differences between monopodial and sympodial orchids, as well as other terms used throughout this book.

Climates for Orchids

For practical purposes, this book refers to four different climatic regions for orchid growing in the garden. The first region is tropical and incorporates coastal districts north of the Tropic of Capricorn in the Southern Hemisphere and south of the

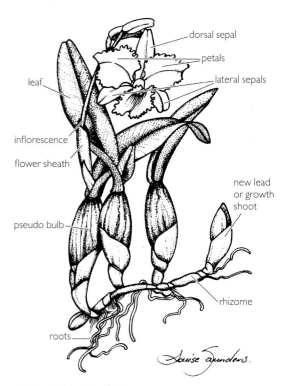

A sympodial orchid—*Cattleya.*

Tropic of Cancer in the Northern Hemisphere. The second region is subtropical, encompassing coastal and near-coastal districts from the Tropic of Capricorn to about latitude 30° south and from the Tropic of Cancer to about latitude 30° north. The third region comprises the cooler, frost-free coastal and near-coastal areas between about latitudes 30° and 37° both north and south of the Equator. The fourth region, the temperate zone, is subject to freezing temperatures and snow cover for several weeks in winter or Mediterranean climates, with warm to hot summers and cool, wet winters (see chapter 3 for more details on the temperate garden). It includes parts of the United States, Canada, and Australia; the Mediterranean region itself; and southern Africa.

In North America the only tropical regions are the islands of Hawaii and Puerto Rico. The subtropical regions include the peninsula part of Florida south of about latitude 30° north and the coast of southern California. The cooler region includes the Gulf coasts of Texas, Louisiana, Mississippi, and Alabama, the balance of Florida's coastal districts and the Atlantic coasts of Georgia and the Carolinas. To the west, orchid gardens on the Californian coast run from dry subtropical San Diego north to cooler San Francisco. Gardeners in southern states may note that the native epiphytic orchid *Epidendrum magnoliae*, more commonly known as *Epidendrum conopseum*, grows naturally across Florida and southern Louisiana to as far north as North Carolina. The rest of continental United States and the lower portion of Canada fall into the temperate, or fourth region.

In Australia, the tropical region takes in the coastline north from Rockhampton on the east coast. The subtropical region runs from the coastline at Rockhampton south to about Coffs Har-

bour, including near-coastal areas. The third region comprises the rest of coastal mainland southeastern Australia. The temperate region includes most of southern and southwestern Australia.

Growers in the Northern Hemisphere will need to take account of climatic conditions in their own locales. This applies particularly to continental coastal areas north of about latitude 30° north. Cold snaps and prolonged periods of cold weather seem to be more common in the Northern Hemisphere than in the Southern. Dubai, on the Persian Gulf, may fall within the subtropical zone by virtue of lying on latitude 25° north, but its desert climate mitigates against growing orchids in the garden without considerable landscaping modifications.

The division of garden orchid growing regions into these four climates is in many respects arbitrary. There are overlapping areas in both hemispheres where orchids from both warmer and cooler climates may thrive. Such overlaps can comprise small areas, usually coastal and often, in the Northern Hemisphere, south facing, where the mean winter temperature is higher than that of nearby districts. Many tropical orchids thrive in subtropical Florida while many subtropical species grow happily outdoors in coastal Californian gardens although nominally within the cooler region. Australian examples include, among many others, north- and northeast-facing valleys in coastal Sydney suburbs such as Manly, Dee Why, Bayview, Avalon, Cronulla, and Port Hacking. Here many subtropical and some tropical genera may grow successfully in the garden. Overlaps can also comprise montane areas, which provide cooler mean temperatures than nearby districts that are at lower altitudes. Australian examples include the Atherton Tablelands in

The pendulous stems of *Dendrobium anosmum* display blooms in spectacular fashion in the American Orchid Society garden.

Andy Phillips grows *Epidendrum parkinsonianum* at his nursery at Encinitas, California. Note the short stems and long, fleshy sword-shaped leaves.

tropical Queensland, the Blackall Range and Mount Tamborine in southeast Queensland, and the Dorrigo Plateau and the Blue Mountains in New South Wales. Orchids generally recommended for cooler regions may grow successfully in gardens in such areas.

Choosing the Right Orchid

Before choosing orchids for landscaping in your garden, it is important to understand two sets of restrictions. The first is imposed by the climate on your particular garden. For instance, if you reside in a cool coastal region, near latitude 40° north or south, your particular climatic restriction may include cold, wet, dull weather in winter. This will preclude the choice of warm-growing orchids such as *Aerides*, *Brassavola*, *Caularthron*, *Grammatophyllum*, and the like. However, if you reside in a warm coastal region, say near either the Tropic of Cancer or Capricorn, your summer climate may be hot, humid, and sunny. This particular climatic restriction will make it hard for you to grow cooler genera such as *Cochlioda*, *Lycaste*, *Masdevallia*, *Odontoglossum*, and others in your garden. In each case your climate limits the range of orchids which will grow in your particular garden.

The second set of restrictions is the limitations that apply to each particular orchid and its optimum growing conditions. What are its requirements for temperature, water, humidity, and sunlight? What are its patterns and methods of growth? Is it an epiphyte, a lithophyte, or a terrestrial? Is it deciduous? Can you provide suitable conditions for it in your garden?

Choosing the right orchid for the right position in your garden landscape is the first and most important step, but this is a good deal easier than it may seem. If orchids are found in almost every country, it is highly probable that some species grow (or used to grow) near where you live. The word *orchid* triggers in many an image of a gorgeous *Cattleya* corsage-type flower, a spray of colorful dendrobiums, or an upright stem of round, waxy *Vanda* blooms. We picture these sprouting from a tree in Pernambuco, a garden in Port Moresby, or a jungle in Thailand. We do not stop to consider that perhaps our home too, before the neighborhood became urbanized, was the native home of orchids just as lovely.

Orchids native to temperate and cold regions have adapted to cope with harsh winter climates by growing as terrestrials, deciduous in the snowy season. Orchids native to regions with hot, dry summers also grow terrestrially, remaining underground and dormant until the approach of cool, wet, winter weather. There is an absolute wealth of these terrestrial species found throughout the world. Many have large, gorgeous, colorful, and showy flowers that bear any comparison with cattleyas, dendrobiums, or vandas. Only now are we learning to cultivate some of these orchids. Some are available as seed-raised nursery stock, and information is becoming available through specialist growers and regional orchid societies. If

you can procure them from such sources, try some orchids native to your region in your garden. Of course, if you live in a tropical or subtropical region, native orchids may be more readily available. Do grow some of these in your garden. They have the advantage of being "locals," bred to your climatic conditions.

Remember, naturally occurring orchid species are protected by legislation in most countries as well as by international treaties. There are heavy penalties for collecting, damaging, or disturbing orchids growing in the wild. Do not collect wild orchids. Almost all species that are worthwhile to grow are available from specialist orchid nurseries. Many commercially available orchids have been raised from seed. They are easier to grow and have better quality flowers than their wild counterparts. The existence of wild orchids is threatened in many regions. Help support their conservation and continued existence by growing seed-raised species in your garden. A number of specialist orchid nurseries grow local species and those from similar climates naturally in their gardens. Do visit these to observe which genera will grow in your particular garden and how they are grown in your locality.

The optimum time to establish an orchid in your garden is just as the orchid starts to produce new root growth. This applies no matter whether you are attaching an epiphyte to a tree, securing a lithophyte in your rockery, or planting a terrestrial in your garden. New root growth indicates the orchid is commencing a growth cycle, which will allow it to become firmly established on or in its new home. Most orchids produce new root growth in spring and autumn. Attaching, securing, or planting orchids in spring, say from late August until November in the Southern

Hemisphere, late February until June in the Northern Hemisphere, allows them at least several weeks of mild weather for growing before summer's heat arrives. In autumn, broadly from late February until May in the Southern Hemisphere, late August to November in the Northern Hemisphere, the orchids have several weeks of good, mild growing conditions before the onset of winter. Subject to these generalizations, if the orchid you wish to attach, secure, or plant is producing new roots, then attach, secure, or plant it right now.

Orchid growers spend one-tenth of their time performing hands-on tasks with their orchids. They spend the other nine-tenths of their time simply enjoying their plants. This sounds deceptively simple and in the simple contemplation of our plants lies one of the greatest pleasures in horticulture. In their observations growers do many things. They may be assessing the plant's condition. Does it need more water? More fertilizer? More light? They may be assessing its stage of development. Is it about to flower? About to produce a new growth? Are its roots actively growing? Is it about to produce a flush of new roots from the base of that latest growth? Experience is our best teacher, and the best way to gain it is to start immediately.

Just like humans, orchids can suffer from too much sun and they can benefit from applications of their own "sunscreen" lotions. Take care when removing an orchid destined for the garden landscape from a shadehouse or nursery. It is probably a little soft and could become burned and damaged by sunlight in the garden, regardless of the time of year. If you paint its leaves and stems with plant sunscreen, the orchid will survive unharmed. You can make plant sunscreen from any harmless substance that will give the plant a white coating. Growers have successfully used milk, water-based white paint thinned with water, weak limewash, and the old white-powdered household cleaner Bon Ami. Even a mild fungicide in the form of a white wettable powder can provide sun screening.

You can add anti-transpirant sprays and white oil made from vegetable oils to the sunscreen lotion to help it spread and stick. The lotion will gradually wash off over several weeks by which time the orchid will have become hardened to the light in its new position. To make a useful white oil, simply beat a vegetable oil in your food processor until it emulsifies, thinning it with water in the processor as necessary. Orchids are no different from other plants in their seasonality. They each have a season for growth, one for maturation, one for flowering, and for some species, a

The first time I visited these hills was in the beginning of February. The trees had dropped their leaves, the jungle grass was burnt up, even to the elevation of 1500 feet [458 meters]. The hills were bare. The stems of the leafless trees were charred and scorched, giving the whole country thereabouts a burnt, black, desolate appearance. Here the heat was almost insupportable, and I do not think I shall be exaggerating in stating that the thermometer could not have been less than 120°F (49°C) in the shade at this season; yet this is the spot selected by Vanda coerulescens, Dendrobium bensonae, *and other orchids.*

—Colonel Robert Benson

An orchid enthusiast, Benson collected many valuable species while stationed in Myanmar (then Burma) in the 1860s. Knowledge of a particular orchid's habitat, climate, and seasons of growth will help to grow it successfully in the garden.

season for rest. Experience gained from observing your orchids throughout the seasons will help you help them to grow to their best.

Surprisingly few of the 20,000 to 30,000 orchid species have common names. They all have botanical names of which the first, usually in Greek, is the generic name, and the second, usually in Latin, is the specific name. The convention is that botanical names are italicized. Hence *Dendrobium nobile*, a commonly grown species, has a generic name, *Dendrobium* (from the Greek meaning "living on a tree"), which it shares with all other members of the genus *Dendrobium*, and a specific name, *nobile* (from the Latin meaning "illustrious" or "magnificent"), which is peculiar to it and cannot be applied to any other *Dendrobium* species. In hybrids, such as *Papilionanthe* Miss Joaquim, only the generic name is italicized.

As knowledge of plant relationships increases botanists reclassify and rename plant genera and species. For instance, an old favorite orchid originally named *Odontoglossum grande* has been reclassified as *Rossioglossum grande*. Under the rules of botanical nomenclature the specific name originally applied to an orchid species is the correct name and should be used. A popular tropical Australian species, *Dendrobium discolor*, was known for decades as *D. undulatum*, an apt name describing its wavy flower segments. However, the earlier name is the correct one. You may find an orchid you want is grown commercially under a different name. Fortunately most orchid suppliers try to keep up-to-date with name changes and can identify the plant you seek.

Finally, for your first orchids choose ones which are in flower, in bud, or at least of flowering size. This way either you see what you are getting or you don't have long to wait. Seedling orchids are cheaper than flowering size ones, but they do have drawbacks. They are harder to grow, needing a more protected environment and more equable conditions than adult plants. Even if you grow them well you will have to wait at least three years and maybe much longer before they first flower for you. No one can guarantee the true color that an unflowered hybrid orchid will produce. It would be a shame, as well as extremely annoying, to plant an unflowered but supposed dark red *Cymbidium* in pride of place in your rockery only to have it flower a washed-out pink.

You will not go wrong if you make your first orchids flowering ones—you won't buy them if you don't like their flowers! Do not buy seedling orchids for your garden until you have had some experience of growing adults in your particular conditions. This will save disappointments and add to your gardening pleasure. By all means cut flowers from your garden orchids to enjoy in a vase in your house. Allow a day or two for the flowers to become firm after opening. Use a sharp blade to cut the stem, then, holding the

Orchis italica is a good choice for gardeners in Mediterranean climates. (Courtesy Richard Manuel)

You could grow a *Phalaenopsis* hybrid like this on a garden tree if you live in the warm tropics.

The adaptable *Dendrobium nobile*, portrayed here in the American Orchid Society garden at Delray Beach, grows just as well in cool montane climates, as its home range reaches nearly to the snowline in the eastern Himalayas.

Epidendrum stamfordianum flourishes in this tree at RF Orchids in subtropical Homestead, Florida.

Dactylorhiza species and hybrids, like this one grown in England at Wisley, are good choices for temperate region gardens. (Courtesy Dick Cavender)

Cypripedium californicum is often a feature of gardens in the western United States. Most *Cypripedium* species are too cool growing for the subtropics but do well in temperate regions. (Courtesy Susan Keenan)

base of the stem under water, slice off a segment before transferring the flower to a vase. This will stop air bubbles from preventing the flower from taking up water.

How to Use This Book

This book is designed both to be read through from beginning to end, and also to go straight to a specific section which interests you. If you are a grower new to orchids you might read first part one, "Types of Orchids," for information about how to grow epiphytes, lithophytes, and terrestri-

als, then the relevant chapter in part two, "Types of Gardens," which relates to your particular garden. You could turn then to the Table of Recommended Orchids to select plants that interest you.

If you are already an orchid grower and would like to grow some plants naturally in your garden, you would read part one to decide whether and how you will use trees, a rockery or wall, or a garden bed (or all of them). You might then look at the Table of Recommended Orchids to decide which of your collection might suit a particular place in your garden.

If you must grow orchids in containers for some reason, such as renting your home, living in a difficult climate, or wanting to be able to bring the best flowering plants in the world into your house, you would read first part three, "Containers in the Garden," for information about using containers in the garden and indoors. You could select orchids that would suit your conditions from the Table of Recommended Orchids.

If you live in a cold climate but would like to grow tropical and subtropical orchids naturally on trees, you would read first chapter 13, "Growing Orchids Indoors," for information about growing orchids on container-grown host trees in your garden room, sunroom, or conservatory.

After you have established orchids successfully in your garden, this book will serve as an ongoing reference to help you look after your plants and plan new ways of using one of nature's best creations.

PART ONE

Types of Orchids

1

The Epiphytes:
Growing Orchids on Trees

Orchids that grow naturally on trees are known as epiphytes. They are not, as people sometimes assume, parasitic. A host tree provides structural support, but suffers no damage from epiphytic orchids.

Requirements of Epiphytes

Epiphytic orchids prefer a position protected from the hot midday sun but exposed to direct early morning and late afternoon sunlight. In the Southern Hemisphere the best positions have a northeast aspect. In the Northern Hemisphere the best aspect is southeast. When the summer sun is directly overhead, the host tree's leaves will shade the orchid. The winter sun, with its weaker light intensity and lower angle, may shine more directly on the orchid to its benefit. In both hemispheres the next best aspect is the east.

In the Southern Hemisphere the northern aspect is good, though the west can sometimes be too hot and dry. The southerly aspect can be too cold and dark, especially if it is in the lee of a building. In the Northern Hemisphere the southern aspect is good. In east coast climates the western aspect can be hot and dry in summer and cold in winter. The northern aspect in the Northern Hemisphere may be too cold and dark, being on the sunless side of the garden. If the only suitable trees or the only suitable areas in your garden have apparently unfavorable aspects, do not despair. You can modify both hot and cold areas by planting trees or shrubs carefully positioned to act as windbreaks or hedges. You can admit more light to dark garden areas by pruning overhanging or shady trees.

Epiphytic orchids have preferences in their host trees, the most important of which is that the tree must have permanent bark. If a tree sheds its bark, then any epiphyte attached to the bark also will be shed. Epiphytic orchids prefer trees with roughened bark, although the degree of roughness does not seem to be terribly important. Roughened bark fulfils two vital functions. First, it retains more water on its surface for longer than smooth bark does. Try spraying water on vertical sheets of sandpaper and shiny cardboard respectively to see the difference. This capacity for holding water longer meets the orchid's need. Second, orchid seed, which is the only source of propagation of orchids in nature, is tiny, dustlike, and wind-borne. It needs to lodge in a position from which it will not be washed easily by rain or blown by wind. The interstices in the bark of a rough-barked tree provide such a position.

Good orchid host trees have open crowns of leaves, which let through filtered sunlight and the rain. Most epiphytic orchids require between 30% and 50% of natural summer sunlight. Too much more light in midsummer might burn epiphytic orchids and dry them out too quickly. Too little light might limit their ability to flower. If you are unsure how much light 30% to 50% represents, check with your local garden center to see the amount of light 70% and 50% shadecloth admits. Open-crowned trees let the air circulate freely around their trunks and branches and hence around the epiphytes growing on them. So, open-crowned trees meet three of the four requirements common to all orchids: light, filtered by the leaves of the open crowned tree; water from the rain which penetrates the open leaf canopy; air from the breezes circulating through the open canopy.

The fourth requirement is food. Epiphytic orchids obtain their food from two principal sources. The first is the decaying leaves, twigs, flowers, and other vegetation that builds up around their stems as they grow on their tree. Some epiphytic orchids even produce special basketlike networks of roots to catch this food source as it falls around them. Added to the decaying vegetable matter are the bodies of dead insects and other animals together with their droppings. While food from this source may be miniscule, it is constantly available. The second source of food for epiphytic orchids is the rain itself. As rain washes through the tree's leaves and down its bark, it leaches small amounts of chemicals and minerals that the tree has brought up from the earth. This sustenance is available to the orchid, albeit in minute amounts, via its root network spreading over the tree's bark. Open-crowned trees that let the rain in are ideal for this reason.

Fortunately, many popular garden trees have the characteristics necessary for epiphytic orchids. Growers in Florida select native trees including southern live oak (*Quercus virginiana*) which is probably the best host, mahogany (*Swietenia mahagonii*), buttonwood (*Conocarpus erectus*), satinleaf (*Chrysophyllum oliviforme*), and geiger (*Cordia sebestena*). The Floridian native sabal or cabbage palm (*Sabal palmetto*) is a popular orchid host as are the queen palm (*Syagrus romanzoffiana*), the coconut (*Cocos nucifera*), the dwarf date palm (*Phoenix roebelenii*), and the silver saw or Everglades palm (*Acoelorrhaphe wrightii*). The sabal and silver saw retain their leaf bases giving a rough surface into which orchids and other epiphytes can root and to which they are easy to attach. However these leaf bases eventually fall, taking with them any epiphyte that is not securely attached to the palm trunk itself. The

Despite the importation and cultivation of orchids in the West for more than two hundred years, some individuals still believe epiphytic orchids are parasites. Hans Sloane lived in Jamaica from 1687 till 1689 and discovered epiphytic orchids including those we now know as *Brassavola cordata*, *Broughtonia sanguinea*, *Oncidium guttatum*, and *O. luridum*. He had no proper botanical frame of reference for orchids. Because the orchids he discovered grew on trees and because he knew that mistletoe also grows on trees, Sloane recorded them under the generic name for mistletoe, *Viscum*. Perhaps this was the foundation for that often-held but erroneous belief.

dwarf date palm has a wonderfully knobbly stem on which orchids soon take root. The queen palm and the coconut have smoother naked trunks as do Alexandra and Bangalow palms (*Archontophoenix alexandrae* and *A. cunninghamiana*) and other suitable palm species. Useful rougher-stemmed palms include the Australian cabbage palm (*Livistonia australis*) and the Washington palms (*Washingtonia filifera* and *W. robusta*).

Of all the trees which I have seen in my travels, the gourd tree (Crescentia), *seems to have a bark which is best adapted for the growth of cattleyas and other epiphytal orchids, and this is the reason that the species is very valuable for cultivation in countries where orchids can be grown in the open air. More than once I have seen sturdy schomburgkia mingling their long floral racemes with those of some beautiful cattleya, magnificent specimens partly shaded by the upper branches of this strange tree, which are themselves splendidly decorated with rodriguezia, ionopsis, small oncidium, and other less-luxuriant plants. The gourd tree does not grow to a very great height (the highest I have seen was scarcely 23 feet [7 meters] high); therefore, it is admirably adapted for the culture of orchids in the open air. The vigor and health of plants which grow on this tree are marvellous. Its bark certainly contains some substance exceedingly favorable to the nutrition of roots and plants which grow upon it, as upon no other tree is the same vigor of roots and shoots observable.*

—Eric Bungeroth, *Journal des Orchidées*,
15 March 1891

An orchid hunter employed by Linden's nursery L'Horticulture Internationale in Belgium, Bungeroth traveled widely throughout South America and passed on much useful information.

Gardeners new to the habits of palms should be aware that some palm species are "self-cleaning"—they drop entire dead fronds—while others produce fronds which persist for a time, hanging like a curtain after they die before falling, leaving the frond base attached to the trunk. In either case it is sensible to remove dead and dying fronds before they fall as they can damage epiphytes, especially orchid flower racemes, as they fall. Some species, notably the queen palm (*Syagrus romanzoffiana*), produce heavy canoe-shaped spathes at the base of each inflorescence. These become quite woody as they age so remove them before they fall as they too can damage epiphytes (and perhaps gardeners who may be working below). Indeed, some palms produce inflorescences heavy with seeds (drupes) which are messy and attract pests to the garden. It makes sense to remove such inflorescences, too, before they can become a nuisance.

Of the Australian genera, *Banksia*, bottle-brush bush (*Callistemon*), cypress-pine (*Callitris*), Australian pine (*Casuarina* including *Allocasuarina*), spider flower (*Grevillea*), paperbark (*Melaleuca*), and some of the longer-lived wattle (*Acacia*) species are frequently used with great success to grow orchids in gardens. In Florida, the Australian pine and paperbark are pests, but they do make excellent orchid host trees. Many Australian rainforest species are also suitable including the red cedar (*Toona australis*), pink euodia (*Mellicope eleryana*), many lilly pilly (*Syzigium*) species, hoop pine (*Araucaria cunninghamii*), and, although not strictly a tree, the tree ferns. Interestingly, epiphytes seldom grow on the quick-growing pioneer rainforest trees. Of the exotics, the African tulip tree (*Spathodea campanulata*), frangipani (*Plumeria*), *Citrus*, *Erythrina* (especially

E. crista-galli), *Eugenia*, *Jacaranda*, *Liquidambar*, and *Poinciana* are among the best. The lovely yellow-flowered *Tabebuia* with deep-fissured, corky bark and sparse leaves, is superb while the tropical species *par excellence* as an orchid host is the calabash or gourd tree (*Crescentia cujete*). Species with fibrous bark, such as *Tibouchina*, have proven to be excellent host trees and can be pruned if their crowns become too dense.

Less suitable species include the rubber tree (*Ficus elastica*) and umbrella tree (*Schefflera actinophylla*), some specimens of which are too densely leaved and too densely crowned to support epiphytes. As already pointed out, many palms have the right canopy and bark characteristics, although some gardeners will give careful thought to the aesthetic appeal of orchids and other epiphytes growing on tall, smooth, upright palm trunks. It is difficult to find a smooth-trunked palm in Florida that does not have a quota of native air plants (*Tillandsia* species) growing naturally on it. If there are no suitable trees in your garden, you could plant some, choosing the optimum position in your garden. With regular watering, feeding, and some care, many trees grow astoundingly rapidly in cultivation.

Another option is to use container-grown trees. This enables even those whose space is

Permanent rough bark like this *Casuarina* trunk is a requirement for epiphytic orchids.

In a subtropical Queensland garden, this vandaceous intergeneric thrives on a queen palm (*Syagrus romanzoffiana*).

This dwarf date palm (*Phoenix roebelenii*) at RF Orchids, Florida, provides perfect conditions for *Cattleya skinneri*.

Maxillaria meleagris growing well on *Erythrina crista-galli*, another good host tree.

Southern live oak (*Quercus virginiana*) such as this bearing *Cattleya guatemalensis*, is probably the most popular host tree for epiphytes in Florida.

×*Ascocenda* Su-Fun Beauty enjoys the epiphytic life at RF Orchids, Florida.

limited to a courtyard or patio to grow some orchids in a natural way. Frangipani and citrus are often grown as feature plants in large ornamental containers. Both are great hosts for epiphytic orchids as are large specimens of *Dracaena* and screw pine (*Pandanus*). Another plant much in demand for courtyard decoration and a good orchid host is the ornamental *Yucca elephantipes*. Its trunk has the rough consistency that epiphytes love. Even though the frangipani is deciduous, it loses its leaves in winter when epiphytic orchids can take more of the weaker sunlight. It produces its new

A little care and attention to your orchid garden will pay dividends like this *Dendrobium thyrsiflorum* growing on a queen palm (*Syagrus romanzoffiana*) at RF Orchids, Florida.

Questions to ask before attaching orchids to your garden tree:

- How will the plant look in that position?
- Will it look reasonably natural when it is established?
- Will it look attractive in the garden landscape?
- Can it be seen easily?
- Can it be reached easily with the hose when it needs water?
- Is it in the optimum position for morning and late afternoon sun?
- Is it sheltered from the hot summer midday rays?
- Is it on a part of the trunk or limb wet by the rain, giving the orchid the best chance for natural feeding?
- If all the answers are positive, you and your orchid should both be happy!

Attaching Epiphytic Orchids

Remove the orchid from its container. Take this opportunity to trim off any old or broken roots and dead bulbs or canes. Old roots are usually dark brown and soft-textured. Newer, healthy roots are creamy white or light brown and firm in texture. Remove any large lumps of potting medium that will come off easily. Determine which is the forward or youngest part of the plant, often called the lead. This part of the plant needs to be closest to the tree because it will produce the new roots to anchor the plant. The new growth will proceed from this point to grow naturally onto the tree.

Place the orchid in position on the tree. At this stage it is often helpful to tie the orchid temporarily in position with plastic-coated wire. You can twist the wire tight with one hand while holding

foliage in spring as the sunlight intensifies and the orchids need more shade.

Epiphytic orchid species frequently colonize citrus plantations in the tropics. Most citrus species tend to grow as shrubs rather than trees in the garden. The line between trees and shrubs is blurred. Many of the "tree" species mentioned are actually shrubs and many will stay at shrub size in the home garden, particularly in containers. This is no disadvantage for most epiphytic orchids. Indeed, it is easier to attach, tend, and observe orchids on shrubs or small trees than on forest giants.

the orchid with the other hand. Tie the orchid firmly in its final position with strips of nylon. Very small plants can be tied on with wool. Remove any temporary ties. Old stockings or pantyhose strips make ideal ties because they stretch and are easy to tie tightly. They also hold a little moisture to assist the orchid's new roots to get established. They expand with the natural growth of the tree and finally rot away or are easily removed when the orchid has become established. You can use nylon fishing line or wire, plain or plastic coated. Be aware, however that these materials can cut into the bark as the tree grows. They need to be monitored carefully and removed as soon as possible. You can also use string or twine to tie on the orchid, but ensure it is not the soft type that rots quickly when exposed to the elements.

Some gardeners glue orchids to host trees. This method of attaching epiphytes works well on small, lightweight plants with a short root system. It does not work for heavy or tall-stemmed plants, which need extra support to keep them firmly affixed. Silicone cement and the type of glue sold as "liquid nails" are suitable. They are easy to use, dry to a hard consistency although orchid roots grow through them, and they weather away after several months exposed to constant sun, rain, and watering. Simply squeeze a generous dollop of silicone or glue on the trunk or branch where you intend to place the orchid, push the orchid onto the glue spreading any long roots over the tree and hold it in place, either by hand or with a tie, until the glue hardens. This could take thirty minutes or so. Do not use casein-based glues, which may dissolve with watering, or resinous glues, which may burn the plant. Be aware, too, that host trees with deep-fissured bark such as oaks (*Quercus*) and *Tabebuia* will need a lot more glue to fill the fissures than smoother-surfaced trees such as most palms.

It is vital for the orchid's quick establishment on the tree that you attach it so firmly that at least its lower half, especially its root mass, cannot move. The orchid will be subject to both wind and water, and making it immobile allows the roots to grow onto the tree so that the orchid attaches and ultimately supports itself. When you examine a healthy orchid with active roots, you will notice the roots are white with small green or yellowish green tips. This tip, which is quite brittle and easily damaged, is the actively growing part of the root. If it is damaged that root cannot grow any further, at least until it produces a branch, and the plant suffers a setback. If the orchid and its root mass wobble while new roots are growing, the chances are that the new root tips will be damaged and the orchid cannot attach itself to the tree. So make sure you tie it on securely. Tie a strip or two of nylon around the orchid's root mass and another one or two securing its bulbs or canes to the tree so it cannot move at all. It is easy to remove ties once the roots have grown, but it takes a long time for the orchid to replace broken roots.

It is not good practice to place other material, such as sphagnum moss or fern fiber, around an orchid's roots when attaching it to a tree. This is sometimes suggested as a means of supplying the orchid with a reservoir of moisture until its new roots become established. However, often the moss or fiber dries out too quickly to be of any assistance to the orchid. Sometimes, if it stays wet, the phenomenon of tropism comes into play. Tropism is the turning of part of a plant in response to an external stimulus. For instance, orchids' new growths and flower racemes turn towards the strongest light source, making it important to keep potted plants facing in one direction once their growths or racemes are length-

The first step in preparing to attach this *Laeliocattleya* Damayanti to a host tree is to remove it from its container. Here the potting medium has been removed along with old dead and broken roots.

Secure the orchid to the tree with strips of nylon material that stretch with the tree's growth. Here the roots straddle the branch, preventing the plant from wobbling and thus damaging newly emerging roots.

Securely attached, the orchid is dressed with Spanish moss to provide congenial conditions in its new position.

ening. Epiphytic orchids' root tips exhibit tropism by turning towards the external stimulus of water. Thus, if you put moisture-holding material between the orchid roots and the surface to which you want them to attach, or if you place it as a layer over the top of the roots, tropism will cause the growing tips to turn towards and stay in that material, preventing rapid attachment to the tree, rock, or other host. This added material could form a hiding place for orchid pests too. Orchids placed directly against the host tree's bark send their new roots directly onto it.

The most beneficial companion for a newly attached orchid is a drape of the so-called Spanish

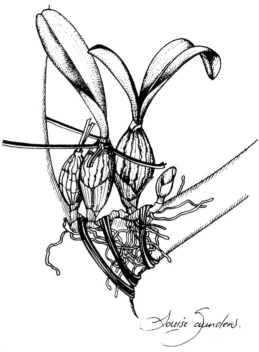

Sympodial orchid securely tied to a tree. Note new shoot next to branch surface where it will attach readily.

Oncidium sphacelatum divisions wired onto a host will establish quickly, being in direct contact with the trunk, but the gardener must take care that the wire does not cut into and kill the trunk.

This *Dendrobium* has been badly affixed and is not growing well. It would have been better to remove all the old material from its rootball and tie it directly to the branch.

moss, which is really the bromeliad *Tillandsia usneoides*. This most useful plant, which consists of a tangle of curly, mosslike strands, provides a humid, nurturing microclimate around the newly affixed orchid. It also provides a modicum of shade and wind protection when draped around the base of the plant from which new growths and roots will emerge. It is worthwhile cultivating amounts of Spanish moss in the garden. It provides a languid, tropical look, hanging in swathes from trees. Secure bunches on wire hooks, then hang them from shady tree branches where they receive constant airflow and lots of water. They will grow rapidly. Do not try to grow Spanish moss in very windy, sunny sites as it will dry out too rapidly. Birds use it when dry as a nesting material.

Companion Planting in the Tree

It is just as easy to care for a number of orchids growing on a tree as it is to care for one. Try attaching several orchids and some epiphytic companion plants. Orchids seldom grow on trees in nature in splendid isolation from other plants. They usually grow in association with companion plants including epiphytic cacti, mosses, lichens, ferns, creepers, and aroids such as anthuriums and philodendrons. In Florida, Central America, and South America epiphytic orchids often grow with bromeliads.

Companion plants add to the orchid's comfort zone. Sometimes they assist the orchid in measurable ways, such as by creating the humid microclimate that orchids relish, or by promoting the growth of beneficial fungi that help the orchid to assimilate nutrients. They also assist the orchid in ways we do not yet understand. We have all seen examples of how, in the natural world, certain species flourish in association with other apparently unrelated species but languish when the other species are removed. The dog becomes disconsolate when the family cat goes missing. Onions grow vigorously with marigolds planted as companions, but often decline if the marigolds are removed. Orchids are the most highly evolved plants. They seem to grow better with companion plants than in isolation.

Epiphytic orchids do grow better with the Spanish moss referred to earlier. It needs no fastening. Simply wind or drape some strands of it round and over epiphytic orchids after you attach them. It loves frequent watering and air moving through it. Be prepared to thin it out, as it can grow so quickly as to hide the orchids it is nurturing. The vase–type bromeliads such as *Aechmea*, *Billbergia*, and *Vriesea* species make excellent com-

I had not far to go before I was rewarded with the object of my search, in the myriads of Bromeliaceae and orchids which literally cover the stunted short trees, and the bare points of rocks, where scarcely an inch [less than 3 centimeters] of soil is to be found. The most magnificent sight for even the most stoical observer is the immense clumps of Cattleya mendelii, *each new bulb bearing four or five of its gorgeous rose-colored flowers, many of them growing in the full sun or with very little shade.*
—Albert Millican, *Travels and Adventures of an Orchid Hunter*, 1891

Late in the nineteenth century a wealthy Scottish amateur orchid grower, R. Brooman White of Arddarroch, sent Millican, an orchid hunter, to South America to collect the beautiful *Cattleya mendelii*. Millican wrote about finding his quarry on the eastern range of the Andes.

panions for epiphytic orchids. The *Tillandsia* species with their often silvery leaves and bright flowers make lovely counterpoints of color in the treescape. Attach the bromeliads in the same way as the orchids. Note that some of the thinner-leaved bromeliad species may like a bit more shade, so try them on the shadier side of the tree.

If you ensure that the bromeliads always have water in their vases, enough will seep out from their bases to keep the nearby sections of the tree damp. This will encourage mosses and lichens to grow. In turn, the orchid roots will be attracted to these areas. The network of orchid roots spreading over the bark ensures the orchid's secure attachment to the tree and forms an expanded resource for its nutrition.

Epiphytic ferns such as the staghorns and elkhorns (*Platycerium*) and bird's nest ferns (*Asple-*

Platycerium bifurcatum is one of the best orchid companions.

A *Neoregelia* hybrid, newly attached to a ficus.

Epiphytic cacti can make interesting orchid companions if you do not let them become too invasive.

nium) are excellent companion plants for epiphytic orchids. They form pleasing components of a treescape in their own right. These ferns need to be attached securely to the trunk or major branches of the tree. They grow into large specimens and become very heavy when saturated. An orchid attached 3 feet (about one meter) or so above one of these epiphytic ferns soon sends its roots down into the fern's roots where it finds a good source of food and moisture. The humidity created by the epiphytic ferns also assists in maintaining the microclimate that epiphytic orchids love.

Using climbers and vines in a treescape requires some careful thought. While they are an integral part of many epiphytic gardens, some species such as the jasmines and wonga vines (*Pandorea* species) tend to be too strong growing on the same trees as orchids. They can hide and indeed smother epiphytes. Lighter climbers such as some *Dischoridia*, *Hibbertia*, and *Hoya* species will twine through the tree and embellish the treescape with their blooms and perfume in season. Many philodendrons produce creeping stems, which climb the trunk of the supporting tree with small, flat leaves lying close to the trunk. These provide a nice background for other epiphytic plantings.

It seems every palm trunk in Florida carries its share of tillandsias. Your palm host may already bear companions for your orchids.

Companion plants such as resurrection fern (*Polypodium polypodioides*) may have foliage that contrasts with and sets off orchid blooms on the same limb. Others such as anthuriums, bromeliads, and gesneriads may flower when the orchids are not in bloom or may provide flowers that complement the orchids. Epiphytic night-blooming cacti provide fragrance. You might use growth forms that contrast with your epiphytic orchids—a stiff rosette of bird's nest fern (*Asplenium*) near a clump of pendulous *Dendrobium* canes, aroids with soft hanging leaves near erect cattleyas. Use companion plants to

create interest in the treescape, leading the viewer's eye from one focal point—a flowering orchid or a colorful bromeliad—to another. You can increase your knowledge and your pleasure and expand the beauty of your epiphytic garden by experimenting with companion planting.

Aftercare of the Treescape

The four requirements common to all orchids are light, water, air, and food. You have taken care of light by selecting the right type of open-crowned tree for your epiphytic orchids. Of course, you can prune any heavily leaved branches on the tree or any overhanging tree that may provide too much shade. Your host tree will not remain static and your orchids are not static either. They will grow away from the original site to which you attached them. In some cases, this growth will be slow and clumping. In others, it will be quite fast, extending by several inches at a time. Orchids seem to have the facility for getting themselves into the places they like best to grow.

Consider water and air together. Epiphytic orchids like water. A cursory glance at an atlas that shows rainfall patterns will reveal how much rain falls in the main epiphytic orchid habitats of the world. What it will not show you is how that rain

The climate of Khasia is remarkable for the excessive rainfall . . . Mr. Yule stated that in the month of August 1841, 264 inches [660 centimeters] fell . . . Dr. Thomson and I also recorded 30 inches [75 centimeters] in one day and night, and during the seven months of our stay, upwards of 500 inches [1250 centimeters] fell.

—Sir Joseph D. Hooker,
Himalayan Journals, 1891

Don't be afraid to water your epiphytes!

falls—in what season and at what time of day or night. Nor will it show you what amount of moisture the epiphytes receive from other sources such as clouds, mist, and dew. In nature, these form an important part of epiphytic orchids' water supply. While few of us live in areas where clouds or even mists occur frequently, dew does form on the plants in our gardens to their great enjoyment. Look on the dew as a refreshing bonus, not as a replacement for regular watering.

As a rule of thumb, epiphytic orchids like to be thoroughly drenched, then allowed to dry almost completely, then to be drenched again. This is known as a wet/dry cycle. The art of growing epiphytic orchids successfully is linked to this cycle, and to ensuring the plants do not become completely dry before their next drenching. It is easy to apply water to provide that thorough drenching. The simplest way is to use a hand-held hose, or a sprinkler fixed to the hose. You could design your own sprinkler system for rigging in the tree to deliver individual sprays of water where required. At the other extreme from the hand-held hose are fully automated systems incorporating thermostats, humidistats, and timers designed to give gardeners full climate-control. You can make your watering system as simple or as sophisticated as you desire.

A word about water quality, which varies considerably from site to site let alone country to country. Most orchids prefer soft water with a pH slightly on the acid side of neutral, or about 5.6 pH. Your local water authority should be able to tell you the pH and the mineral content of your particular water. If you use well or bore water, it is worthwhile having it checked by a laboratory. Hard water, that with a pH higher than 7 which is the point of neutrality, can cause problems for

your orchids because of its usually high level of calcium salts which can throw unsightly deposits and prevent the orchid from taking up essential trace elements. If possible, store sufficient rainwater to use on your orchid garden. If you live in a low rainfall area and your water quality is poor, consider installing a reverse osmosis system or one that allows you to inject chemicals such as phosphoric acid into the water to correct the pH. If excessive chlorine in your water causes problems, fill a separate reservoir and let the water stand for 24 hours before using it on your orchids. The difference between a thriving orchid garden and one which looks scruffy and run down can often be put down simply to the quality of the water used on it.

Whatever system you use, nothing beats your own observations of your orchids and the conditions in which they are growing. Look at your orchids' roots before watering. You will see they are a creamy white color. Now water them thoroughly. They change to a greenish brown color as they absorb the water. Ensure when watering that all your orchids' visible roots have changed to the greenish brown color. If they are still white, they have not absorbed enough water. Go back and drench them again.

It is easy to take care of the wet part of the cycle, but how about the dry part? In nature most epiphytic orchids grow where they are exposed to a great deal of air movement from gentle zephyrs to seasonal strong winds. So it is in the garden. Just as a breeze dries the washing on the clothesline, so air movement round epiphytic orchids dries up the water with which they have been drenched. Newly attached epiphytes will require water every day to dampen the tree's bark at the point of attachment. This will encourage them to grow new roots. As the roots lengthen over the bark, they will gather more moisture from rain and condensation. When the plant is securely attached, with roots spreading out over the bark, it will be able to make full use of the conditions in which it is growing.

If all this watering sounds like hard work, you will be surprised to find that watering your epiphytic orchids is a real pleasure. Time spent with your orchids is a bonus, something to look forward to each day. Whether on cool winter mornings or balmy summer evenings, watering enables you to regard them closely while doing something practical for them. The spray of water from the hose to the treescape is a bridge between you and your orchids. To be in communion with living plants in this way is one of the special joys of growing orchids naturally. Epiphytic orchids always look better, fresher, and perkier when they have just been watered.

The fourth requirement of epiphytic orchids is food. When your plants have become well established on the tree, they will have grown an extensive root network. At that time, which may take perhaps a year or two, they will obtain some of their food the natural way. Until then, help them along with some judicious feeding. While your epiphytes are establishing, feed them weekly but weakly. Use a soluble plant fertilizer because it is difficult to get insoluble fertilizers, such as the manures and slow-release pellets, to stay on the tree. A thorough spray of fertilizer weekly, prepared at half the manufacturer's recommended strength, will speed plant growth. Water the plants thoroughly, then apply the fertilizer over leaves and roots while the plants are still wet.

Purchase an efficient sprayer with a capacity of from about two pints to one gallon (approxi-

Maintaining a successful wet/dry cycle:

- Water newly attached epiphytes every day until they have produced new roots which have grown at least 4 inches (10 centimeters) over the tree's bark.
- Water at least four times per week until the epiphytic orchid's roots have grown from 4 to at least 10 inches (10 to 25 centimeters) over the tree's bark.
- Water daily during hot, dry, windy weather, twice daily if it is very hot and dry, no matter how long the orchid roots are.
- Water in the evening during warm or hot weather.
- Water in the morning during cold weather. This allows the plant to become dry by nightfall, thus lessening the risk of damage if the weather turns cold.
- Orchids can take advantage of the condensation that occurs on cool nights.
- Water more frequently during windy weather. Increased air circulation dries out the epiphytes more quickly.

Compared to North American trees, all tropical trees are grimy. Liverworts, mosses, ferns, and many other epiphytes grow on the vertical surfaces of trunks and the upper sides of limbs. Their roots twist along bark grooves to secure a footing and to search for nutrients, yet they do not become parasites on the tree. Eventually the roots form a mat that can become a foot [30 centimeters] or more thick. The mat in turn traps falling particles that accumulate and eventually decompose into a nutrient-rich humus that supports many organisms. Humus on limbs is often even thicker than the rapidly decomposing layer on the ground.

—Donald Perry,
Life Above the Jungle Floor, 1988

Bromeliads on a log provide a comfortable microclimate for nearby orchids and hold reservoirs of water for other epiphytes.

This semiterete *Vanda* grows well with ferns and lichens as companions sharing a palm trunk.

mately one to five liters) to use for fertilizing. An alternative is a siphon attachment to the hose. Some gardeners fix small mesh bags containing manure pellets or slow-release fertilizer pellets near the newly affixed orchid's base. Apart from looking somewhat unsightly, this system could cause an oversupply of fertilizer to an orchid's tender new roots in periods of excessive rain. If the bag is not wetted, no fertilizer becomes available. Some forms of plastic coated slow-release pellets can crack in sunlight, releasing all the contents to the orchid's detriment. If you have a sprinkler system, consider running fertilizer through it weekly. A soluble fertilizer sprayed over

leaves and roots is the best method of feeding your epiphyte. So long as your epiphyte is growing, feed it. Container-grown orchids often stop growing in cooler weather but those growing in the landscape can grow year-round. Your care in preparing and applying fertilizer regularly will be repaid tenfold by the increase in your orchids' growth, vigor, and health. You will receive tremendous pleasure from the consequent increase in the size, color, and production of your orchids' blooms. The "flow-on" effect of your orchids' fertilizer on the companion plants, the host tree itself, and any understory plants will benefit the whole area of your orchid garden.

It really is as straightforward as that. With some prior planning, judicious placement, and attention to water and feeding, you can have a fulsome display of orchids in your garden that will outshine any potted specimens.

A Selection of Epiphytic Orchids

A vast range of orchid species and hybrids in many genera is epiphytic in nature and therefore suitable for planting in trees in the garden landscape. The limiting factor, apart from the cost of purchasing some of the rarer types, is the climate in your particular area. Orchids are found in all types of climates and at all altitudes. The orchids which would succeed in a treescape in Singapore or in Cairns (Australia) would be those from similar climates, namely, warm tropical lowlands. Orchids originating from cooler regions such as the Papua New Guinea highlands, the Andes of Colombia, the Himalayas, or the rain forests of New South Wales would be much less likely to succeed in a warm tropical lowland treescape. Conversely, epiphytic orchids from those cooler regions would be likely to succeed in coastal California or even in protected pockets of coastal northeastern Tasmania but not in Singapore, Cairns, or southern Florida.

There are overlapping areas where orchids from tropical, subtropical, and cooler regions may thrive. Proximity to a large body of water can help to keep the ambient temperature more even and humidity levels higher. So coastal climates in Florida, California, the Mediterranean, eastern Australia, and South Africa are more moderate than inland climates. Do not be put off by the opinions of doomsayers who say, "You can't grow that species in your garden here." Because of its tropical background, *Phalaenopsis* does not grow outside where temperatures regularly fall between 30° and 39°F (−1° and 4°C); however, there are plenty of subtropical species which will thrive in those conditions. Try inexpensive species such as *Bifrenaria harrisoniae, Dendrobium nobile,* or *Laelia anceps,* and out-dated *Cattleya* or *Cymbidium* hybrids to experiment in your particular garden. If these grow for you, expand your collection by adding others that appeal to you. Yellow-flowered vandas usually will not thrive in cool conditions whereas the blue *Vanda coerulea* from high altitudes in India, Myanmar, Thailand, and southern China prefers cooler climates. If it grows in your conditions, many of the blue-flowered hybrids derived from it may do so too. Orchids can't read thermometers, but they can and do adapt to conditions which experts might consider less than ideal.

It will help in achieving an interesting balance in your orchid landscaping if you are aware of the tremendous diversity of form that orchids take. Australia's *Bulbophyllum minutissimum* and *B. globuliforme,* with chains of tiny pinhead-sized pseudobulbs, contest the title of the world's smallest orchid. *Grammatophyllum speciosum,* a candidate for larger tropical gardens, produces sturdy 6- to 10-foot (about 2- or 3-meter) canes in clumps that can weigh over a ton! Here are some examples of orchid plant forms between these extremes:

Certain fat-stemmed cattleyas and bifrenarias grow stems like bunches of bananas.

The aptly named hardcane dendrobiums have stiff upright stems.

Some dockrillias and scuticarias have bunches of tight, pencil-like leaves.

Lockhartias, called braided orchids, have leafy stems that look as though they have been plaited.

Some coelogynes look like fat green pears.

Stanhopeas resemble the aspidistras so favored by our forebears of Victorian times.

Many of the smaller-growing maxillarias and oncidiums look like pincushions as their growth encircles the branch.

Small bulbophyllums, laniums, mediocalcars, and neolauchias, among others, are diminutive, creeping plants, which can be grown as fillers in spaces between larger specimens like an "orchid grass"—the lawn in the tree garden. They add another sphere of interest to the orchidscaped tree.

A sampling of epiphytic genera for all regions follows. These are suggestions only and this list is by no means exhaustive. Remember, if any of the terms used in the following descriptions are unfamiliar, turn to the glossary and plant diagrams (in the introduction). It is worth becoming familiar with the make-up of your orchids. You will soon start talking like an expert.

Ada

Natural habitat: Andes in Colombia, Ecuador, and Peru.

Plant form: Sympodial. Thin pseudobulbs and leaves. Arching racemes with many bright orange flowers.

Culture: 70% shade. Keep these damp. They create very bright spots of color on trees.

Climate: Cool climate gardens.

Species: The best and the only one commonly available is *Ada aurantiaca*.

Aerides

Natural habitat: From India and Sri Lanka through Yunnan and Southeast Asia to the Philippines and Papua New Guinea.

Aerides Hermon Slade, one of the lovely hybrids in this genus.

Orchids were abundant and often occupied positions in which the growers of these plants in England would little expect to find them, but in which they gave an indescribable singularity and charm to the landscape.
　　　　　—Reverend William Ellis,
　　　　　Three Visits to Madagascar, 1859

Ellis, one of the early botanical explorers in Madagascar, introduced the spectacular *Angraecum sesquipedale* to English greenhouses in the first half of the nineteenth century.

Plant form: Monopodial. Stems often branch, forming large, pendulous clumps with gracefully hanging leaves. Their flower racemes are arching to pendulous, sometimes branched, with many usually rosy purple, fragrant flowers. They have heavy, fleshy roots that ramble for meters up and down the host tree's trunk.

Culture: 50% to 70% shade. Attach as high as possible on the trunk so you can appreciate the effect as they grow down and out from the tree.

Climate: Tropical, subtropical, and cool regions.

Species: Tropical species include *A. falcata, A. falcata* var. *houlletiana, A. lawrenceae, A. leeana* (syn. *A. jarckiana*), *A. odorata,* and *A. quinquevulnera.* Some beautiful hybrids have been bred, the most famous of which is *A.* Hermon Slade. While the previously mentioned species live at lower elevations, several species come from moderate to very high elevations in the tropics, including *A. crassifolia, A. crispa, A. maculosa, A. multiflora, A. odorata* (the most popular all-round species), and *A. rosea* (syn. *A. fieldingii*). These would be more suitable for subtropical gardens. Cooler climates could host *Papilionanthe vandara,* until recently known as *Aerides vandara.* This lovely, sweetly fragrant species has terete leaves and grows well in 70% shade, flowering in spring.

Angraecum

Natural habitat: Tropical Africa, Madagascar and nearby islands.

Plant form: Monopodial. Some species are small growers, others very large. Stems usually branch as the main plant ages. Some bear many flowers on each inflorescence, others only one or two. Flowers, usually in the white tones, are mostly fragrant at night.

Culture: Grow most species in 50% shade, the larger ones in 30% shade. Because of their flower tones, these look good against dark-barked tree trunks and dark foliage.

Climate: Tropical and subtropical.

Species: Warmer growing species include *A. eburneum,* a large, imposing plant with long racemes; *A. eichlerianum* and *A. infundibulare,* both almost vinelike; *A. leonis,* is short with thick fleshy leaves; and *A. sesquipedale,* the famous comet orchid, which has huge white flowers with very long spurs. Several hybrids are available including the old timers *A.* Alabaster and *A.* Veitchii which, with *A.* Lemforde White Beauty, are sturdy plants for the tropical treescape. The subtropical species with long, broad leaves like more light than the smaller growers. Among them are *A. bicallosum, A. comorense, A. compactum, A. didieri, A. elephantinum, A. leonis, A. scottianum, A. sesquipedale* (the best epiphytic angraecum), and *A. vigueri.*

Ansellia

Natural habitat: Widespread in tropical and subtropical Africa.

Plant form: Sympodial. Vigorous clumping type with 3-foot (one-meter) long, canelike pseudobulbs leafed near the top. Flower stems from the apex of the pseudobulbs are paniculate with many spreading branches. When established they form a basket of upright, litter-catching roots.

Culture: Grow them in no more than 30% shade. They take full sun if attached in early spring so new growth can become acclimatized. Use a crotch or stout branch because of the plant size.

Climate: Tropical and subtropical.

Species: There is a single species, *Ansellia africana* (syns. *A. gigantea, A. nilotica*), which, because of its huge geographical range, has many color forms from almost blackish brown to pale yellow. The yellow-flowered forms do not grow as robustly

> *In cattleyas, especially, I have always remarked the strength and size of the roots which the plants send out most abundantly in all directions, and which twine closely round the branches and trunk. I saw, some years ago, in the botanic garden in Demerara [Guyana], a very fine collection of orchids, many of which were cultivated on gourd trees. Several long avenues of these elegant trees were devoted to the growth of epiphytal orchids, and the plants seem to thrive well under this simple and inexpensive mode of treatment. The great secret of success in all systems of cultivation is to follow Nature herself.*
> —Eric Bungeroth, *Journal des Orchidées,*
> 15 March 1891

or as tall as do those that are heavily barred and marked with chocolate.

Arpophyllum

Natural habitat: Mexico and Central America to Colombia.

Plant form: Sympodial. Thin stems with fleshy leaves and densely flowered, erect inflorescences, rose-purple in color.

×*Ascocenda* Princess Mikasa, a colorful intergeneric hybrid that will bloom in subtropical gardens.

Culture: 50% shade. These form large clumps and withstand wind well if kept damp. Attach in forks and to thick branches.

Climate: Subtropical and cool climates.

Species: *Arpophyllum alpinum* and *A. spicatum* (syn. *A. giganteum*) have thin, wiry roots that attach themselves tenaciously to the host tree.

Ascocentrum

Natural habitat: From northeast India through Southeast Asia to the Philippines.

Plant form: Monopodial. Short, often-branching stems form upright clumps. Flower racemes are erect and densely flowered. Colors are brilliant orange, red, and yellow.

Culture: Grow them in 50% shade, attached to a stout horizontal branch or a crotch at the junction of trunk and branch.

Climate: Tropical, subtropical, and cooler regions.

Species: Two species, *Ascocentrum curvifolium* and *A. garayi* (syn. *A. miniatum*), are readily available. Hybrids between this genus and *Vanda*, making the combination ×*Ascocenda*, are common and are highly recommended for tropical treescaping. For subtropical gardens try the above two species and *A. ampullaceum* and *A. aurantiacum*. In bright light these develop tiny purple spots on their leaves, which adds to their attraction. *Ascocentrum ampullaceum* comes from higher elevations in cooler regions than the other *Ascocentrum* species. It should grow well on trees in the less-tropical parts of the Florida coast, southern California, and at least as far south as Sydney on latitude 34° south.

Bifrenaria

Natural habitat: Brazil.

Plant form: Sympodial. Tough, four-angled pseudobulbs and broad, leathery leaves. One to four flowers on short, upright stems, white to purple, fragrant.

Culture: 30% to 50% shade. These make good specimens, crawling round branches. Affix plants where you can take advantage of their perfume.

Climate: Subtropical and cool climates.

Species: Subtropical species include *Bifrenaria harrisoniae* (the best), *B. inodora*, *B. tetragona*, and *B. tyrianthina*. A couple of hybrids are even more vigorous than the species. For cool regions, this genus includes some of the most indestructible orchids known, especially *B. harrisoniae* and *B. tyrianthina*.

Brassavola

Natural habitat: Mexico, Central America, and the West Indies south to Brazil.

Plant form: Sympodial with unusual terete, slightly channeled leaves arising from tiny stemlike pseudobulbs. Flowers are medium sized to large, usually green or cream with a white trumpet-shaped lip. Fragrant at night.

Culture: 30% to 50% shade. They grow into large clumps. Those with pendent leaves look good on trunks or near-vertical surfaces.

Climate: Tropical and subtropical.

Species: *Brassavola acaulis* and *B. cucullata* have long pendulous leaves and large flowers. *Brassavola cordata* has many slightly smaller flowers and *B. nodosa*, the best, flowers year-round when established. Several species, including the latter, called lady of the night for its nocturnal perfume, are suitable for the subtropics. Consider the fragrance when positioning them. Common species besides those already mentioned include *B. flagellaris* and *B. perrinii*.

Brassia

Natural habitat: Mexico, the West Indies, Central and South America.

Plant form: Sympodial. Often flattened pseudobulbs and arching racemes with large spider-shaped flowers in cream, green, and purple spots. Very attractive.

Culture: 50% to 70% shade. The flowers look effective against dark foliage.

Climate: Subtropical.

Species: *Brassia arcuigera* (syn. *B. longissima*), *B. caudata*, *B. gireoudiana*, *B. maculata*, and *B. verrucosa* (the best). A number of hybrids including the huge, vigorous *B. Rex* and wonderful intergeneric hybrids such as ×*Brassidium*, ×*Degamoara*, ×*Maclellanara*, ×*Miltassia*, and ×*Odontobrassia* some of which are even more adaptable than the species and all of which are excellent for the garden treescape.

Bulbophyllum

Natural habitat: Worldwide through the tropics and subtropics. This is the largest orchid genus although botanists are splitting it into several separate genera.

Plant form: Sympodial, creeping types, some with prominent pseudobulbs, some with tiny ones. Large-flowered species usually with one or a few flowers, but smaller flowers often occur many per stem. All colors, some fragrant, some unpleasantly so!

Culture: 70% or more shade, this and their creeping habit makes many species good fillers between larger orchids.

Climate: Tropical and subtropical.

Species: In warmer areas *Bulbophyllum barbigerum*, *B. biflorum*, *B. blumei* (syn. *B. masdevalliaceum*), *B. coriophorum*, *B. lobbii*, *B. macranthum*, and *B. medusae*, among many hundreds including some fabulous Indonesian species relatively new to cultivation such as *B. echinolabium* with 13-inch (33-centimeter) flowers. Although many tropical species will grow well in subtropical trees, the following come

Bulbophyllum macranthum is a tropical species that creeps around mossy branches in moist, shady conditions.

from higher altitudes and will perform better in the subtropics: *B. amesianum, B. dayanum, B. dearei, B. fascinator, B. gracillimum, B. leopardinum, B. makoyanum, B. ornatissimum,* and *B. rothschildianum.* Botanists are revising this genus and you may find some desirable species listed under other names, including the genus *Cirrhopetalum.*

Cattleyas, the most beautiful of all American orchids, are found in the most varied positions, sometimes on the branches of giant trees in the virgin forests of the low ground, sometimes on the rocks and steep slopes of mountainous regions, at elevations ranging from 3250 to 4225 feet [985–1280 meters] above sea level. When they grow on trees, as is almost always the case in the low-wooded regions, it is usually on certain species of trees the bark of which seems to be particularly well suited to their requirements, and usually on the border of forests or in clearings, where daylight and sun can freely penetrate.

—Eric Bungeroth, *Journal des Orchidées,*
15 March 1891

Cattleya

Natural habitat: Central and South America.

Plant form: Sympodial. Club-shaped, unifoliate (single-leafed) or canelike bifoliate (two-leafed or multileafed) pseudobulbs. Unifoliates have one to a few large, showy "corsage" flowers; bifoliates are usually clusters of smaller flowers. Many are fragrant, all are showy plants.

Culture: 50% shade. Place where the large flowers will be most effective. Bifoliates can grow to over 3 feet (one meter) tall.

Climate: Tropical, subtropical, and cooler regions.

Species: Truly tropical species are *Cattleya eldorado, C. lueddemanniana, C. rex,* and *C. violacea.* Several others such as *C. aurea, C. amethystoglossa,* and *C. dowiana* are good. Thousands of hybrids including ×*Brassocattleya,* ×*Brassolaeliocattleya,* ×*Cattleytonia* (wonderful miniatures), ×*Laeliocattleya,* ×*Sophrocattleya,* and ×*Sophrolaeliocattleya* as well as other combinations make good subjects for subtropical treescapes. Most species grow beautifully in the subtropics. See some in flower at nurseries and orchid shows to help in making your selection. These are simply a representative selection from some fifty species: *C. aclandiae, C. aurantiaca, C. bicolor, C. intermedia, C. gaskelliana, C. labiata, C. loddigesii, C. mossiae, C. percivaliana, C. skinneri, C. trianaei, C. walkeriana,* and *C. warneri.* For cooler climate gardens, including southern California, try the species from high altitudes such as *C. trianaei* and *C. warscewiczii* (syn. *C. gigas*) and those from southern Brazil including *C. forbesii, C. harrisoniae, C. intermedia,* and *C. loddigesii.* In cool climates it's also worth trying those species and hybrids which grow and flower in summer and early autumn as they start growing in spring, flower from the new growth in the warm months, then rest in the colder months. Hybrids with the genus *Sophronitis* (×*Sophrocattleya,* abbreviated as *Sc.,*

Cattleya amethystoglossa '85' has tall stem-like pseudobulbs. It makes a strong accent plant in a large tree crotch.

Glorious *Cattleya aurea* grows well on hardwood trees in the tropics and warm subtropics.

Cattleya harrisoniae from southern Brazil is one of the cooler growing species, worth trying as an epiphyte in cool regions near the coast.

and ×*Sophrolaeliocattleya*, abbreviated as *Slc*.) prefer cooler conditions than most.

Caularthron

Natural habitat: Northern South America and some Caribbean islands.

Plant form: Sympodial. Spindle-shaped, hollow pseudobulbs, flower stems to about 18 inches (about 45 centimeters), with white, very beautiful flowers.

Culture: 30% shade if acclimatized gradually. Stems are upright and show up against dark backgrounds.

Climate: Tropical.

Species: Formerly classified as *Diacrium*. The only one to grow is *Caularthron bicornutum*. Hybrids with *Cattleya*, usually listed as *Diacattleya*, are great.

Cochlioda

Natural habitat: Andes of Colombia, Ecuador, and Peru.

Plant form: Sympodial. Small plants with arching racemes of brilliant orange to rose flowers 2 inches (5 cm) in diameter.

Culture: 70% shade. Keep these moist. They love mossy branches.

Climate: Cool climate gardens.

Species: Several are sometimes classified in the genus *Mesospinidium* or *Symphoglossum* but are usually sold as *Cochlioda*, including *C. noezliana* (the best species), *C. rosea*, and *C. vulcanica*. Some lovely intergeneric hybrids are available including ×*Burrageara*, ×*Miltonioda*, ×*Oncidioda*, ×*Vulstekeara*, and ×*Wilsonara*, some of which will grow in subtropical gardens too.

Coelogyne

Natural habitat: Himalayas, southern China through Southeast Asia to the Philippines and Papua New Guinea.

Tropical *Coelogyne meyeriana*, an orchid for planting just above head height.

Plant form: Sympodial. Usually round or pear-shaped pseudobulbs on a creeping rhizome. Flowers from new growth with arching to pendulous racemes, few to many, white and pastel colors, often fragrant.

Culture: 70% shade. The smaller growers make good fillers between larger orchids on trunks or branches. They like to be kept moist. Affix the pendulous-flowered species like *C. dayana*, *C. flaccida*, and *C. pandurata* very high for best effect.

Climate: Tropical, subtropical, and cool climates.

Species: For tropical gardens, *C. asperata*, *C. cumingii*, *C. meyeriana*, and *C. pandurata*, one of the so-called black orchids. For the subtropics, try the above as

well as *C. dayana*, *C. flaccida*, *C. fragrans*, *C. mooreana*, *C. speciosa*, and *C. tomentosa* (syn. *C. massangeana*). In cooler climates, use species of Himalayan origin such as *C. amoena*, *C. barbata*, *C. cristata* (the best species), *C. elata*, *C. flaccida*, *C. nitida*, and *C. ochracea*.

Cymbidium

Natural habitat: Himalayas, southern China, Southeast Asia to the Philippines, Papua New Guinea, and Australia.

Plant form: Sympodial. Round to conical pseudobulbs with long, thin but tough leaves. Erect, arching, or pendulous racemes, flowers in many different colors, often fragrant.

Culture: 50% shade. Best planted in hollow limbs, also in forks and crotches. They also grow well in epiphytic ferns.

Climate: Tropical, subtropical, and cool climates.

Species: Tropical gardens can use *C. aloifolium*, *C. atropurpureum*, *C. bicolor*, and *C. finlaysonianum*. These will also grow in the subtropics along with *C. canaliculatum* (grow on the dry side), *C. dayanum*, *C. erythrostylum*, *C. madidum*, *C. sanderae*, and *C. tracyanum*. Some enlightened hybridists are making warm-growing *Cymbidium* hybrids. This genus really comes into its own in the cooler regions such as the coastal districts of southern California and southeastern Australia. Many species live at considerable altitude in subtropical regions where the climate is distinctly cool. Select from *C. eburneum*, *C. floribundum* (syn. *C. pumilum*), *C. iridioides* (syn. *C. giganteum*), *C. hookerianum*, *C. lowianum*, and many thousands of hybrids.

Dendrobium

Natural habitat: India to Samoa, Japan to New Zealand.

Plant form: Sympodial. Extremely diverse. The plants most frequently grown have canelike pseudobulbs. Inflorescences carry from one to many flowers of many colors. Many species are fragrant.

Culture: 50% shade, but many will take more sun if acclimatized. Affix pendulous types like *D. anosmum* well above head height so you can look up into their blooms. Affix tall hardcane types like *D. discolor* low on the tree and medium-sized plants towards the outside where they get plenty of light.

Climate: Tropical, subtropical, and cool climate gardens.

Species: In tropical gardens use *D. affine, D. anosmum, D. bigibbum, D. canaliculatum, D. crumenatum, D. discolor, D. helix, D. johannis, D. lasianthera, D. lineale, D. macrophyllum, D. nindii, D. spectabile, D. stratiotes, D. striaenopsis* (syn. *D. phalaenopsis*), the natural hybrid *D. ×superbiens,* and *D. taurinum.* Thousands of hybrids, many of which are compact and colorful, are ideal for highlighting the garden treescape. For the subtropics, use species from higher altitudes, including *D. anosmum, D. aphrodite, D. atroviolaceum, D. chrysanthum, D. dearei, D. densiflorum, D. farmeri, D. fimbriatum, D. formosum, D. johnsoniae, D. lindleyi, D. moschatum, D. nobile, D. parishii, D. polysema, D. primulinum, D. pulchellum, D. speciosum, D. tetragonum,* and *D. thyrsiflorum* and hundreds of hybrids, particularly Australian native hybrids and softcane hybrids. Some of these grow in monsoon climates with definite wet and dry seasons. Water these heavily while they are growing, but don't try too hard to differentiate. Tree culture, good light, and air circulation prevent them from staying too wet when their growth finishes. In cooler regions, use species from high elevations in the subtropics or in temperate regions like southern Queensland and New South Wales. These include *D. adae, D. aemulum, D. amoenum, D. bellatulum, D. chrysotoxum, D. curvicaule* (syn. *D. speciosum var. curvicaule*), *D. falcorostrum, D.*

Stout-stemmed *Dendrobium sanderae* is a long-lasting Philippine species for the tropics and subtropics.

×gracillimum, D. jonesii, D. macropus (syn. *D. gracilicaule*), *D. moniliforme, D. monophyllum, D. nobile* (the best), *D. pendulum* (syn. *D. crassinode*), *D. tarberi* (syn. *D. speciosum var. hillii*), *D. tetragonum, D. victoria-reginae,* and *D. wardianum.* Also try the many hybrids from Australian natives and from softcanes.

Dockrillia

Natural habitat: Australia, Papua New Guinea, and New Caledonia.

Plant form: Sympodial. These were segregated from the genus *Dendrobium.* They comprise pseudobulbless forms including the pencil-leaved types.

Dockrillia striolata growing naturally in Tasmania with lichens and mosses protecting its roots.

Culture: 50% to 70% shade for most. The pendulous types make wonderful specimens and will hang from the underside of a branch as well as the main trunk.

Climate: Cool climates.

Species: *Dockrillia bowmanii, D. calamiformis, D. cucumerina* (best host is the Australian pine, *Casuarina*, attach on shady side of tree), *D. fairfaxii, D. fuliginosa* from Papua New Guinea (will grow in warm climates), *D. linguiformis, D. pugioniformis, D. rigida, D. striolata* from Tasmania, and *D. teretifolia.*

Encyclia

Natural habitat: Florida, Mexico, West Indies, Central and South America.

Plant form: Sympodial. Mostly walnut- to tennis-ball-sized pseudobulbs, with erect or arching racemes, sometimes branching, and few to many flowers, often fragrant. Colors mostly in the honey brown, cream, yellow, and rose shades.

Culture: 50% shade. Place so the arching racemes clear the host tree's foliage.

Climate: Tropical, subtropical, and cool climate gardens.

Species: Tropical species include *E. cordigera, E. dichroma, E. longifolia, E. osmantha, E. patens* (syn. *E. odoratissima*—the name says it all), *E. phoenicea* (redolent of chocolate), and *E. selligera*. Hybrids with *Cattleya*, strangely called ×*Epicattleya*, are worth growing in tropical treescapes. This is a huge genus and botanists have split several groups from it in recent years. You may find some species listed in the genera *Anacheilum* and *Prosthechea*. Many of the Mexican and Central American species like subtropical climates because they grow naturally at a fair height above sea level. Try *Encyclia alata, E. aromatica, E. baculus, E. brassavolae, E. cochleata, E. cordigera, E. fragrans, E. guatemalensis, E. polybulbon, E. radiata,* and *E. tampensis*. As well as several of the subtropical species, three spectacular species from high country in Mexico merit space on cooler region trees: *E. citrina* (syn. *Cattleya citrina*), *E. mariae,* and *E. vitellina*. Some botanists place *E. citrina* and *E. mariae* in the genus *Euchile*.

Gongora

Natural habitat: Mexico to Central and South America.

Plant form: Sympodial. Clustered, ridged pseudobulbs with large, thin, plicate, ribbed leaves. Mostly pendulous racemes with many colorful, oddly shaped flowers, usually fragrant.

Culture: 70% shade. To enjoy the perfume, try horizontal branches or crotches where the flowers will hang at head height.

Climate: Tropical and subtropical.

Species: *Gongora armeniaca, G. atropurpurea, G. bufonia, G. galeata, G. maculata, G. quinquenervis,* and *G. portentosa* are reasonably easy to find.

Grammatophyllum

Natural habitat: Southeast Asia, the Philippines, Papua New Guinea, and Fiji.

Plant form: Sympodial. Clustered ovoid to very tall pseudobulbs with strap-shaped leaves. Large growers, arching racemes with many flowers with mostly yellow to chocolate tones. Spectacular orchids.

Culture: 30% shade to full sun. They love air movement but need thick branches or a stout main trunk. Plant *G. speciosum*, the world's bulkiest orchid, with pseudobulbs to 10 feet (about 3 meters) long, in a fork where its long racemes can arch down.

Climate: Tropical.

Species: *Grammatophyllum measuresianum*, *G. scriptum*, *G. stapeliaeflorum*, and, in large gardens, *G. speciosum* are commonly grown. There are a couple of intraspecific hybrids available which are very handsome.

Holcoglossum

Natural habitat: Southern China, Myanmar, Thailand, Vietnam, Laos, and Cambodia at considerable elevations.

Plant form: Monopodial. Very long fleshy leaves grooved lengthwise. Very thick roots. Flowers on erect or arching racemes, large and beautiful, pastel colors, fragrant. Graceful plants some of which are charming miniatures.

Culture: 50% to 70% shade. Keep moist while roots are active.

Climate: Cool climates.

Species: These were formerly classified as *Vanda* and are sometimes still listed as such. *Holcoglossum amesianum*, *H. flavescens* (a miniature, raised from seed by some suppliers as *H. yunnanense*), *H. kimballianum*, and *H. subulifolium*.

Laelia

Natural habitat: Mexico and Brazil.

Plant form: Sympodial. Some resemble unifoliate

This blue-lipped form of *Laelia purpurata* is a strong-growing species for subtropical trees.

cattleyas; others have smaller, more succulent pseudobulbs. Inflorescences are erect, with a few large to many smaller flowers, colored yellow through orange to purple. sometimes fragrant.

Culture: 50% shade for unifoliates, 70% for slender types.

Climate: Subtropical and cool climates.

Species: In the subtropics try unifoliates *L. anceps*, *L. autumnalis*, *L. crispa*, *L. gouldiana*, *L. grandis*, *L. perrinii*, *L. purpurata*, *L. rubescens*, *L. tenebrosa*, and *L. xanthina*. *Laelia fidelensis*, *L. harpophylla*, *L. jongheana*, and *L. pumila* all like to be kept damp. In cooler regions use species from high elevations in Mexico which enjoy cool winters. These include *L. albida*, *L. anceps* (arguably the best orchid to try first on a tree in your garden), *L. autumnalis*, *L. furfuracea*, *L. gouldiana*,

Laelia xanthina displays its subtly colored blooms on medium-sized plants.

Cool-growing *Lycaste skinneri* needs protection from sun and strong winds.

and *L. speciosa* (syn. *L. majalis*). *Laelia albida* and *L. speciosa* in particular struggle to grow well outside cool montane areas.

Lemboglossum

Natural habitat: Mexico and Central America.
Plant form: Sympodial. Quite small, compressed pseudobulbs with arching racemes and large, colorful flowers.
Culture: 70% shade. Must be kept moist.
Climate: Cool climates.
Species: *Lemboglossum bictoniense, L. cervantesii, L. cordatum, L. nebulosum,* and *L. rossii.* These were classified formerly as *Odontoglossum* and are sometimes listed as such.

Lycaste

Natural habitat: Mexico, Central and South America.
Plant form: Sympodial. Clustered pseudobulbs with broad, thin, plicate leaves. Flowers borne one per stem but several stems per bulb, in yellows, greens, and pastels, fragrant. Some species are deciduous, others evergreen.

Culture: 50% shade for deciduous types, 70% for evergreens. Let deciduous types become a bit dry in winter after they lose their leaves. Keep evergreens damp year-round. Give both types a lot of wind protection.
Climate: Cool subtropical and cooler climates.
Species: Deciduous types include *Lycaste aromatica, L. consobrina, L. cruenta,* and *L. deppei.* Evergreens include *L. macrophylla* and *L. skinneri* (the best species). Many hybrids are available that are good, vigorous growers.

Maxillaria

Natural habitat: Mexico, the West Indies, Central and South America.
Plant form: Sympodial. Some grow in clusters, others ramble. Most have small pseudobulbs and single flowers per stem but many stems per bulb. Flowers come in many colors and are fragrant.
Culture: 70% shade. Small species make good fillers, larger ones make great specimens. Often come in nice, compact forms that contrast well with monopodials.

Maxillaria elatior makes large, scrambling specimens in cool climate and subtropical garden trees.

Intergeneric hybrids in the *Oncidium* alliance grow vigorously in the subtropics. This one is ×*Miltonidium* Bartley Schwarz 'Highland' AM/AOS.

Climate: Subtropical and cool climates.

Species: Subtropical species to try include *M. houtteana, M. marginata, M. meleagris, M. nigrescens, M. picta, M. porphyroglossa, M. rufescens, M. tenuifolia,* and *M. variabilis.* Some species live in cool cloud forest areas at great altitude and should be kept shady and damp in your garden treescape. Among these are *M. eburnea, M. grandiflora, M. luteoalba,* and *M. sanderiana,* which is the most spectacular species.

Miltonia

Natural habitat: Brazil.

Plant form: Sympodial. Clustered pseudobulbs with thin leaves, upright inflorescences, and sev–

Brightly colored *Miltonia citrina* is an easy-growing epiphyte.

eral flowers. Most have erect or arching scapes with several large blooms

Culture: 50% to 70% shade. Most grow into clustered specimens quite quickly. Several grow upwards and are good on ascending branches or walls.

Climate: Subtropical.

Species: *Miltonia Bluntii, M. citrina, M. clowesii, M. cuneata, M. flavescens, M. moreliana, M. regnellii,* and *M. spectabilis.* There are many excellent intergeneric hybrids, including *×Beallara, ×Blackara, ×Colmanara, ×Miltassia,* and *×Miltonidium.*

Odontoglossum

Natural habitat: Venezuela, Colombia, Ecuador, and Peru at high altitude.

Plant form: Sympodial. Rather succulent pseudobulbs and leaves, with arching, often branched inflorescences bearing many good-sized flowers. Mostly pastel shades, and fragrant.

Culture: 70% or heavier shade. The species are best suited to montane areas like the New South Wales Blue Mountains and coastal Oregon and Washington because of their liking for constant moisture, cool temperatures, and high humidity. High summer temperatures are the bane of odontoglossums. Try them on mossy branches, kept damp.

Climate: Cool climate gardens.

Species: Rather than attempting to grow *Odontoglossum* species, try some intergeneric hybrids, which are usually more vigorous and more tolerant of warm conditions. *×Beallara, ×Colmanara, ×Odontioda,* and *×Wilsonara* are four hybrid genera worth trying. The closely related *Osmoglossum pulchellum,* with fragrant white flowers, is a good subject for treescapes in both subtropical and cooler regions.

Oncidium

Natural habitat: Florida, Mexico, West Indies, Central and South America.

Plant form: Sympodial. A huge genus varying from clustered pseudobulbous types to tereteleaved types with tiny bulbs and some with small bulbs and large, fleshy leaves shaped like mules' ears. Flowers mostly in the yellow, brown, cream, and purple tones. Some are fragrant.

Culture: 50% shade. Most have arching racemes that will hang down. Attach them quite high in the tree.

Climate: Tropical, subtropical, and cooler regions.

Credited with starting the orchidmania that gripped England in the first half of the nineteenth century, *Psychopsis papilio* is a tropical species.

Showers of gold highlight *Oncidium ampliatum* in bloom.

Oncidium hastilabium, a cool moist grower, exhibits attractive color contrasts.

Segregated from the genus *Oncidium*, the small fan-shaped plants now called *Tolumnia* grow well on trees, shrubs, and driftwood mounts in warm, sunny courtyards. This one is *T. pulchella* 'Skippy' FCC/AOS.

Strong-growing *Oncidium strobelii*.

Species: *Oncidium ampliatum, O. carthagenense, O. cebolleta, O. lanceanum, O. luridum* (syn. *O. guttatum*), *O. panamense, O. stipitatum,* and *O. stramineum* should all grow and flower in tropical regions. The fabulous butterfly orchids, *Psychopsis kramerianum* and *P. papilio,* used to be classed as oncidiums and are well worth trying in tropical regions with a little more shade than the other species. For cool areas try *O. cheirophorum, O. concolor, O. crispum, O. forbesii, O. gardneri, O. marshallianum, O. sarcodes,* and *O. varicosum* (possibly the most spectacular species) as well as many beautiful hybrids both within the genus and with other closely related genera. Some of these *Oncidium* species and hybrids don't like growing in pots but flourish on trees in subtropical and cooler coastal and montane gardens.

Renanthera

Natural habitat: Eastern India, southern China, Southeast Asia, and the Philippines to Papua New Guinea.

Plant form: Monopodial. Several are short growers, but *R. coccinea* and *R. storiei* are real scramblers growing to 26–30 feet (8–10 meters). Inflorescences are much branched, spreading, with very bright flowers in orange to red tones.

Culture: 30% to 50% shade for the short growers, full sun for the large ones.

Climate: Tropical and warm subtropical.

Species: *Renanthera imschootiana, R. matutina, R. monachica, R. philippinensis, R. pulchella,* and the closely related *Renantherella histrionica* are quite short growers while *Renanthera coccinea* and *R. storiei* are large.

Rhyncholaelia

Natural habitat: Mexico, Honduras, and Guatemala.

Plant form: Sympodial. Short, thick, glaucous pseudobulbs with fleshy leaves. Single spectacular flowers (*R. digbyana* with a fantastically fringed lip) which are fragrant.

Culture: 50% shade. They will take tough conditions provided they have good light, plenty of water and are in an exceedingly well-drained position.

Climate: Tropical and subtropical.

Species: There are only two species, both formerly classified as *Brassavola. Rhyncholaelia digbyana* grows in the tropics while *R. glauca* prefers cooler conditions. Many hybrids are available under the names ×*Brassocattleya,* ×*Brassolaelia,* and ×*Brassolaeliocattleya,* usually abbreviated to *Bc., Bl.,* and *Blc.*

Rhynchostylis

Natural habitat: Eastern India, Southeast Asia, and the Philippines.

Plant form: Monopodial. Short-stemmed but long leaved, forming clumps as they mature. Upright, arching sometimes pendulous inflorescences. Fragrant flowers from blue to amethyst-purple.

Culture: 50% shade. Use stout branches or forks to allow for its clumping habit. Attach *R. retusa* above head height to enjoy its pendulous "foxtail" of blooms.

Climate: Tropical and subtropical.

Species: *Rhynchostylis coelestis* (blue), *R. gigantea, R. retusa,* and *R. violacea.* Many hybrids between these and vandaceous genera such as *Aerides, Ascocentrum, Renanthera,* and *Vanda* are very suitable.

Rodriguezia

Natural habitat: Central and South America.

Plant form: Sympodial. Scramblers with small pseudobulbs and long rhizomes, they seldom have more than a couple of roots attached to the host with a shower of roots hanging free. Flowers white, chocolate, and red on many-flowered racemes.

Culture: 70% shade. Affix these to quite thin branches.

Climate: Subtropical.

Species: *Rodriguezia decora, R. lanceolata* (*R. secunda*), and *R. venusta* (*R. fragrans*).

Schomburgkia

Natural habitat: Mexico, the Caribbean, Central and South America.

Plant form: Sympodial. Large, tough plants. Some species have hollow pseudobulbs; others have spindle-shaped ones. Flower stems are usually very long, sometimes more than 10 feet (3 meters). Flowers are curly, shiny in shades of yellow, honey brown, pink to purple, sometimes fragrant, segments crisped or wavy.

Culture: 30% shade to full sun, ideal for exposed branches on trees.

Climate: Tropical and subtropical.

Species: Some species are still listed commercially under the genus *Laelia*. Tropical species include *Schomburgkia crispa*, *S. fimbriata*, *S. lyonsii*, *S. splendida*, *S. thomsoniana*, *S. tibicinis*, and *S. undulata*. Hybrids with other members of the *Cattleya* alliance, particularly ×*Schombocattleya*, are also good in tropical treescapes. Subtropical species include *Schomburgkia elata*, *S. exaltata*, *S. moyobambae*, *S. rosea*, *S. superbiens* (will also grow in cooler regions), and *S. tibicinis*. Give these robust growers plenty of light and room. They are spectacular orchids for landscaping.

Sophronitis

Natural habitat: Brazil, mostly on mountains at about 6500 feet (2000 meters) elevation.

Plant form: Sympodial. These resemble diminutive unifoliate cattleyas (to which they are related) with pseudobulbs only an inch or two (a few centimeters) tall. Flowers are proportionately large and brilliant, in orange to red shades.

Culture: 70% shade. Attach reasonably low on main trunk, particularly if moss-covered.

Keep cool and humid; do not let surroundings become totally dry. In nature they receive much moisture from clouds, mists, and condensation.

Climate: Cool subtropical to cool climate regions.

Species: *Sophronitis brevipedunculata*, *S. cernua*, *S. coccinea* (the best), and *S. mantiqueirae*.

Stanhopea

Natural habitat: Mexico, Central and South America.

Plant form: Sympodial. Clustering pseudobulbs with broad, thin, ribbed leaves. Inflorescences descend sharply. Large flowers in many colors last three or four days. Very fragrant and spectacular.

Culture: 50% to 70% shade. Protect from strong winds. Attach to main trunk or trunk and branch junctions above head height so you can examine the fabulous flowers at close range.

Climate: Tropical, subtropical and cooler regions.

Species: Tropical species include *Stanhopea candida*, *S. connata*, *S. ecornuta*, *S. grandiflora*, and *S. reichenbachiana*. Most stanhopeas come from subtropical regions or from forested tropical mountains

Sophronitis coccinea tetraploid form, a glowing decoration for humid courtyard trees or shrubs in cool to subtropical climates.

Spectacular in flower, *Stanhopea connata* 'Everglades' is a warm grower.

Stanhopea oculata var. *ornatissima* atones for its short blooming season with its ease of growth and abundance of flowers.

One of the less-common strap-leaf species *Vanda celebica* would be a talking point in tropical gardens.

where the climate is milder than tropical lowlands although several of these will grow in tropical climates and several listed above will grow in cooler conditions. In subtropical and cooler climates try *S. devoniensis, S. graveolens, S. hernandezii, S. insignis, S. nigroviolacea* (probably the best to try first on your tree), *S. oculata, S. saccata,* and *S. tigrina* which is often confused with *S. nigroviolacea* however both are worth growing.

Trichopilia

Natural habitat: Mexico, Central and South America.
Plant form: Sympodial. Compressed, clustered pseudobulbs with short racemes of large flowers, white, purple, green, and red in combination. Fragrant.
Culture: 70% shade. These like to be kept damp as they have fine roots. Best planted on main trunk or branches carrying mosses and lichens.
Climate: Subtropical.
Species: *Trichopilia fragrans, T. hennisiana, T. laxa, T. marginata* (*T. coccinea*), *T. suavis* which is possibly the nicest species, and *T. tortilis.*

Vanda

Natural habitat: Himalayas, Sri Lanka, China through Southeast Asia and the Philippines to Papua New Guinea and Australia.
Plant form: Monopodial. Size varies from small to very large, often clumping when mature, with thick, long, rambling roots. Flower stems are erect, horizontal, or arching. Flowers have many colors, are usually well displayed and often fragrant.
Culture: 50% shade. Attached to trunk or sloping branch, plants will ultimately droop gracefully down and out. Water and fertilize frequently except in cool weather.

Climate: Tropical, subtropical, and cool regions.

Species: *Vanda brunnea, V. dearei, V. denisoniana, V. hindsii, V. insignis, V. limbata, V. liouvillei, V. luzonica, V. sanderiana* (now *Euanthe sanderiana* but sold as a *Vanda*), *V. tricolor, V. tricolor* var. *suavis,* and the many intergeneric hybrids of ×*Aeridovanda,* ×*Ascocenda,* and ×*Rhynchovanda* are suitable for tropical treescapes. Species from considerable altitude are suitable for subtropical and cooler regions. These include *V. bensonii, V. coerulea* (a beautiful blue, the best of the cooler species), *V. coerulescens, V. cristata* (now classified as *Trudelia cristata* but sold under the former name), *V. javieriae, V. lilacina,* and *V. roeblingiana.*

Do orchids have aphrodisiac qualities? Consider this description of the use of *Grammatophyllum scriptum* in the Moluccas, Indonesia: *In Ternate, according to Rumphius, the matrons, and especially the wives, sisters and daughters of the kings (who are all called "putri" in Malay, and "boki" in the Moluccas) so entirely appropriate these flowers to themselves that a common woman and especially a slave would offer them a great affront if she were to put them on her head. The flowers are reserved exclusively for the great ladies, who cause them to be sought for in the forests, and braid them in their hair, saying that nature herself has shown that such flowers are not fit for people of low degree, since they grow nowhere but in high places; hence they are called "bonga boki" and "bonga putri," or the princesses' flower. It would also appear that the Malay gentlemen make from the seeds a philtre, which has a surprising effect upon ladies who swallow it.*

—John Lindley and Joseph Paxton,
Flower Garden, 1851–1852

Georg Rumphius was a young naturalist and botanist in the employ of the Dutch East India Company in the far-off days of 1653. History does not record that he was in a hurry to return to the Netherlands.

2

The Lithophytes: Growing Orchids on Rocks and Walls

We sometimes think rock faces, ledges, and cliffs must be the most inhospitable places for plants to live, but some plants forms have evolved to flourish in places where others would perish. A surprising number of orchids have adapted themselves to a rock-dwelling life. An even greater number of orchids will grow well on or among rocks in gardens.

The hard granite of the top was covered with matted mosses, lichens, lycopodiums, and ferns, among which were many curious and beautiful air plants. Eria, Coelogyne (wallichii, maculata, *and* elata), Cymbidium, Dendrobium, Sunipia, *some of them flowering profusely; and though freely exposed to the sun and wind, dews and frosts, rain and droughts, they were all fresh, bright, green, and strong, under very different treatment to that to which they are exposed in the damp, unhealthy, steamy orchid-houses of our English gardens.*
—Sir Joseph D. Hooker,
Himalayan Journals, 1891

Hooker is describing the Kollong Rock in Assam, a large red granite dome rising some 700 feet (about 215 meters) above the valleys.

The Rockery

The position and aspect of the rockery in your garden are important. In the Southern Hemisphere, the northeast aspect is the best for orchids in the rockery. In the Northern Hemisphere, the southeast aspect is the best. Consider whether overhanging trees or shrubs shade the rockery. If the site does not receive at least 30% of midsummer sun filtered through the trees then it is probably too shady for most lithophytic orchids. Can any overhanging, too-shady trees or shrubs be pruned? Is the rockery too exposed? If so, you may be able to plant trees or shrubs in strategic positions to modify the rockery's microclimate. Is it well drained or is it at a low point in your garden? Not many orchids like to grow in waterlogged soil, so it is important to make sure your rockery is well-drained before placing lithophytic orchids in it. You can do this by siting it at a high point in your garden or by laying a drain to keep runoff away from it. Simply building the rockery tall enough will ensure that no excess water lies in it. Use plenty of rubble, broken brick, and stone as the foundation for the rockery so it drains rapidly after watering and after heavy rain.

Dendrobium kingianum makes a good subject to glue or tie to a rock.

Planting *Cattleya bowringiana* in a rockery pocket. Remove potting medium from the rootball, insert stake in pocket, and tie plant securely to it.

A sympodial orchid (*Encyclia* species) attached to a stone wall using masonry nails and nylon strips.

A rockery usually affords a number of different sites that are suitable for different types of orchids. If it has some large boulders, then lithophytic orchids can be grown both on their horizontal and vertical surfaces as well as in the crevices between. If the rocks are smaller, they will form convenient pockets for lithophytic orchids. Use leaf mold and coarse gravel as a planting medium in the rock pockets. Lithophytic orchids most often grow on sandstone, limestone, or basalt rocks. Sandstone can be quite porous and soft. It may be easier to fix orchids to sandstone rocks, but these rocks are more liable to break or crumble, especially when

An *Angraecum sororium* seedling taken from a 2-inch (50-millimeter) tube and tied on a granite rock. It established quickly, kept shady and watered daily.

A few rocks to hold it firmly on a boulder and this *Dendrobium tarberi* backcut has all the start it needs.

Dendrobium tarberi and *Cymbidium madidum* in their natural habitat on the Lamington Plateau, Queensland.

This tropical *Cymbidium* species grows securely in a boulder crevice in Hawaii.

waterlogged. However, many very attractive and successful rockeries are formed of sandstone. Basalt is harder and not as porous as sandstone. Orchids like to grow on it too. In other countries, notably Brazil and Southeast Asia, lithophytic orchids grow on limestone rocks and on outcrops of ironstone. Use the type of rock that appeals to you. Lithophytic orchids usually are not too fussy.

Planting Orchids in the Rockery

If your lithophytic orchid is growing in a container, you must remove it. Trim off any old roots and dead bulbs. Remove all potting medium which will come off easily, especially below the older part of the plant. Inspect the plant for pests. The orchid is now ready for planting. It is vital to ensure newly planted lithophytic orchids cannot

The gardener placed this *Laelia sanguiloba* on a well-shaped granite rock, then secured it firmly with nylon strips.

Spanish moss both hides the nylon ties and provides a humid microclimate round the roots of *Laelia sanguiloba*.

Questions to ask before planting lithophytic orchids:

- How will the plant look in that position?
- Will it look reasonably natural when it is established?
- Will it look attractive in your garden landscape?
- Is it easily visible?
- Is it within easy reach of a hose?
- Is it in the optimum position for morning and late afternoon sun?
- Is it sheltered from the hot summer midday rays?
- Does the rain run down the rock face round the plant?

If the answers are positive, you have the makings of a successful and attractive orchid rockery.

move and damage their newly emerging roots. A little ingenuity helps in achieving this immobility. For instance, to grow a lithophytic orchid on a horizontal rock, try placing another rock carefully over the orchid to hold it firmly in place until it becomes established on the horizontal surface. The top rock will give the orchid some protection and concentrate some moisture around the orchid while it is taking hold. However, do not use a rock so large and heavy that it squashes the orchid it should be holding down. No orchid likes to be between a rock and a hard place.

To plant orchids in rock pockets you may need to pack in some smaller rocks to hold them firm, or force a stake into the pocket to which you can tie the orchid while it becomes established. You can wedge lithophytic orchids into crevices in the rockery and tie them to rocks in much the same way you would tie an epiphyte to a tree. Strips of nylon stocking or pantyhose make the most effective ties. If you can maneuver a rock then you can tie an orchid to it before placing the rock in its final position in the rockery. To attach a lithophytic orchid to the face of a very large rock, drill some holes in the rock, hammer in masonry nails, and secure the orchid by strips tied from nail to nail. Remove the strips and nails when the orchid has attached itself firmly to the rock. Some growers use glue to attach smaller or lightweight orchids to rocks. Try one of the glues mentioned in chapter 1, ensuring that it is waterproof and nonharmful to plants and that the rock face is dry before using it.

Place the lithophytic orchid's new lead next to the rock face, so the orchid's new root growth will attach directly to the rock and its next growth will nestle naturally against the rock. If you fasten the orchid with its newest growth facing away from the rock, the roots will struggle to reach back to the rock. The next growth will dangle, dangerously unsupported, in the air. Do not place any material round a lithophytic orchid's roots before planting or attaching it. Not only does material such as sphagnum moss or fiber look unsightly on a rock face, it also dries out too quickly and can provide a hiding place for pests such as cockroaches, slugs, and snails. If the moss retains too much moisture, tropism will cause the orchid's roots to remain in the material rather than attaching to the rock. Spanish moss draped round orchids affixed to rock faces looks more natural and helps to provide a favorable microclimate.

On the borders of this orchid garden [at Demerara, Guyana] are rocks, suitably arranged on which species which in tropical regions grow on rocks and in stony places can easily be cultivated. Cattleyas can be managed in two ways, as they grow upon the rocks as well as upon the trees. Many times have I seen splendid plants of cattleya, in the mountainous regions of America, growing on enormous perpendicular rocks, where the specimens are accessible only to the most intrepid of the natives, whose only support when gathering them is a strong rope fastened to the summit of the precipice. When cattleyas grow in forests, they are usually found in more shady places than those which grow upon rocks, consequently, the leaves and bulbs are almost always darker in color and less firm in texture; while, on the other hand, exposure to the sun colors the leaves and bulbs of the others with clearer hues, and renders the substance of the foliage much firmer and stiffer.

—Eric Bungeroth, Journal des Orchidées,
15 March 1891

Madagascan species *Jumellea major* is at home as an epiphyte in about 70% shade or on a mossy boulder.

When plant collecting in Hubei Province, western China, Ernest H. Wilson noted the use to which local people put the lithophytic orchids *Pleione henryi* and *P. pogonioides* which grew there on damp, mossy, humus-covered rocks between 3500 and 6000 feet (about 1000 to 1830 meters) elevation. The pseudobulbs were pounded and boiled with dried orange peel and sugar to make a concoction used as a cure for tuberculosis and asthma. Orchids in many countries have been used for various medicinal purposes for centuries. Western scientists have started to study such potentially useful properties in orchids. Surely, this is a reason in itself for preventing the destruction of orchid habitats before their denizens' usefulness is known.

Use your ingenuity when fastening lithophytic orchids to rocks or when planting them in the rockery. The single rule that cannot be broken is that the orchid must be fixed so firmly that it cannot move in any circumstances. If it moves, its roots will be broken and it will not thrive. If the orchid is so secure that it cannot move, then it will establish itself quickly.

Growing Orchids on Walls

One of the most impressive gardens I have seen featured orchids growing on the stone foundations of a hillside house. The orchids were attractive and gave the stone pillars and the whole house an informal look, very different from the classical appearance of bare stone. These days, few new homes have either stone foundations or stone walls. If you do have stone construction, an "orchid wall" or orchids planted on stone foundations make wonderful focal points. You have a ready-made site for a lithophytic orchid garden. If you do not have a stone foundation, wall, or rockery but you still want to grow some lithophytic orchids naturally, use that most modern building material, the concrete block. Concrete blocks are quite alkaline in their chemical composition. As many lithophytic orchids grow naturally on limestone rocks, they are quite at home growing on concrete. Concrete blocks are easily handled. They can be formed into many shapes—straight or curving walls, pillars, semicircles, free forms. They can be cemented together or laid with gaps or overlaps to provide pockets for planting. The ways in which you can use concrete blocks to make walls for orchids are limited only by your imagination.

To attach orchids to the vertical faces of stone or concrete block walls, use masonry nails to secure the plants, or glue for lightweights. If your wall has gaps, you may be able to wedge orchids in them. You can attach orchids to the top of block walls by anchoring them with a rock. If you leave well-

Judging from what I have observed, an excess of shade is far more injurious to cattleyas than excessive light. In a South American village, I saw hundreds of cattleyas planted on the tops of walls of earth, exposed to the full sun, and flourishing splendidly.

—Eric Bungeroth, *Journal des Orchidées*, 15 March 1891

drained pockets at the base of the block wall, you can plant orchids in them. Tall-growing genera such as epidendrums and vandas love to scramble up block structures with their roots running over the surface into the cracks and crevices. It is best to attach orchids to stone or block pillars by tying them on with nylon stocking or pantyhose strips. The cardinal rule is that you must attach the orchid so firmly that it cannot move.

Companion Planting in Rockeries and Walls

In nature, lithophytic orchids frequently grow in association with other plants. Such companions may be grasses, ferns, gesneriads, mosses, lichens, or shrubs. In Central and South America, companion plants of lithophytic orchids are often cacti or bromeliads. In the rockery, shrubs are useful both for their ornamental value and for the beneficial microclimates they can provide. Strategically placed shrubs can provide windbreaks, shade, and extra humidity for the orchids in the rockery. Consider the characteristics of the shrubs you intend to plant. Choose densely leafed types where shade for the rockery orchids is needed, and more open types where more light is required. Avoid shrubs with rampant, invasive root systems that can provide too much competition for the orchids. Decide whether flowering shrubs will complement or detract from your flowering orchids.

Ornamental grasses and ferns in the rockery can assist also in maintaining a beneficial microclimate. Ensure that any grasses you plant are not so vigorous that they choke out or smother the lithophytic orchids. Clumping types are easier to manage than running types. Several species of fern are vigorous clumpers and climbers. You can train them to scramble through rockeries and up garden walls. Watch that they, too, do not choke orchids over which they may climb.

Plant ferns towards the lower levels of the rockery. These levels often are more damp than the higher levels and the orchids will appreciate the extra humidity the ferns create. Many ferns like to be kept damp while most orchids prefer a wet/dry cycle. This is a good reason for planting ferns below the orchids, where you can water them without having to wet the orchids too. Use Spanish moss on rockeries and walls. Draped around newly planted orchids, it assists their quick attachment to the rock face or wall. It also provides them with extra shade and humidity. You can thin it out or remove it if necessary once the orchid has become established.

Bromeliads make wonderful companion plants for lithophytic orchids. The vase types retain water in their vases, helping to create the extra humidity which lithophytic orchids love. Rock faces and cliffs do not usually contain water storage areas other than in the plants that grow naturally on them. Seepage from the bases of vase-type bromeliads will encourage the growth of mosses, lichens, and small ferns. These add to the beneficial microclimate that lithophytes need.

Bromeliads, several creeping types of ferns, small-growing vines, staghorn and elkhorn (*Platycerium*), and bird's nest ferns (*Asplenium*) in shady areas are among the few types of plants which will grow with the lithophytic orchids on garden walls. They are as easy to attach to the wall as orchids.

Bromeliads feature in this Hawaiian rockery.

A single *Tillandsia* as a feature plant in the American Orchid Society garden, Delray Beach.

Aechmea Little Mary thrives in a lakeside rockery in Fairchild Tropical Garden, Miami.

Aftercare for the Rockery and Wall

Most lithophytic orchids commonly grown in rockeries have high light requirements. Many will take full sun provided they are acclimatized to it gradually. Some lithophytes will also grow and flower happily with only about 30% sunlight. If your rockery is under densely shady trees, you may need to do some pruning to let enough light on the orchids. Most orchids suitable for growing on garden walls and house foundations have the same high light requirements as those in rockeries. Some members of certain genera, including *Bulbophyllum* and *Coelogyne*, like quite shady conditions. Many epiphytic orchids grown as lithophytes in rockeries or on walls do better with 50% to 70% shade as well. As a general rule to which there are exceptions, orchids with wide, soft, or thin leaves prefer shade to sun. Orchids with hard, thick leaves and hard, waxy pseudobulbs prefer sun to shade.

The more you can learn of your orchid's habitat and growing conditions in nature, the easier it will be for you to grow it in the right place in your garden. Because of their vertical nature and their limited porosity, garden walls and house foundations tend to dry out rapidly. Orchids planted on them need daily watering in the warmer months, perhaps every second day in cooler weather. You will need to water even more frequently during hot, dry weather. Rocks and walls become much hotter and retain surface heat longer than tree trunks and branches. You can easily set up sprinkler systems in rockeries and over wall plantings. Once they are established, your lithophytic orchids will benefit from the natural condensation that collects on them at night.

You need to consider the drainage characteristics of your particular rockery in conjunction with watering your lithophytic orchids. If the rockery is well-drained and exposed to the drying influences of the sun and wind, then you can water frequently—every day in hot, dry weather, every second day when conditions are milder—until your orchids show good root growth. As your orchids become established, you can reduce watering to perhaps three times each week in summer and once each week in winter. Water less frequently if the weather turns cold, and more frequently (even daily) during hot spells. However, if your rockery retains moisture, with deeper pockets, more shade, and less than full sun exposure, you will need to reduce the frequency of watering. It is important to ensure lithophytic orchids have the wet/dry cycle that they like. Those planted in pockets with some leaf mold and gravel will stay damp much longer than those higher in the rockery, on bare rock or in vertical crevices. Orchids on bare walls dry out the quickest. Nothing is as important as your own observation in deciding whether your orchids need watering. As a rough rule of thumb, during the cooler months, if in doubt do not water until tomorrow, but in summer when those hot, drying winds blow, give your lithophytes a thorough watering every evening.

Air circulation is not a problem with orchids growing on garden walls and foundations. Breezes blow about them unhindered. However, consider whether a newly planned garden wall should run east–west or north–south. From which direction do the fiercest winds blow in your garden? Can you provide a windbreak to reduce the wind's force? Hot, drying winds can be tempered by planting a windbreak. Well-watered leafy shrubs filter hot dry winds and add humidity to the air on their lee side. If the worst wind blows from the south in your garden, any orchids planted on the south side of a wall running east–west will have two disadvantages. They will be exposed to the strong, cold southerly wind and they will be on the shady side of the wall. In the Northern Hemisphere strong, cold winds are likely to blow from the north, which also will be the shady side of the wall. Your orchids might be better served growing on a wall running north–south where you can give them shade and humidity on the west side by judicious companion planting.

In nature rock growers obtain their nutrition in much the same way as do the tree dwellers. Decaying vegetable matter becomes trapped around the bases of the plants, releasing nutrition as it breaks down. Lithophytes absorb minute quantities of minerals from the very rocks on which they grow, assisted by the leaching effect of rainfall. Decayed vegetable matter in the form of leaf mold, no doubt enriched by minute quantities of minerals from the rocks, forms in pockets and crevices in rock faces, ledges, and cliffs. Lithophytic orchids grow with extraordinary robustness where they are able to send their roots into such nutritionally rich areas.

While your lithophytes are becoming established, feed them with a soluble fertilizer weekly but weakly. Spray it thoroughly over leaves and roots after watering, using the fertilizer at half the manufacturer's recommended strength. Use soluble fertilizers. It is difficult to make the insoluble fertilizers, such as manures and slow-release pellets, stay on vertical or steeply sloping surfaces. Keep feeding the lithophytes while they are in active growth. Congenial conditions in a well-made rockery or garden wall often allow lithophytic orchids to grow right through the year.

A Selection of Lithophytic Orchids

Orchids growing on rocks are found in the same regions as orchids growing epiphytically. Indeed,

a number of orchids that we think of as epiphytes grow equally well in nature as lithophytes. In North Queensland, the golden orchid (*Dendrobium discolor*) grows right down to the beach and on rocks on offshore islands. The warm tropical lowlands to Australia's immediate north are home to several other species which are found both as epiphytes and lithophytes including *D. lineale* which grows on rocks at the water's edge and on trees on some islands of Papua New Guinea. In Brazil species of *Bifrenaria* are equally at home as epiphytes and as lithophytes on precipitous rock faces in bright sunlight. *Cattleya schilleriana* and *C. walkeriana*, while principally epiphytes, have adapted to lithophytic life in some areas of Brazil. In Australia, New South Wales and southern Queensland are home to the tongue or thumbnail orchid (*Dockrillia linguiformis*) and the lily-of-the-valley orchid (*Dendrobium monophyllum*). Both species grow as lithophytes, usually closer to the southern extremes of their natural range. Towards the more northerly parts of their range, particularly near the coast, they grow as epiphytes.

Many purely lithophytic orchid species have a unique vegetative shape that helps to identify them as lithophytes. Such species have flask-shaped pseudobulbs or stems, widest at the base then tapering to a much thinner neck. Perhaps this form is nature's adaptation, allowing a bottom-heavy plant to hug its rock home more securely than a top-heavy shape would do. Most of us are familiar with Australia's pink rock lily (*Dendrobium kingianum*), a true lithophyte. It grows on the rocks and cliff faces of the Great Dividing Range and its eastern spurs from about central New South Wales to central Queensland. The length of its pseudobulbs may vary from more than 12 inches

(30 centimeters) when growing in shady damp areas to about 2 inches (5 centimeters) in exposed sunny sites. However, it retains a constant bottom-heavy flask shape.

Several Brazilian *Laelia* species grow only as lithophytes, having similar flask-shaped pseudobulbs to those of *Dendrobium kingianum*. Orchid growers often call this group the rupicolous laelias. *Rupicolous* and *lithophytic* mean the same thing, namely, growing on rocks. The lithophytic laelias include *Laelia cinnabarina*, quite tall-growing with spectacular cinnabar-orange flowers, and the sturdy *L. caulescens*, with sparkling lavender-pink flowers. *Laelia milleri*, another flask-shaped lithophyte with wonderful red flowers, grew on ironstone ridges in Brazil. It may be extinct in nature, because of the destruction of its habitat by mining. Fortunately this species has been raised from seed and is quite readily available in the nursery trade.

In addition to the orchids that grow only as lithophytes, in nature many epiphytic species adapt quite readily to life as a lithophyte. Most cattleyas, for example, are epiphytic in nature but can grow well in rockeries. We would not expect an orchid like a *Cattleya*, which grows naturally with its roots creeping over the surface of a rough-barked tree, to enjoy life in a rockery with its roots buried in a pocket of leaf mold and gravel. However, attach the same *Cattleya* to a vertical wall or sloping rock face; give it good light, air movement, and water and its roots will spread vigorously over the rock surface, growing as Bungeroth has described.

Sympodial lithophytes such as *Dendrobium kingianum*, *D. speciosum*, and the laelias mentioned above grow in clumps or clusters. They have almost no space between the pseudobulbs, and the rhizomes are scarcely discernible. This makes them easier to plant in pockets and crevices in the rockery or in holes in the garden wall. Other lithophytic species such as some bulbophyllums and coelogynes grow with extended rhizomes, having several inches (a few centimeters) between pseudobulbs. These types make good filler plants, creeping over the rock faces between other plantings. Many monopodial orchids will grow well in a rockery, adding interest and contrast in their plant forms as well as their flowers. The larger-growing monopodials eventually become top-heavy in a rockery. Supported with stakes they look unnatural. Unsupported they sprawl over the rockery and can look untidy. Choose the compact growers to start.

Here is a sampling of orchids that will grow lithophytically in tropical, subtropical, and cool climate gardens.

As regards size, I do not believe that any other orchid attains to such enormous proportions as do cattleyas when placed in a favorable situation, and at the same time have plenty of warmth and moisture. I have seen plants weighing more than 150 pounds [68 kilograms] each and bearing more than 300 bulbs. It must have been many years before, even in their native land, plants could have grown to such a size, and in this case it was only under conditions the most favorable to their development.

—Eric Bungeroth, *Journal des Orchidées*, 15 March 1891

Angraecum

Natural habitat: Tropical Africa, Madagascar and nearby islands.

Plant form: Monopodial. Some species are small growers, others very large. Stems usually branch as the main plant ages. Some species bear many flowers on each inflorescence, others only one or

Angraecum magdalenae is a superb lithophyte for subtropical gardens.

Most tropical and subtropical gardens have room for a rockery bed of ×*Ascocenda* hybrids.

two. Flowers, usually in the white tones, are mostly fragrant at night.

Culture: Grow most species in 50% shade, the larger ones in 30% shade. *Angraecum eburneum* grows in the wild into huge plants in full sun. Train it up a wall or rock face. Plant smaller growers in small pockets.

Climate: Tropical, subtropical, and cool climate gardens.

Species: In tropical gardens, try *Angraecum comorense, A. eburneum* and its subspecies *xerophilum* (a large-flowered small grower), *A. humbertii, A. longicalcar,* and *A. sesquipedale,* plus hybrids including *A. Alabaster, A. Lemforde White Beauty,* and *A. Veitchii.* These will grow outdoors also in the warm subtropics–north of Brisbane in Australia and in southern Florida. Lithophytic species from higher altitudes that are suitable for the subtropics include *A. magdalenae, A. protensum,* the tiny *A. rutenbergianum,* and the wonderful *A. sororium,* the best of the lithophytic angraecums. In cooler areas, try *A. magdalenae* and *A. sororium,* both of which grow naturally on boulders at altitudes of about 4900 to 6500 feet (about 1500 to 2000 meters), where they are exposed to bright light and some frosts in winter. Plant them on or near large boulders or walls; these retain some residual heat after sunny days.

Arundina

Natural habitat: Himalayas and southern China through Southeast Asia. Naturalized in many tropical regions such as Hawaii.

Plant form: Sympodial. Thin, canelike, leafy stems to 6 feet (nearly 2 meters) tall, successive *Cattleya*-like white to pale rose fragrant flowers.

Culture: Full sun. This true terrestrial species adds height and dimension to the tropical rockery planted in a pocket at ground level. It grows well in rockeries with full sun and plenty of fertilizer while in active growth.

Climate: Tropical and warm subtropical.

Species: Just the one, *Arundina graminifolia* (syn. *A. bambusifolia*).

Ascocentrum

Natural habitat: From northeast India through Southeast Asia to the Philippines.

Plant form: Monopodial. Short, often-branching

stems form upright clumps. Flower racemes are erect and densely flowered. Colors are brilliant orange, red, and yellow.

Culture: 50% to 70% shade. Try these in small pockets or on wall shelves.

Climate: Tropical.

Species: *Ascocentrum garayi* and smaller-growing intergeneric hybrids such as ×*Ascocenda*, ×*Kagawara*, ×*Mokara*, and ×*Renancentrum*.

Bifrenaria

Natural habitat: Brazil.

Plant form: Sympodial. Tough, four-angled pseudobulbs with broad, leathery leaves. One to four flowers on short, upright stems, white to purple, fragrant.

Culture: 30% shade to full sun when acclimatized. Try sloping rock faces, walls, and the top of boulders.

Climate: Subtropical and cool climates.

Species: The best subtropical species are *Bifrenaria harrisoniae*, which has several color forms, *B. tyrianthina*, and, if you can obtain it, *B. magnicalcarata*. *Bifrenaria harrisoniae* and *B. tyrianthina* grow just as well, if not better, in cooler regions as they do in the subtropics.

Brassavola

Natural habitat: Mexico, Central America, and the West Indies south to Brazil.

Plant form: Sympodial with unusual terete, slightly channeled leaves arising from tiny stemlike pseudobulbs. Flowers are medium size to large, usually green or cream with a white trumpet-shaped lip. Fragrant at night.

Culture: 30% to 50% shade. These do well on rock faces and walls.

Climate: Tropical.

Species: *Brassavola cordata* has many smaller flowers. *Brassavola nodosa* flowers year-round when established.

Calanthe

Natural habitat: South Africa, India, China, Japan, through Southeast Asia, Philippines, Papua New Guinea, and Australia to Tahiti.

Plant form: Sympodial. Small to prominent pseudobulbs with large, broad, thin, plicate leaves. Erect to arching inflorescences, with flowers in most colors and with intricate lips. Species with big bulbs are deciduous. The evergreen species are more suitable for garden culture.

Culture: 50% shade for deciduous, 70% shade for evergreens. All must be protected from the wind. Plant these in sheltered pockets low in the rockery where their size helps the rockery's balance. They are very shallow rooted and love to grow in leaf mold.

Climate: Tropical, subtropical, cool, and temperate regions.

Species: Evergreens for the tropics and subtropics include *Calanthe ceciliae*, *C. madagascariensis*, *C. pulchra*, and *C. sylvatica*. The most common evergreen species, *C. triplicata* (syn. *C. veratrifolia*), ranges from Madagascar through India and southern China to Australia and some Pacific Islands. Protect its leaves from any wind stronger than moderate breezes. The evergreen species from Japan and montane subtropics, which do well in cooler regions, even in temperate gardens, include *C. brevicornu*, *C. caudatilabella*, *C. discolor*, *C. fimbriata*, *C. hizen*, *C. masuca*, *C. sieboldii*, and *C. tricarinata*. A number of Japanese hybrids are worth seeking out for temperate gardens.

Cattleya

Natural habitat: Central and South America.

Plant form: Sympodial. Club-shaped, unifoliate (single-leafed) or canelike bifoliate (two-leafed or multileafed) pseudobulbs. Unifoliates have one to a few large, showy "corsage" flowers; bifoliates are usually clusters of smaller but showy flowers. Many are fragrant.

Culture: 50% to 70% shade. Fix to rock faces or start on top of boulders, walls, or shelves in walls.

Climate: Tropical, subtropical, and cooler regions.

Species: The best tropical lithophytic species is *Cattleya violacea* (syn. *Cattleya superba*). *Cattleyas amethystoglossa* and *C. bowringiana*, both very robust, tall bifoliates, are excellent in pockets. Many hybrids in different shapes, sizes, flower forms, and colors are worth using in rockeries and walls. Most cattleyas are subtropical and grow well on walls and rock faces. *Cattleya aclandiae* and *C. walkeriana*, both Brazilian species, sometimes grow lithophytically in the wild. In cool climates, use the species and hybrids that flower in summer and early autumn and rest during the colder months. In particular, try hybrids made with *Sophronitis* such as ×*Sophrocattleya* and ×*Sophrolaeliocattleya*. Plant at the top of rockeries and walls to ensure quick drainage in winter.

Caularthron

Natural habitat: Northern South America and some Caribbean islands.

Plant form: Sympodial. Spindle-shaped, hollow pseudobulbs, flower stems to about 18 inches (45 centimeters), with white, very beautiful flowers.

Culture: 30% shade. This grows naturally on rocks right on the coast in some areas.

Climate: Tropical.

Species: *Caularthron bicornutum* and its hybrids registered under the former genus name, *Diacrium.*

Coelogyne

Natural habitat: Himalayas, southern China through Southeast Asia to the Philippines and Papua New Guinea.

Plant form: Sympodial. Usually round or pear-shaped pseudobulbs on a creeping rhizome. Flowers from new growth with arching to pendulous racemes, few to many, white and pastel colors, often fragrant.

Culture: 70% shade. Start in crevices or on shelves where they can grow down walls or rock faces; many of these are scramblers. Keep moist.

Climate: Subtropical and cool climates.

Species: In subtropical areas, *Coelogyne asperata, C. fimbriata, C. fuliginosa, C. nervosa* (often listed as *C. corrugata*), *C. ovalis, C. primulina,* and *C. rossiana.* In cooler climates, try the high altitude species such as *C. barbata, C. cristata* (especially beautiful), *C. fimbriata, C. fuliginosa, C. nervosa* (syn. *C. corrugata*), *C. nitida,* and *C. ovalis.*

Cymbidium

Natural habitat: Himalayas, China, Japan, Southeast Asia, and the Philippines to Australia.

Plant form: Sympodial. From tufted leafy types to those with prominent pseudobulbs and long, strap-shaped leaves. Erect to arching inflorescences, many colored flowers, mostly pastel tones, often fragrant.

Culture: 50% to 70% shade. Plant in pockets with enough room to let roots spread just under surface layer.

Climate: Subtropical and cool climates.

Species: The best rockery species for the subtrop-

Cymbidium Gladys Whitesell 'No.3', a charming plant for a cool climate rockery.

Although usually epiphytic, *Cymbidium finlaysonianum* looks imposing in rock in the Foster Botanic Garden, Hawaii.

ics are the warmth-tolerant *C. eburneum*, *C. ensifolium*, and *C. insigne*, which grow terrestrially in the wild, as well as *C. sanderae* and *C. tracyanum*. Hybrids will grow in the subtropics but flower best in cooler climates. These lovely orchids come into their own in cooler region gardens. *Cymbidium devonianum*, *C. ensifolium*, *C. erythraeum* (often listed as *C. longifolium*), *C. lowianum*, *C. sanderae*, *C. sinense*, and *C. tracyanum* do well in rockeries as do most of the thousands of hybrids available. Plant *C. devonianum* on a shady shelf or ledge where its pendulous racemes can cascade.

Dendrobium

Natural habitat: India to Samoa, Japan to New Zealand.

Plant form: Sympodial. Extremely diverse. The best species for tropical rockeries are medium to tall types with canelike pseudobulbs—the so-called hardcanes—with long, colorful sprays of twisty, curly flowers and petals like antelope horns.

Culture: 30% to 50% shade. Plant tall types in shallow, well-drained pockets or the base of a wall with gravel. Put smaller growers on the top of boulders or walls and in crevices or rock faces.

Climate: Tropical, subtropical, and cooler regions.

Species: For tropical areas, try *D. bigibbum* and its lithophytic relative *D. lithocola* (often listed as *D. bigibbum* var. *compactum*), *D. discolor*, *D. lineale*, *D. rennellii*, *D. striaenopsis*, *D. tangerinum*, and *D. tokai* together with many hardcane hybrids. In the subtropics, *D. aphrodite*, *D. bensoniae*, *D. chryseum*, *D. chrysotoxum*, *D. densiflorum*, *D. farmeri*, *D. jonesii*, *D. nobile*, *D. rex*, and *D. speciosum* all have something different and special to offer, as do four tall-growing species—*D. fimbriatum*, *D. gibsonii*, *D. moschatum*, and *D. pulchellum*. *Dendrobium bigibbum* and its variants

One of the absolute best rockery plants, especially in cool climates, is *Dendrobium kingianum*, grown beautifully at Andy's Orchids, Encinitas.

will also do well in the warmer subtropics in rockeries and on walls. An almost bewildering range of dendrobiums is available for cooler regions. It would be hard to go past lithophytic Australian species such as *Dendrobium ×delicatum*, *D. fleckeri*, *D. ×gracillimum*, *D. jonesii*, *D. kingianum*, *D. macropus* (syn. *D. gracilicaule*), *D. monophyllum*, the *D. speciosum* complex, and hundreds of hybrids now available. Four Australian species of *Dockrillia*, formerly known as dendrobiums, do well attached to large boulders or walls—*D. linguiformis*, *D. pugioniformis* (grow this shady), *D. striolata*, and *D. teretifolia*. Of the exotic species, that old standby *Dendrobium nobile* and its countless hybrids look good in small rock pockets or attached to walls.

Encyclia

Natural habitat: Florida (United States), Mexico, West Indies, Central and South America.

Plant form: Sympodial. Some lithophytic species have pseudobulbs of the characteristic flask shape, with narrow, tough leaves. Long, erect or arching inflorescences, usually branching. Fragrant flowers in many colors.

Culture: 30% to 50% shade. Plant on rocks rather than in pockets as none like waterlogged soil, and some come from almost arid climates.

Climate: Tropical, subtropical, and cool climate gardens.

Species: In tropical gardens try *Encyclia altissima* (a very dry grower, sometimes listed as *E. hodgeana*), *E. gracilis*, *E. nematocaulon* (syn. *E. xipheres*), *E. phoenicea*, *E. plicata*, and *E. selligera*. Mexico offers a number of species for subtropical rockeries, including *E. aromatica*, *E. boothiana*, *E. bractescens*, *E. cochleata*, *E. michuacana*, and *E. polybulbon*. A section of this genus has been classified now as the genus *Prosthechea*, but they will continue to be known as

Tall hardcane dendrobiums are good rockery orchids in well-drained pockets in the tropics and warm subtropics.

encyclias for some time in the trade. Several are good candidates for rockery pockets in 50% to 70% shade in cooler gardens. These include *Prosthechea baculus* (sometimes listed as *P. pentotis*), *P. brassavolae*, *P. chacaoensis*, *P. cochleata*, *P. prismatocarpa*, and *P. radiata*. *Anacheilum vespa* (syn. *Encyclia vespa*) is another good one.

Epidendrum

Natural habitat: Florida, Mexico, West Indies, Central and South America.

Plant form: Sympodial. Most species have thin, canelike stems, but some have short to medium-sized pseudobulbs. Flowers from few to many, sometimes on panicles, many colors, sometimes fragrant.

Culture: 70% shade for small, soft-leaved types to full sun for the reedstem type, also known as crucifix orchids because of the shape of their prominent labellums. The reedstem types grow well planted against a wall, the smaller ones in crevices or shelves.

Climate: Tropical, subtropical, and cooler regions.

Species: *Epidendrum cinnabarinum, E. ibaguense, E. schomburgkii*, and hybrids from them are reedstem types. A new range of shorter-growing, large-flowered reedstem hybrids is becoming available. *Epidendrum ciliare* grows like a *Cattleya* with large white butterfly-looking flowers.

Eria

Natural habitat: Himalayas, China, India, Sri Lanka, Southeast Asia, Philippines, Papua New Guinea, and Australia to Samoa.

Plant form: Sympodial. Some have round pseudobulbs on creeping rhizomes, others have tall, leafy canes. Racemes are often branching, with flowers in many colors. Erias are sometimes

Epidendrum stamfordianum produces clouds of showy flowers in warm subtropical and tropical gardens.

The Madagascan genus *Gastrorchis* contains some of the most beautiful terrestrial orchids in the world. Shown here is *G. schlecterii*.

sweetly fragrant, sometimes unpleasantly so.

Culture: 70% shade. Keep moist. Creeping types do well on shady walls and rocks.

Climate: Tropical, subtropical, and cool climates.

Species: In tropical and subtropical areas, try *Eria albido-tomentosa*, a real scrambler; *E. bractescens*; *E. floribunda*, with tall stems; *E. hyacinthoides*, sweetly fragrant; and *E. javanica*, a robust creeper. Species that grow and flower in cooler gardens, adding interest and a lot of fragrance, include *Eria barbata, E. coronaria, E. hyacinthoides, E. rhynchostyloides*, and *E. spicata* (syn. *E. convallarioides*).

Gastrorchis

Natural habitat: Madagascar.

Plant form: Sympodial. Small pseudobulbs, with tall, broad, thin, plicate leaves, upright inflorescences, and a dozen or so gorgeous flowers.

Culture: 70% or more shade. Must be protected from breezes that damage the leaves. Plant in a shady rockery, in medium-sized, well-drained pockets with leaf mold and gravel, and keep just damp.

Climate: Subtropical and cool climates.

Species: *Gastrorchis francoisii, G. humblotii, G. schlecterii, G. simulans*, and *G. tuberculosus* are available. They are worth trying in coastal climate rockeries north from at least the Illawarra region south of Sydney, coastal central to southern Florida, southern California, and their equivalents in other countries.

Laelia

Natural habitat: Mexico and Brazil.

Plant form: Sympodial. The rupicolous (rock-dwelling) types have squat to tall flask-shaped pseudobulbs, single tough leaves, and erect racemes with few to many flowers in cream, yellow to rose colors, sometimes fragrant.

Culture: 50% shade. Plant rupicolous types in small pockets or crevices or affix to walls. Keep them on the dry side in cold weather and when they are resting.

Climate: Subtropical and cool climates.

Species: For the subtropics, try *L. anceps*, especially on large boulders and walls, *L. blumenscheinii, L. cinnabarina* (a tall rupicolous type), *L. crispata, L. flava*, and *L. milleri*. *Laelia lobata* likes lots of sun, while *L. purpurata* is a large grower like a *Cattleya*.

Laelia crispata grows naturally on rock formations in the Brazilian mountains.

Laelia liliputana, another Brazilian rock dweller, established on a rock at Andy's Orchids, Encinitas.

Laelia sincorana, a Brazilian species from a high, arid area, is a lithophyte in nature and should do well on rocks and walls in cooler regions. Several of the rupicolous laelias, including *L. liliputana* and *L. reginae*, will do equally well in cooler region rockeries or on walls.

Lycaste

Natural habitat: Mexico, Central and South America.

Plant form: Sympodial. Clustered pseudobulbs with broad, thin, plicate leaves. Flowers borne singly but several per bulb, in yellows, greens, and pastels, fragrant. Some species are deciduous, others evergreen.

Culture: 50% shade for deciduous, 70% shade for evergreen. Plant in small to medium-sized pockets and large crevices or holes in walls. Let deciduous types become a bit dry in winter after they lose their leaves. Keep evergreens damp year-round. Give both types a lot of wind protection.

Climate: Cool subtropical and cooler climates.

Species: Deciduous types include *Lycaste aromatica*, *L. consobrina*, *L. cruenta*, and *L. deppei*. Evergreens include *L. macrophylla* and *L. skinneri*. Many hybrids are available which are good, vigorous growers.

Maxillaria

Natural habitat: Mexico, West Indies, Central and South America.

Plant form: Sympodial. Some grow in clusters, others ramble. Single flowers per stem but many stems per pseudobulb, sometimes fragrant.

Culture: 70% shade. Rambling types are good planted at the foot of walls or rock faces.

Climate: Subtropical and cool climates.

Species: For the subtropics, *M. houtteana*, *M. marginata*, and *M. tenuifolia* are ramblers, while *M. picta*,

Lycaste costata, which may be removed to a new genus *Ida*, is a high-elevation Andean species suited to protected rockeries in the cool subtropics.

M. porphyrostele, and *M. rufescens* are more clumping types for elevated pockets or shelves. Several species occurring naturally in montane areas in Brazil grow well in rockery pockets in cooler regions as well as in subtropical gardens. These include *M. ochroleuca*, *M. picta*, *M. porphyrostele*, *M. seidelii*, and the Central American *M. cucullata*.

Neobenthamia

Natural habitat: Tropical East Africa.

Plant form: Sympodial. Tall, leafy stems bear erect inflorescences from the top. Fragrant flowers are white, in clusters.

Culture: Will grow in full sun. A terrestrial, plant it

For floral display, it's hard to beat *Oncidium sphacelatum*.

in pockets at the base of the rockery or wall on the sunny side. Likes plenty of fertilizer when growing.
Climate: Tropical and subtropical.
Species: There is only one—*Neobenthamia gracilis*.

Oncidium

Natural habitat: Florida, Mexico, the West Indies, Central and South America.
Plant form: Sympodial. A huge genus. The lithophytes are mostly tough looking with hard pseudobulbs and leathery leaves. Inflorescences are upright to arching, sometimes branched, and the flowers range through shades of yellow and brown. Often fragrant.
Culture: 30% to 50% shade. Several grow as terrestrials in very stony ground, so plant in very well-drained pockets using stones and pebbles as a medium.
Climate: Tropical and subtropical.
Species: *Oncidium baueri, O. blanchetii, O. ensatum, O. gracile, O. floridanum, O. hydrophyllum, O. sphacelatum, O. spilopterum, O. splendidum,* and *O. warmingii.*

Phaius

Natural habitat: Africa, Himalayas, China, tropical Asia through Papua New Guinea to Australia and Fiji.
Plant form: Sympodial. Robust, sometimes elongated pseudobulbs with broad, thin, plicate leaves. Erect inflorescences with large, colorful, often fragrant flowers.
Culture: 70% shade. These are terrestrials and

Pleiones are first choices for sheltered rock gardens in temperate regions. (Courtesy Dick Cavender)

Pleione formosanum at home in an old log in Washington. (Courtesy Dick Cavender)

must be protected from breezes that could damage their luxuriant foliage. Plant in large pockets at the base on the shady side of the rockery.

Climate: Tropical and subtropical.

Species: Not many species are common in cultivation. *Phaius amboinensis*, *P. mishmensis*, and *P. tankervilliae* are available and several species from Madagascar and the Philippines are worth seeking out including *P. luteus* and *P. pulchellus*.

Pleione

Natural habitat: Himalayas, China, northern Myanmar, northern Thailand, and Taiwan.

Plant form: Sympodial. Small flask–shaped pseudobulbs with thin, plicate leaves which are deciduous. Single, large, beautiful flowers arise in spring with the new growth. Colors are mostly pastel shades to deep, rich purple, mostly fragrant.

Culture: 70% shade. In nature they grow on mossy, humus-covered rocks and trees. Duplicate this by securing them on mossy rocks, ledges, shady wall shelves, or even old, moss-covered logs and stumps. They will also grow in light, well-drained soil under evergreen trees. They do not mind natural winter rain provided the weather is cool. They are deciduous and dormant in winter.

Climate: Cool to temperate gardens.

Species: *Pleione bulbocodioides*, *P. formosana*, (the easiest), *P. limprichtii*, and *P. speciosa* are usually available along with increasing numbers of hybrids which are equally good.

Polystachya

Natural habitat: Worldwide in the tropics and subtropics.

Plant form: Sympodial. Usually small clustered pseudobulbs, erect racemes with many flowers. White, green and yellow colors predominate, often fragrant.

Culture: 50% to 70% shade. Keep moist while growing. Plant in crevices and small pockets or shelves and ledges in walls.

Climate: Tropical and subtropical.

Species: *Polystachya adansoniae*, *P. bella*, *P. maculata*, and *P. pubescens*.

Schomburgkia

Natural habitat: Mexico, the Caribbean, Central and South America.

Plant form: Sympodial. Large, tough plants. Some species have hollow pseudobulbs; others have spindle-shaped ones. Flower stems are usually very long, sometimes more than 10 feet (3 meters). Flowers are curly, shiny in shades of yellow, honey brown, pink to purple, sometimes fragrant, segments crisped or wavy.

Culture: 30% shade to full sun, ideal for well-drained rockeries and walls.

Climate: Tropical and subtropical.

Species: *Schomburgkia crispa*, *S. fimbriata*, *S. lyonsii*, *S. splendida*, *S. superbiens* (probably the best, and it will grow cool), *S. thomsoniana*, *S. tibicinis*, *S. undulata*, and hybrids especially ×*Schombocattleya*.

Sobralia

Natural habitat: Mexico, Central and South America.

Plant form: Sympodial. Clusters of tall, reedlike, leafy stems with no discernible rhizome. Flowers from stem apex sequentially, with large flowers lasting one to a few days but replaced immediately throughout the warm months. Often fragrant.

Culture: 30% shade. Plant these in large pockets at the base of rockeries and walls. Keep their very fleshy roots moist.

Climate: Tropical, subtropical, and cool climates.

Species: *Sobralia callosa* (a blue–purple miniature), *S. decora*, *S. leucoxantha*, *S. macrantha*, *S. violacea*, *S. xantholeuca*, and the hybrid *S.* Veitchii. Given good drainage and no more than 50% shade these sobralias will also grow in cooler regions. In particular, try *S. decora*, *S. macrantha*, *S. xantholeuca*, and *S.* Veitchii.

Thunia

Natural habitat: Northeastern India, Myanmar, and Thailand.

Plant form: Sympodial. Tall, leafy deciduous stems, flowers from the top, with drooping

Now in one place I found Coelogyne sanderiana *or a variety of it—flowers not seen. It was also, although growing, very much shrivelled. It grows on the tops of the highest rocks very often inaccessible even for a gnat.*

—Wilhelm Micholitz,
in a letter to F. Sander

An orchid hunter employed by the famous English orchid nursery Sander and Sons, Micholitz collected some plants of this *Coelogyne* species in Sumatra in 1891. Many orchid hunters were very secretive about where they found valuable plants and the conditions in which their finds grew. Secrecy prevented competitors from cashing in on their discoveries. When Micholitz discovered *Dendrobium sanderae* in the Philippines in 1909, Sander did not disclose its origin, or the name of its discoverer, because his movements could have been traced.

racemes and white to magenta, fragrant blooms.

Culture: 30% to 50% shade. Plant in pockets with rich leaf mold. Keep dry after leaves drop until new growth starts in spring.

Climate: Tropical, subtropical, and cooler regions.

Species: Only one species, *T. marshalliana*, is common but *T. alba*, *T. bensoniae*, and a couple of old-time hybrids are sometimes available. The members of this genus live in nature at considerable altitude in areas with monsoonal climates and they are not demanding as far as temperature goes. Feed and water them well as soon as they start to grow in spring, then taper the watering off as their leaves fall in autumn.

Zygopetalum

Natural habitat: South America.

Plant form: Sympodial. Well-defined pseudobulbs with long, very broad leaves. Erect inflorescences

Dramatic blooms on compact plants are the hallmark of intergeneric *Zygopetalum* hybrids, such as this one of *Z.* Titanic ×*Hamelwellsara* June 'Gold Dust'.

with several good–sized flowers, usually green and brown with large purple and white lips, fragrant.

Culture: 70% shade. Plant in pockets with enough room for their fleshy roots to spread out. Keep moist.

Climate: Subtropical and cool climates.

Species: *Zygopetalum crinitum* which is smaller and neat, *Z. intermedium*, *Z. mackaii*, and many hybrids, including some smaller colorful intergeneric hybrids, do equally well in subtropical and cool areas. The hybrids may be even easier to procure than the species.

3

The Terrestrials:
Growing Orchids in the Ground

The vast majority of orchids in popular cultivation are epiphytic. However, surprising numbers of genera grow as terrestrials in nature and are showy, easy-growing subjects in the garden, even in gardens that are snowbound during winter. Terrestrial orchids grow under the same range of conditions as the epiphytes and lithophytes, from exposure to full sun to deep shade on the forest floor. Some terrestrial species are wide-ranging, growing under several different sets of conditions. For instance, the widespread Asian and Pacific species *Calanthe triplicata* is found in northern New South Wales in deep shade beside rainforest streams. Within a couple of miles (kilometers) it grows well on lightly timbered, sunny, grassy, north-facing hillsides.

The Temperate Garden

This chapter includes several deciduous terrestrial genera suitable for gardens in temperate regions. These regions fall into two types. The first includes Northern Hemisphere gardens where temperatures drop below freezing and snow cover for several weeks in winter is common. The second includes gardens in Mediterranean climates, with warm to hot summers and cool, wet winters. In the Northern Hemisphere, as well as the Mediterranean region itself, central western and northwestern California, western Oregon, and western Washington have a Mediterranean climate. In the Southern Hemisphere, most of southern and southwestern Australia and southern Africa also have this type of climate.

Terrestrial orchids from these regions follow patterns of growth adapted to their particular climates. Those from areas in the Northern Hemisphere with winter snow become dormant underground during that season. As spring approaches, the orchids commence their growth season, producing leaves and flowers from spring to late summer. As autumn arrives, they start shedding their leaves in preparation for their period of winter dormancy. The layer of snow that covers them actually insulates them from extreme cold. *Calypso bulbosa*, which is found throughout the Northern Hemisphere, exemplifies an orchid that is covered by snow in winter. It grows principally in northern coniferous forests, appearing in bloom after the spring snow melt.

Terrestrial orchids from Mediterranean climates produce their vegetative growth and bloom under the influence of autumn and winter rain and mild spring weather. Many grow and flower from winter through spring then shed their leaves and retreat into underground dormancy during the hot, dry summer. Typical is the genus *Caladenia*, Australian spider or fairy orchids, with small underground tubers, dormant in summer. When rain falls in autumn, the tubers produce a leaf, followed by an inflorescence, which blooms in late winter or spring.

A considerable number of terrestrial orchids simply are not amenable to cultivation, although they grow vigorously in their natural habitats. Many have a relationship with mycorrhizal fungi in nature that is hard to replicate in the garden. As we learn more about raising different terrestrial genera from seed and thus obtain material with which to experiment, we will be able to provide in our gardens the conditions they require in nature. There are not many suppliers of deciduous terrestrial genera at present. Most countries have passed laws protecting terrestrial orchids and these cannot be collected in their natural habitats. The survival of many terrestrial genera worldwide is threatened by cultivation and development of the land, by competition with weed species, by grazing animals, and by introduced pests like the rabbit. The sooner we raise all terrestrial orchids readily from seed, the sooner we will discover that many will grow in and enhance our terrestrial garden landscapes with their unique beauty, even in the coolest climates. Programs are in place worldwide to raise many terrestrial orchids from seed.

European orchid growers have long recognized the delights of growing native terrestrial orchids in their gardens. Northern Hemisphere terrestrials may be divided loosely into three groups according to the natural conditions under which they grow. The first comprises species growing in open, sunny positions in gravelly soil. The second is made up of species growing in more shady woodlands, and the third includes those growing in boggy areas. With a little ingenuity gardeners in temperate climates, including areas subject to frost and snow, can grow representatives of each type in their gardens. Here are a few ideas to help intending growers in temperate areas to get started.

Terrestrial orchids in the first group are mostly tuberous and many appreciate alkaline soil. If your garden does not provide ideal conditions, try building a raised bed in the sunniest position possible, filling it with light, well-drained, gravelly, limed soil. Unlike many Southern Hemisphere terrestrial orchids, these Northern Hemisphere terrestrials commence their growth cycle in spring, flowering from spring through summer to autumn, then shedding their leaves and falling dormant through the cold months.

The second group, terrestrial orchids growing in shady woodlands, prefers well-drained, moist soils containing leaf mold and other organic matter. Most like neutral soil so, if you have alkaline soil in your garden, build a well-drained bed and fill it with the correct material. Ensure you line it with plenty of stony material to stop alkaline water flooding it. The best of all temperate garden orchids, the cypripediums or lady slippers, thrive in shady woodland situations as do *Calanthe* species from temperate climates.

The third group, which prefers boggy conditions, includes some *Cypripedium* species, the European *Dactylorhiza majalis*, and the American *Epipactis gigantea*. Not many gardens have natural boggy areas. However, ingenious American orchid growers have built their own bogs by digging out an area to a depth of about one foot (30 centimeters), lining it with impervious material such as black plastic sheeting, filling it with water, then heaping rich, open soil on top. Orchids planted in the soil can send their roots down to the constant moisture while their leaves and flowers reach for the full sun above.

Most Southern Hemisphere terrestrials are too tender for frosty, snowy climates as they commence growing in autumn and winter, flowering in late winter and spring, then falling dormant during the hot, dry summer months. Coming from climates with warm to hot summers and cool, wet winters, Southern Hemisphere terrestrials grow well in Mediterranean climates. Finding a suitable soil type can be a matter of some trial and error. In the first instance, research each species you wish to grow, finding out its habitat, local climate, and the type of soil in which it grows. This gives you some understanding of the conditions you should attempt to duplicate. For instance, in the Australian genus *Thelymitra*, the blue-flowered *T. nuda*, although widespread, grows in colonies in heathlands in well-drained sandy loam. It flowers in spring after autumn rains following a warm, dry summer. Yet, *T. cyanea*, from southeastern Australia and New Zealand, grows in sphagnum moss colonies and wet peat bogs at considerable altitude where it remains damp year-round.

Gardeners wishing to try temperate Australian terrestrial orchids could start with a soil mixture in the garden bed containing sandy loam, coarse sand, and leaf mold in approximately equal proportions. Leaf mold obtained beneath *Eucalyptus* and *Casuarina* species is the best as it is likely to contain mycorrhiza necessary for the health of terrestrial orchids. Surface the bed with a mulch of either pine or casuarina needles. Temperate Australian terrestrial species grow from small tubers. Your supplier will send tubers in the dormant season. Plant them while they are still dormant, at a depth of no more than 1 to 1.5 inches (about 3 centimeters). Water them in, then wait for your region's autumn rains to spur them into growth. The growth cycle of deciduous Australian terrestrials

I want to show you a little of the country around Miraflores. There are no valleys here to any extent, mostly high hills, with depressions between, also narrow openings along the streams. There are also a number of treeless hills covered with grass. On some of these I saw some of the most beautiful sights. The entire hills from foot to summit were literally covered with Sobralia violacea *in full bloom, in all shades from pure white to dark lavender. The best time to see this show was in early morning, before the sun became too strong; with the night dew still lingering on the foliage and with the galaxy of colors on such a large scale, the sun finally rose higher and higher reflecting the colors in a way impossible for me to describe. Towards midday thousands of flowers began to drop off. This continued throughout the day, but early the next morning there was a new display. At the foot of these hills where the soil was rich and the plants partly shaded by trees they attained 5 to 6 feet [1.6–2 meters] in height. In ascending the hills the plants gradually diminished in height, until at the top they were only a few inches high. There was no difference however in the size of the flowers.*

—John E. Lager, *Orchid Review*

An American nurseryman and orchid hunter, Lager addressed the Massachusetts Horticultural Society in 1907 about his time collecting orchids in South America and Panama late in the nineteenth century.

consists of six to eight months growing from autumn to spring followed by four to six months dormancy in hot, dry late spring and summer.

Try to avoid exposing your terrestrials to warm, wet, humid conditions during their dormant period because this can rot the tubers. In subtropical regions you may need to put up a rain shelter to keep the bed dry during summer. Fertilize Australian terrestrials sparingly and avoid phosphates, which are naturally deficient in Australian soils. Organic foods such as bloodmeal and bonemeal are suitable if used lightly. Sprinkle your dormant terrestrials every week to ten days during warm, dry summer weather to ensure the tubers don't desiccate while they are resting. Ensure grasses and other groundcover plants do not compete with or smother your terrestrials.

Probably the best Australian genera to start in your Mediterranean orchid garden are *Diuris*, especially hybrids, *Lyperanthus*, and *Pterostylis*, again with vigorous free-flowering hybrids. It is a myth that the beautiful blue sun orchids in the genus *Thelymitra* need sunshine to open. They do close at night but open the next day when the temperature rises above 70°F (20°C). Some beautiful *Thelymitra* hybrids are becoming available. Enjoy experimenting with terrestrial orchids in your temperate garden and do not hesitate to ask your supplier for specific cultural advice about the genera that you wish to try.

The Garden Bed

In Southeast Asia and in Hawaii, huge cut-flower industries are based on orchids growing in the ground in garden beds. The orchids grow wonderfully and look spectacular in full flower. The most casual nonorchid-grower cannot help but be amazed at the beds of orchids in Singapore Botanic Gardens. These beds are specially pre-pared and the orchids are regimented in neat rows with stakes for ease of handling. Imagine how orchids suitable for your conditions would look growing naturally in feature beds in your garden. The term *garden bed* covers any area for terrestrial orchid planting. This could be a classic, large, rectangular bed extending for many feet (meters), or a small area prepared specially for perhaps just one plant.

Whatever the size of your garden bed, a northeastern aspect in the garden is the best in the Southern Hemisphere, a southeastern aspect in the Northern Hemisphere. If you intend to grow a range of terrestrial orchids, then the garden bed (or beds) will need a range of sunlight from about 30% to full sun all day long. Usually, it is easy to modify the garden surrounds to provide orchids in garden beds with the optimum conditions. Modifications might include planting sheltering shrubs, trees, and windbreaks or constructing rockeries or walls. You can erect temporary windbreaks of shadecloth or lattice screens until windbreak plants are tall and thick enough to be effective. Container-grown trees or shrubs can provide shade for orchids. Palms in containers are particularly useful as their leafy crowns can shade the garden bed during the hottest hours. Move the containers to provide different angles and areas of shade according to the season. Perhaps you could incorporate a pond or water feature already in the garden in the orchid bed design. Ponds have their own microclimates that terrestrial orchids relish.

Generally, orchids are comfortable in the temperature ranges and humidity levels that are comfortable for humans. Orchids, like humans, cannot tolerate "wet feet." This means simply that, wherever they grow, orchids must have good drainage so that their roots do not sit in water. When plan-

Dendrobium tarberi, like other orchids, can refresh even the plainest-looking garden bed. (Courtesy Mary Pollard)

An effective massed planting of *Dendrobium stratiotes* in a well-drained, raised garden bed.

Phaiocalanthe Charlie Klehm grows in the American Orchid Society garden where it is protected from winds that would shred its broad, thin leaves.

The leaves of *Phaiocalanthe* Kryptonite require protection from hot sun and strong winds.

ning a garden bed for orchids it is essential to site it properly in the garden. Do not build your garden bed at the foot of a slope where all drainage from the slope will gather. Orchid garden beds built across slopes will drain satisfactorily. Construct them as terraces—the steeper the slope, the better they will drain.

Constructing a garden bed for terrestrial orchids is straightforward. It can be any shape pleasing to your eye. Use the hose to try layouts of free-form outlines until you find a suitable one. Dig the bed out to a depth of at least 6 inches (15 centimeters). Replace the soil with inert drainage material such as broken bricks and stones. This material will not break down to cause drainage problems. If the bed is in a lawn, place edging round it to exclude grass. This saves much hard work removing grass from the bed in the future. Add enough planting medium to raise the level of the bed at least 6 inches (15 centimeters) above

Fragile-looking *Ludisia discolor* var. *dawsoniana* is at home in a shady subtropical setting.

A tropical and subtropical species, *Eulophia pulchra* needs a little shelter from hot sun and leaf-shredding wind in the garden.

the surrounding ground level, ensuring good drainage and air circulation. Use a mixture of say 40% leaf mold, 40% light, fluffy peat moss (not caked as it sometimes is supplied), and 20% coarse sand as a planting medium. This provides an open, well-drained, long-lasting, easy-to-use medium. Add food, both organic and inorganic, as you plant the orchids. In the more tropical, high rainfall regions, use more drainage material and less planting material. In Hawaii many nurseries use raised beds of pumice for ground plantings of cut-flower orchids. If you need to support some of the orchids to be planted, insert stakes in the bed before adding the planting medium. Use substantial, long-lasting hardwood or metal stakes or solid fiberglass rods. You can paint them a natural color to blend with the garden. Hammer them in firmly.

These principles apply also to the construction of large pockets at the lower levels of rockeries. Large-growing orchids such as cymbidiums and sobralias are very effective planted at these lower levels. Their sheer bulk and solidity help to tie the rockery into the ground and the surrounding garden. Cymbidiums and zygopetalums, both of which are good for garden-bed planting, have thick, branching, somewhat loose roots. They tend to spread their roots out just below the surface of the planting medium. Sobralias have thick, dense, brittle roots. The plants grow in quite a compact manner. I grew *Sobralia macrantha* in the same terracotta tub for twenty years without repotting. Rockery pockets for sobralias need to be deeper but not much wider than the rootball of the plant and their roots do not spread out to the same extent as cymbidiums in the garden bed.

Planting Terrestrial Orchids in the Garden Bed

Remove any container-grown orchid from its container. This is your last chance to clean the plant by trimming old, dead roots, stems, or bulbs before planting. Check that it has no pests and treat any you may find. When preparing cymbidiums for planting, be rigorous in removing all old roots and leafless bulbs. These take up precious space and hinder drainage as they break down to form a soggy mass. Cymbidiums produce roots freely, so err on the side of removing too many rather than too few. If necessary, split the cymbidium into two or more plants to clean it properly. You can plant the pieces together. Ensure the new leads face outwards to obtain a symmetrical specimen as it grows. Prior to planting, clean any dead leaf husks from the older bulbs. They can provide a hiding place for insect pests.

It is vital that the newly planted terrestrial cannot move and damage its new roots. You can achieve this in a couple of ways. If the orchid is monopodial, it will grow quite tall; hence, the need for the stakes referred to earlier. A word of caution here—many monopodial orchids will not flower unless their top sections are free to wave around in the breeze. Keep the stake quite short. You can always topcut any monopodial that grows too tall. It will throw one or more side-shoots, and you can replant the topcut.

Use materials such as raffia, garden twine, or plastic-covered wire to tie monopodial orchids to stakes. Use several ties, depending on the height of the plant. The aim is to keep the main part of the stem immobile so that it can produce new roots to establish itself in the bed. The top 4 or 5 inches (10 or 12 centimeters) of stem can remain unsecured, as the flower stems will come from this section.

Questions to ask when planning a garden bed for terrestrial orchids:

- Will the bed be well drained in that site?
- Does the bed provide the right amount of shade and sun for the orchids you wish to grow?
- Will the bed look attractive in the garden landscape?
- Can you make the bed bigger if you want to try more orchids in it?
- Can you reach plants in the bed easily with the hose?
- Is the bed protected from the worst winds?

Plant the base of the monopodial orchid 3 or 4 inches (8 or 10 centimeters) deep in the planting medium. Cover any roots that reach that depth with the planting medium. Monopodial roots growing into the planting medium become the main feeding roots. Those which cling to the stake or wall are primarily the means of attachment, although they are capable of supplying food and water to the orchid. Roots issuing from monopodial stems are sometimes called aerial roots.

Secure tall-growing sympodial terrestrials by tying them to stakes also. Such orchids include *Arundina, Epidendrum, Neobenthamia, Oerstedella, Sobralia,* and similar tall-caned types. You can remove stakes once these orchids are securely established in the bed. Shorter-growing orchids to be grown terrestrially include *Calanthe, Cymbidium, Gastrorchis, Phaius, Spathoglottis,* and *Zygopetalum.* You can hold these types firmly in garden beds by placing rocks judiciously around the plant. If necessary, remove the rocks when the plant establishes, or leave them as an embellishment. As well as trapping moisture on their lower surfaces, rocks

Reedstem epidendrums enjoy full sun which helps to keep them compact in size and encourages year-round blooming.

A vigorous, medium-sized hybrid, *Oerstedella* Lumita makes a showy display in cool and subtropical climates.

This massed planting of mokaras has been well prepared.

retain the sun's warmth, which can be beneficial to terrestrial orchids. However, ensure that rocks used for support are not placed in full sun where they will reflect heat and burn the broad-but-thin-leafed genera.

To plant the lower-growing types, simply scoop out several handfuls of planting medium, make a low mound in the hole, and place the orchid on the mound with its roots spread. Then re-place and firm the medium so that the bases of the orchid's pseudobulbs are just below the surface. After planting, water the planting medium to settle it in round the orchid's roots.

Companion Planting for the Terrestrials

While many terrestrial orchids grow with grasses in nature, gardeners generally keep grasses out of orchid garden beds. It is extremely difficult to eliminate stoloniferous grasses such as couch (*Cynodon dactylon*) and kikuyu (*Pennisetum clandestinum*) once they become established, so keep them out in the first place. Many gardeners use shrubs as companion plants for terrestrial orchids. If you select shrubs carefully, they can provide shelter from sun and wind as well as a favorable microclimate for the orchids you plant. If you need shrubs to provide dense shade and wind protection, then choose densely leafed types. Shrubs as companions for sun-loving terrestrial orchids may be more sparsely leafed. Select types that prefer similar planting material to the terrestrial orchids, that

This *Billbergia* hybrid and other bromeliads make good contrasts with orchids in garden beds.

If you use the right companion plants, such as pineapple (*Ananas comosus* tricolor form), you can even eat their fruit.

Orchids in garden beds flourish with companions such as ferns and palms, which help create the right microclimate.

being slightly acid rather than alkaline. Consider whether you wish the companion plants or the orchids to have more emphasis in your landscape. Will shrubs with very colorful leaves, such as croton (*Codiaeum variegatum*), detract from terrestrial orchids nearby? Do you want a flowering shrub to compete for attention with orchid blooms in the same bed?

Some plants are so voracious that they put the survival of terrestrial orchids sharing their space at risk. Once I made the mistake of planting a *Zygopetalum* in a pocket in a rockery dominated by a large traveler's palm (*Ravenala* species). The orchid grew very well but after about six months the palm's roots totally invaded its rock pocket. They forced the poor *Zygopetalum* up out of the ground so it was growing "on stilts." I had to remove the orchid and give the traveler's palm the bed. Be mindful of the growth characteristics of companion plants in your landscape. Choose companions that will not send invasive roots to compete with your terrestrial orchids.

Ferns, including tree ferns, are good companion plants in the shady garden beds or rockery

Brownea coccinea, a subtropical large shrub, could provide shade and shelter for more delicate orchids in the garden.

Bromeliads provide humidity for orchids growing nearby.

pockets. Their foliage complements orchid blooms. Bromeliads are also excellent companions for terrestrial orchid plantings. Many of the tougher bromeliad species live naturally in poor, stony soil in full sun. They flourish with the sun-loving terrestrial orchids. Bromeliads planted as terrestrials assist in providing a beneficial microclimate for the terrestrial orchids. Some gardeners include members of the cactus family with terrestrial orchid plantings. The large-growing organ-

pipe cactus (*Pachycereus marginatus*) and tall euphorbias provide different plant forms that can complement orchids growing in garden beds.

Aftercare for Terrestrial Orchids

Most terrestrial monopodial orchids and a few of the tall-caned sympodial types such as *Arundina* and reed-stemmed epidendrums prefer from very bright light to full sunlight. Ensure they are not shaded by overhanging trees or shrubs. These types need maximum exposure to the sun to flower well. Check throughout the year, and when necessary prune trees which would shade them. Orchids that like bright light but prefer not to grow in full sunlight include *Bletilla, Cymbidium, Oerstedella, Peristeria,* and *Sobralia*. Monitor the growth of shade trees and shrubs to ensure these genera receive their light requirements throughout the year. Terrestrial orchids preferring shade to sunlight include *Calanthe, Gastrorchis, Phaius,* and *Spathoglottis* although the latter will accept full sun if acclimatized. Give these orchids heavy wind protection and 70% shade, particularly during the warmer months and the warmer daylight hours.

The terrestrial orchids requiring the most water are the monopodials growing in full sun. The sun's warmth dries them out quite rapidly. They grow under more exposure to the elements than the other terrestrials, so rapid air circulation also dries them. Most produce roots along the length of their stems. Many of these roots dangle free in the air. Monopodial orchids' aerial roots collect both water and food. The quicker such roots dry out the more often you can water them and the more you water them, the quicker they will grow and flower. So when watering your terrestrial monopodials, make sure you spray their stems and aerial roots thoroughly. Orchid roots take up fine droplets more readily than a heavy flow. Water them with fine droplets and you will see the aerial roots change color from white or gray to greenish brown as they take up the water. You can use fixed sprinkler systems giving a fine spray to water large plantings of monopodial orchids effectively. For smaller areas, all you need may be a sprinkler attached to the hose.

The root masses of terrestrial orchids will stay damp for longer than those of their epiphytic or lithophytic relatives because they are covered by the planting medium and so are less exposed to the drying effect of sun and breezes. Most evergreen terrestrial orchids prefer to have their roots just damp most of the time. The frequency with which you water varies from site to site and from garden to garden. Water frequency depends on the drainage, exposure to light, and air circulation peculiar to each site in each garden. Rely on your own observation in determining whether to water your terrestrial orchids. Be prepared to poke your fingers under the planting surface to see if the lower stratum where the orchid's roots grow is still moist. Terrestrial orchids do not like waterlogged soil but neither will they benefit from drought conditions.

Air circulation for terrestrial orchids in garden landscapes is seldom a problem. It is, however, important to watch that the shade-lovers are not so crowded and closely planted that air circulation is stilled. Very few orchids grow in nature where there is no air movement. Make sure you protect those types with broad, ribbed, thin, folded leaves from wind damage without cutting all air movement down to dangerously low levels. You have achieved the right level of air movement and protection for these types if their leaves just wave and nod in a stiff breeze.

I love the little controversy regarding "manures for orchids" and I can heartily support your Singapore correspondent with regard to the value of cow manure for vandas and that class of what I call semiterrestrial orchids; whether it is better used wet or dry I cannot venture an opinion. It is very difficult to get our laborers to handle it wet, so I take the line of least resistance and use it dry.

—From a letter written to the *Orchid Review* by a correspondent from Jamaica in the far-off days of 1935. The grandchildren of those "laborers" are probably now the champion orchid growers of Jamaica.

Terrestrials obtain their food in much the same way and from the same sources as do epiphytes and lithophytes. These sources comprise decaying vegetable and animal matter as well as elements and minerals leached from the surrounding vegetation and from the stratum of soil round the orchid's roots. You can use both soluble and insoluble fertilizers, organic and inorganic, for terrestrials. Add top dressings and light mulches of humusrich vegetable matter such as straw or spent mushroom compost and manure to the orchid bed. These organic fertilizers simulate the constant supply of decaying vegetable matter the orchid would have in nature. Top dressings and mulches also serve to keep down weeds, which compete with the orchids for food, water, and light.

Inorganic, slow-release fertilizer in pellet form is suitable for terrestrial orchids. Some such pellets can break open if exposed to direct sunlight, spilling all their contents at once. This can damage orchid roots, but you can overcome the danger simply by sprinkling a light covering of planting material or mulch over the pellets to protect them from sunlight. Feed terrestrial orchids while they are growing. Cut down or stop feeding if their growth slows down, usually in winter. Residual food will remain in the terrestrial bed so do not overfeed. Ensure you feed lightly. Do not feed the deciduous types while they are dormant. They can't use it, so save your money.

A Selection of Terrestrial Orchids

Select only terrestrial orchids suitable for your particular climate. The Himalayan species of *Cymbidium* are unlikely to thrive in the warm tropical lowlands. Tropical species such as *Arundina graminifolia* and *Papilionanthe* (formerly *Vanda*) *hookeriana* are unlikely to thrive outdoors in a cool garden at, say, latitude 35 degrees north or south. Many monopodial species and hybrids grow brilliantly as terrestrials in 70% to full sunlight in tropical and subtropical regions. Most monopodial hybrids flower year-round. These are eminently suited to a feature bed in a position where a bright display is desired.

Arundina graminifolia, epidendrums and their numerous reedstem hybrids, *Neobenthamia gracilis*, some *Oerstedella* species, and the sobralias are tall-stemmed sympodial, terrestrial orchids. They provide a bridge in plant form between the monopodial genera and the more bulbous, broader-leafed sympodial genera. Several terrestrial genera have particular vegetative characteristics to assist us in determining how and where to grow them. These include *Calanthe*, *Gastrorchis*, *Peristeria*, and *Phaius*, all of which have large, prominently ribbed, thin, plicate leaves. A glance at these leaves will tell us that they cannot stand strong breezes which would shake, twist, and split the leaves, shredding them to the orchid's lasting detriment. These leaves can take quite bright light, but full sunlight would burn them. It is mandatory that you protect orchids with this leaf type from any strong breeze in the garden bed. If you cannot give them sufficient shelter, do not plant them. Other terrestrial orchids are suitable for breezy conditions.

A wonderful species which is well worth trying as a terrestrial in a particularly well-drained, raised bed in tropical regions is *Grammatophyllum speciosum*. This species has earned the sobriquet of the world's largest orchid, so it requires plenty of space. It likes bright light and will gradually become conditioned to full sun, although it should have some shade in the middle of the day.

Cymbidiums come into their own for terrestrial plantings in the cooler regions. The hybrids with miniature- and intermediate-sized flowers are good, particularly as fillers in raised beds, but the stately, standard-sized cymbidiums can look ma-

---

If the world's largest orchid in terms of mass is *Grammatophyllum speciosum*, the claim to being the world's tallest orchid used to be made for a somewhat obscure slipper orchid from Panama called *Selenipedium chica*. Its stems grow some 16 feet (5 meters) in height. However, the discovery of a *Sobralia altissima* in a Peruvian cloud forest early in 1999 has put an end to the slipper's claim. Discoverers of the new species say that when it grows in the sun, its stems reach 16 feet (5 meters) but in shadier conditions they grow to at least 26 feet (8 meters). One stem measured nearly 44.5 feet [13.5 meters] at 44 feet [13 meters] tall! This treasure has massive rose-pink, white-lipped flowers lasting for two weeks. Isn't it wonderful that one of the world's wild places has kept such a huge treasure secret until the end of the twentieth century? How can we let such wild places be destroyed when they contain undescribed and unknown orchids?

jestic in cooler region gardens. In the 1950s, the then-largest commercial orchid nursery in Australia grew thousands of cymbidiums in prepared beds of natural "bush" sand, peat moss, and sheep manure at Dee Why, north of Sydney. The plants grew and flowered superbly in these beds, proving the cymbidium's worth as a premier landscaping orchid. Cymbidiums will grow and flower best in the garden bed in about 50% sunlight. They will certainly take more sun but will look yellow and a little stressed in summer heat. Less than 50% sunlight will make them deeper green with longer, lusher leaves. They will bloom in shady conditions but not so profusely as they do in 50% sunlight.

More orchids from areas such as the Papua New Guinea highlands and the Andes of South America are becoming available, raised from seed. These include new species of *Calanthe*, *Spathoglottis*, and terrestrial *Lycaste* species (some of which may be placed in a new genus, *Ida*), all from considerable altitude. Many such orchids will be suitable for garden planting in the cooler regions but none have been in cultivation for long enough to allow experimentation. Once we understand the climate and conditions they live in naturally, they will succeed in our garden landscapes.

Arachnis

Natural habitat: Himalayas through Southeast Asia to the Solomon Islands.
Plant form: Monopodial. Very stout, erect stems with short, stiff leaves. Arching racemes, often branched with many bizarre, scorpion-shaped fragrant flowers in yellow, red, and purple.
Culture: Full sun. Attach to stakes leaving the top 5 inches (12 centimeters) free. Water and fertilize freely.
Climate: Tropical and warm subtropical.
Species: Tropical species include *Arachnis flos-aëris* (syn. *A. moschifera*), *A. hookeriana*, and the natural

hybrid *A. ×maingayi*. There are many intergeneric hybrids, with ×*Aranda*, ×*Aranthera*, ×*Ascorachnis*, ×*Chuanyenara*, ×*Mokara*, ×*Renanda*, ×*Trevorara*, and ×*Vandachnis* being some of the best for garden beds. Suitable for the warm areas of the subtropics are *Arachnis flos-aëris*, *A. hookeriana*, *A. ×maingayi* and the hybrid genera such as ×*Aranda*, ×*Aranthera*, ×*Ascorachnis*, and ×*Mokara*. Keep garden beds sheltered from biting cold winter winds. Other *Arachnis* species are worth trying in full sun.

Arundina

Natural habitat: Himalayas and southern China through Southeast Asia. Naturalized in many tropical areas such as Hawaii.
Plant form: Sympodial. Thin, canelike, leafy stems to 6 feet (nearly 2 meters) tall, successive *Cattleya*-like white pale rose, fragrant flowers.
Culture: Full sun, plenty of water and fertilizer. Tie to a stake until plants become established. Ease off on watering if winters are cold.
Climate: Tropical and subtropical.
Species: Just the one, *Arundina graminifolia* (syn. *A. bambusifolia*).

Arundina graminifolia is virtually ever blooming in the tropics.

Bletilla

Natural habitat: China and Japan.

Plant form: Sympodial. Flattened, cormlike pseudobulbs with very broad, plicate, deciduous leaves. Erect inflorescences from the center of new growth, with several good-sized white to rose flowers. A very attractive orchid.

Culture: 50% shade in warm regions but needs full sun to bloom in temperate gardens. Extremely hardy. Plant pseudobulbs just under the surface and mulch with straw or leaf mold—they are then impervious to frost and snow. Keep moist while growing, but drier when the foliage falls. Put a stake in the bed so you know where they are and won't disturb them in the winter when they are underground.

Climate: Cool to temperate.

Species: Only one species is commonly cultivated, *Bletilla striata* (syn. *Bletilla hyacinthina*), sometimes called the Chinese ground orchid. A couple of other species and a couple of hybrids are becoming more available and all are worth trying.

Caladenia

Natural habitat: Southern Australia with a few species in New Zealand.

Plant form: Single, usually hairy leaf arising from a small, round tuber. Flower stem from a few to 24 inches (about 60 centimeters) tall. Some species have single flowers; some bear several per stem. Colors range from white through pastels to strong pink and even blue in the smaller-flowered types. The large-flowered types with spidery flowers are often in the yellowish green, red, and brown tones.

Culture: Not all are amenable to cultivation. They

A large-flowered showy *Caladenia* Fairy Princess, for climates with dry summers and wet winters. (Courtesy Les Nesbitt)

A wonderful hardy orchid for temperate and cool climate gardens is *Bletilla striata*. (Courtesy Dick Cavender)

do better in dry climates than in regions with high humidity. Well-drained sandy loams are the best starting point in garden beds. In dry climates, water in autumn and keep moist through winter. Because the leaves die back after flowering, dry the bed but sprinkle it occasionally through hot dry summers.
Climate: Cool, temperate Mediterranean climates.
Species: Of the small but well-colored types, *C. carnea*, which is quite variable, *C. catenata, C. flava, C. latifolia*, and *C. menziesii* are the easiest. Try *C. dilatata* and *C. tentaculata* from the large-flowered section.

Calanthe

Natural habitat: South Africa, India, China, Japan through Southeast Asia, Philippines, Papua New Guinea, and Australia to Tahiti.
Plant form: Sympodial. Small to prominent pseudobulbs with large, broad, thin, plicate leaves. Erect to arching inflorescences, with flowers in most colors and with intricate lips. Species with big bulbs are deciduous. The evergreen species are more suitable for garden culture.
Culture: 50% shade for deciduous, 70% shade for evergreens. All must be protected from the wind. Keep evergreens in tropical and subtropical regions moist year-round. Allow deciduous types to become dry in winter after their leaves fall. Do not water evergreens in winter in temperate regions as winter precipitation will take care of their needs. If deciduous types become overgrown and untidy, lift them in late winter, clean them up, separate the bulbs, trim all roots, and replant.
Climate: Tropical, subtropical, cool, and temperate regions.
Species: Evergreens for the tropics and subtropics include *Calanthe ceciliae, C. madagascariensis, C. pulchra, C. sylvatica*, and *C. triplicata*. Suitable deciduous

species are *C. cardioglossa, C. rosea, C. rubens, C. vestita*, and many colorful hybrids. Several species live at considerable altitude in the Himalayas, the Philippines, and Papua New Guinea. Other evergreen species come from temperate climates in China and Japan, including *C. brevicornu, C. caudatilabella, C. discolor, C. fimbriata, C. hizen, C. masuca, C. sieboldii* (syn. *C. striata*), *C. tricarinata*, and a number of cool to temperate growing hybrids, many emanating from Japanese hybridists. In temperate regions

Cool-growing *Calanthe hizen* is another temperate climate orchid. (Courtesy Dick Cavender)

Calanthe fimbriata thrives outdoors in Red's Hardy Orchids in Oregon. (Courtesy Dick Cavender)

One of the subtropical deciduous species, *Calanthe vestita* Kalimantan form.

Growing terrestrially in nature, *Cymbidium insigne* is a showy orchid for garden beds.

Cymbidium insigne var. *album* compliments its pastel-colored relation.

keep these drier during winter. *Calanthe tricarinata* and *C. reflexa* are reported to have survived 22°F (–5°C) in the garden without damage.

Cymbidium

Natural habitat: Himalayas, China, Japan, Southeast Asia, and the Philippines to Australia.

Plant form: Sympodial. From tufted leafy types to those with prominent pseudobulbs and long, strap-shaped leaves. Erect to arching inflorescences, many-colored flowers, mostly pastel tones, often fragrant. Plant sizes range from miniatures through intermediates to very large standards, some with 5-foot (1.5-meter) stems, long, flowing, sword-shaped leaves, and large pseudobulbs.

Cymbidium sinense is another terrestrial species for cool to subtropical gardens.

Attractive *Cynorkis purpurea* contrasts neatly with larger orchids.

Culture: 50% shade. Keep them moist year-round, easing off watering in winter when it turns cold. Fertilize regularly. Cymbidiums in beds respond well to organic fertilizers.

Climate: Cool climates.

Species: Cymbidiums make wonderful, showy specimens for garden beds in the cooler regions. Species from which hybrids have been bred include the miniatures *C. devonianum*, *C. ensifolium*, *C. floribundum* (syn. *C. pumilum*), and *C. sinense*. Larger plants well worth growing include *C. hookerianum* (syn. *C. grandiflorum*) in cool montane areas, *C. insigne*, *C. lowianum* with very long, arching sprays of green red-lipped blooms, *C. sanderae*, and *C. tracyanum*. *Cymbidium goeringii*, a Chinese terrestrial species, is reputed to be the coolest grower, even surviving temperatures below freezing. It may be worth trying in the temperate garden.

Cypripedium

Natural habitat: North America, Mexico, Europe, and the temperate regions of Asia.

Plant form: Sympodial. Creeping rhizomes and stems with soft, spreading leaves, deciduous in winter. Usually single flowered, with a large, colorful slipper-shaped labellum.

Culture: Woodland orchids. Grow in very shady, peaty, loamy garden beds. Some species appreciate slightly acidic soils and some like a little lime. Your supplier can tell you each species' requirements.

A temperate garden special—*Cypripedium formosanum.*
(Courtesy Dick Cavender)

Dactylorhiza growing in the ground. (Courtesy Dick Cavender)

Dendrobium lancifolium grows terrestrially in peaty swamps in
Southeast Asia. Keep it moist but well drained in the subtropics.

Climate: Cool and temperate (the northern United
States and Europe).

Species: *Cypripedium acaule* (the moccasin flower),
*C. arietinum, C. calceolus, C. californicum, C. formosanum,
C. japonicum, C. macranthum, C. montanum, C. parviflo-
rum,* and *C. reginae.* A few hybrids are available.

Dactylorhiza

Natural habitat: Europe, temperate Asia to North
America.

Plant form: Fleshy tuberous roots give rise to tall
leafy stems bearing densely flowered inflorescences in spring and summer.

Culture: Most species grow naturally in wet areas
and will establish in moist sunny garden beds in
soil containing leaf mold, sand, and peat. Plant
and keep the bed drier in winter when the plants
are dormant.

Climate: Cool temperate.

Species: *Dactylorhiza aristata, D. elata, D. foliosa, D.
fuchsii, D. majalis, D. praetermissa, D. purpurea,* and a
number of hybrids. Check each species' specific
requirements with your supplier.

Dendrobium

Natural habitat: India to Samoa, Japan to New
Zealand.

Plant form: Sympodial. Extremely diverse.

Culture: 30% shade to full sun. Although this genus
is predominantly epiphytic, the hardcane antelope-
flowered types grow well in well-drained garden
beds. Plant in plenty of broken brick, stones, and
inert material to ensure good drainage. Topdress
with a thin layer of leaf mold. Fertilize with organic
materials. Stake firmly until plants are established.

Climate: Tropical.

Species: Try tall-growing species such as *D. conan-
thum, D. discolor, D. gouldii, D. helix, D. lineale, D. streb-
loceras, D. taurinum,* and *D. violaceoflavens*–a true giant

reaching at least 13 feet (4 meters) in height. There are many antelope-flowered hybrids in many different colors, most of which are almost ever blooming in the tropics. *Dendrobium lancifolium* is a true terrestrial species from Indonesian forests, watercourses, and lakesides.

Diuris

Natural habitat: Southern Australia.

Plant form: Several grassy leaves arise from a fleshy tuber. Flower stems to 20 inches (50 centimeters) tall, bearing several showy flowers. The broad, upright petals and pairs of thin, extended lateral sepals give the genus its common names of donkey orchids and doubletails.

Culture: As for *Caladenia*, but using about 30% by volume leaf mold in the bed.

Climate: Mediterranean climates. Several species will grow in the subtropics in areas of low humidity and winter rainfall.

Species: *Diuris alba, D. aurea, D. corymbosa, D. cuneata, D. maculata, D. punctata,* and *D. sulphurea* should be good species with which to start.

Epidendrum

Natural habitat: Florida, Mexico, the West Indies, Central and South America.

Plant form: Sympodial. Although forms are diverse, those recommended for garden beds are thin, tall, reedstem types commonly called crucifix orchids because of the shape of their prominent labellums. Flower stems arise from the apex of each growth, flowering sequentially over a long period with a good number of flowers open together. Flowers are multicolored, occasionally fragrant.

Culture: Full sun. They will grow and flower in shade but become long, lanky, and sprawling. Sunlight keeps them stocky. Fertilize regularly as they seem to grow all year in the garden. Cut

Modern reedstem epidendrum hybrids such as *Epidendrum* Ididit × *E. schomburgkii* exhibit different colors and forms.

Compact reedstem epidendrums are great garden-bed plants.

More large-flowered compact reedstem epidendrums.

Red *Epidendrum* hybrid.

flowers leaving a few nodes on the old stem as these usually produce another flower stem.

Climate: Tropical, subtropical, and cooler regions.

Species: Species suitable for all climates include *E. cinnabarinum, E. evectum, E. ibaguense, E. schomburgkii,* and many hybrids. Provided they have full sun, the reedstem crucifix orchids will grow well in garden beds in cooler regions. Select the rainbow-colored hybrids in flower if possible, so you can see what you are getting.

Epipactis

Natural habitat: Northwestern America south to northern Mexico, Europe, and the temperate regions of Asia.

Plant form: Sympodial. Short rhizomes with thick, fleshy roots, leafy stems to more than 3 feet (one

Epipactis gigantea grows in wet areas. (Courtesy Dick Cavender)

meter) tall carrying about 15 showy flowers which last well. Flowering season is from spring to autumn.

Culture: Woodland plants that enjoy damp but well-drained conditions in neutral soil with a lot of organic material. Often found beside streams. Dappled light allowing about 70% shade suits them well. Plant in raised beds to obtain optimum drainage and soil content. Cover bed with mulch in winter for some protection against freezing conditions.

Climate: Cool, temperate, the northern United States, and Europe.

Species: *Epipactis gigantea* (the best), *E. helleborine*, *E. palustris*, and *E. royleana*.

Himantoglossum

Natural habitat: Europe and Asia Minor.

Plant form: Stems to more than 3 feet (one meter) tall arising from a pair of tubers. Inflorescence from the stem apex, to about 12 inches (30 centimeters) tall, densely flowered, the lizard-shaped individual flowers to more than 2 inches (5 centimeters) long. Flowering season is spring to summer.

Culture: As for *Orchis* in sunny well-drained garden beds of gravelly soil. Keep dry when dormant.

Climate: Cool, temperate.

Species: *Himantoglossum hircinum*, the common name of which is lizard orchid, and *H. longibracteatum*.

Lyperanthus

Natural habitat: Coastal southeast and southwest Australia.

Plant form: Flower stem and leaves arise from very large subsoil tubers. Several reddish to brown, fragrant flowers to 2 inches (5 centimeters) in diameter.

Culture: As for *Caladenia* with plenty of sand in the soil mix. Will take semishade.

Climate: Cool temperate.

A showy plant for temperate gardens is lizard orchid, *Himantoglossum hircinum*. (Courtesy Richard Manuel)

Species: The easiest to grow are *L. serratus* and *L. suaveolens*, both of which flower in spring.

Orchis

Natural habitat: Europe, Asia, and North America.

Plant form: Leafy stemlike growths arise from subsoil tubers. Stems vary from a few inches to 3 feet (almost one meter) tall, bearing short densely flowered inflorescences from their apices.

Culture: These enjoy sunny, relatively dry well-drained garden beds with an open gravelly soil. Many species prefer an alkaline soil; check with your supplier. Most *Orchis* species are dormant in winter, growing and flowering through spring and summer.

Orchis laxiflora (Courtesy Richard Manuel)

Orchis longicornu, another orchid for temperate garden beds. (Courtesy Richard Manuel)

Orchis morio, a lovely temperate garden orchid. (Courtesy Richard Manuel)

Climate: Temperate.

Species: *Orchis aristata, O. coriophora, O. latifolia, O. laxiflora, O. maculata, O. mascula, O. morio, O. palustris,* and several others including some hybrids.

Papilionanthe

Natural habitat: India, Sri Lanka, southern China, and Southeast Asia.

Plant form: Monopodial. Terete-leafed, tall-growing species which scramble up shrubs and trees in nature. Inflorescence erect, with up to 10 large flowers in pink to rose shades, some fragrant. This genus was included in *Vanda* but is florally and vegetatively distinct.

Culture: Full sun (they seldom bloom without it). Attach to a stake allowing the top 5 inches (12 centimeters) or so to wave about in the breeze. Water and fertilize regularly.

Climate: Tropical and subtropical.

Species: Only three species are commonly available, often listed as vandas—*Papilionanthe hookeriana*, *P. teres*, and *P. tricuspidata*. Several hybrids are available including the ever-popular *Papilionanthe* Miss Joaquim (sold commercially as a *Vanda* hybrid). Hybrids with strap-leafed vandas, giving rise to forms with semiterete leaves, are extremely popular. Although tropical in origin, *Papilionanthe teres* will grow in warm garden beds in most subtropical areas. *Papilionanthe hookeriana* and *P. tricuspidata* need more tropical conditions. Try them if you are in a warm area reasonably close to the tropics. *Papilionanthe* Miss Joaquim will grow where *P. teres* succeeds.

Peristeria

Natural habitat: Central and South America.

Plant form: Sympodial. Grapefruit-sized pseudobulbs with long, broad, thin, plicate leaves. Erect inflorescence to 5 feet (1.6 meters) tall, with fleshy, white, fragrant flowers.

Culture: 50% to 70% shade. Plants must be protected from winds that could damage their foliage. Water heavily while growing, but cut down water in winter when growth stops.

Climate: Tropical and warm subtropical.

Species: While there are several epiphytic species, there is only one terrestrial, *Peristeria elata*. Commonly known as the dove orchid or the Holy Ghost orchid, it is the national flower of Panama. It also makes a worthwhile garden subject in warm areas of the subtropics. The warmer the better—do not plant it if you live near the notional subtropic/cooler region divide. Cold, wet winters will kill it.

Phaius

Natural habitat: Africa, Himalayas, tropical Asia to Fiji.

Plant form: Sympodial. Robust, sometimes elongated pseudobulbs with long, broad, thin, plicate leaves. Erect inflorescences with large, sometimes fragrant flowers.

Culture: 70% shade. They must be protected from breezes that could damage their luxuriant foliage. Water and fertilize frequently in warm weather, dry out a bit in cool weather.

Phaius tankervilliae is grown worldwide in the tropics and subtropics.

Species: *Phaius amboinensis, P. pulchellus,* and *P. tankervilliae* (syn. *P. grandifolius*) together with a few hybrids made in the early 20th century but still available from time to time do well in the tropics and subtropics. *Phaius flavus* (syn. *P. maculatus*) with yellow flowers and *P. mishmensis* with pink flowers also make good subtropical garden subjects.

Plantanthera

Natural habitat: Northern temperate regions of Europe, Asia, and North America.

Plant form: Sympodial. Leafed flowering stems arise from thick, fleshy, tuberous roots. Several species have stems reaching 3 feet (nearly one meter) in height, although most are shorter. Inflorescences are usually many-flowered with individual flowers about 0.5 to 1 inch (1 to 2 centimeters) in diameter. Many species are fragrant. Flowering season varies from spring to autumn.

Culture: Many *Plantanthera* species grow naturally in bogs, stream margins, and similar wet areas. Emulate these conditions by building a bog garden with rich well-drained soil through which cold water can percolate. In regions with short summers, allow full sun. Closer to the equator, give shade that is more dappled.

Climate: Cool temperate. This genus is not generally suitable for the subtropics.

Plantanthera bifolia (Courtesy Richard Manuel)

The greater butterfly orchid, *Plantanthera chlorantha,* makes a lovely show in moist temperate gardens. (Courtesy Richard Manuel)

Species: *Plantanthera bifolia, P. blephariglottis, P. ciliaris, P. dilatata, P. fimbriata, P. integra, P. montana, P. nivea,* and many others. Check with your supplier.

Pleione

Natural habitat: Himalayas, China, northern Myanmar, northern Thailand, and Taiwan.

Plant form: Sympodial. Small flask-shaped pseudobulbs with thin, plicate, deciduous leaves. Single, large, beautiful flowers arise in spring with the new growth and are mostly fragrant. Colors are mostly pastel shades to deep, rich purple.

Culture: 70% shade. As well as growing on rocks and trees, pleiones often grow in the ground in leaf litter. Plant them in the garden where they receive shade from a shrub or tree at midday. In temperate climates, place them near an exposed rock, which will retain the sun's heat into the night. Keep damp while growing after the flowers fade, but let them dry out in winter, which is their natural rest period.

Climate: Cool to temperate gardens.

Species: *Pleione bulbocodioides, P. formosana, P. limprichtii,* and *P. speciosa* are usually available along with many modern hybrids in various colors, which are equally as beautiful.

Pterostylis

Natural habitat: Southeast Australia, Western Australia, New Zealand, Papua New Guinea, and New Caledonia.

Plant form: Mostly rosettes of small deciduous leaves arising from subsoil tubers. Some produce leafy flower stems. Some species form colonies, others remain as single plants.

Culture: Most species occur in moist, forested areas where they grow in shady, sheltered positions. A shady garden bed of sandy loam with about 30% leaf mold added should suit them. Allow to dry in summer when the plants are dormant. Recommence watering in autumn.

Climate: Cool temperate.

Species: *Pterostylis abrupta, P. baptistii,* which has the largest flowers, *P. curta, P. nutans, P. pedunculata, P. stricta,* and a number of hybrids, are all worth trying.

Renanthera

Natural habitat: Himalayas, China, through Southeast Asia to the Philippines, and Papua New Guinea.

Plant form: Monopodial. The species to grow as terrestrials have tall, scrambling stems, short, tough leaves, and thick roots. They flower on panicles, in brilliant reds and oranges.

Culture: 30% shade to full sun. Attach to stakes but leave at least the top 5 inches (12 centimeters) waving in the breeze. Water and fertilize frequently.

Climate: Tropical and subtropical.

Species: The tropical terrestrial species are *R. coccinea* and *R. storiei.* There are several hybrids as well as intergeneric crosses such as ×*Aranthera,* ×*Hawaiiara,* ×*Holttumara,* ×*Kagawara,* ×*Limara,* ×*Renanopsis,* and ×*Renantanda. Renanthera coccinea* will grow in the subtropics, as it comes from regions with short but cool winters. *Renanthera storiei* likes warmer temperatures year-round, but succeeds in warmer subtropical regions.

Sobralia

Natural habitat: Mexico, Central and South America.

Plant form: Sympodial. Clusters of tall, reedlike, leafy stems. Flowers from stem apex sequentially, with large, showy flowers lasting one to a few days but replaced immediately throughout the warm months. Great for table decoration used like hibiscus. Often fragrant.

Sobralia decora grows well in sunny subtropical garden beds.

Spathoglottis plicata shows to advantage in massed plantings.

Culture: 30% shade. Ensure they are planted at ground level, not sunk below the surface. Keep moist, but they must be well drained.

Climate: Subtropical and cool climates.

Species: *Sobralia callosa, S. decora, S. leucoxantha, S. macrantha, S. violacea, S. xantholeuca,* and the hybrid *S. Veitchii.*

Spathoglottis

Natural habitat: Himalayas, southern China through Southeast Asia, Philippines, Papua New Guinea to Samoa.

Plant form: Sympodial. Prominent, sometimes flattened pseudobulbs with long, thin, plicate, sometimes deciduous leaves. Erect inflorescences, with many flowers opening sequentially over a long period, in multicolors.

Culture: 30% to 50% shade. They will take full sun, but this sometimes makes the leaves look tatty. Plant pseudobulbs at ground level, not buried. They like good drainage and must have protection from strong breezes. Deciduous species need a dry winter rest; start watering when new growth arises and keep damp until leaves start to drop. Keep other species moist year-round.

Climate: Tropical and subtropical.

Species: *Spathoglottis affinis, S. aurea, S. chrysantha, S. lobbii, S. plicata, S. vanoverberghii,* and *S. vieillardii* are all suitable for tropical gardens, as well as many hybrids. Ask your supplier for color and size recommendations. This genus contains species from highland areas in Papua New Guinea, Thailand, and the Philippines that will grow in cooler conditions than the tropical species. Not many are readily available yet, but ask around and you may locate some. Otherwise, the following species and their innumerable hybrids are suitable for subtropical areas, provided you give them very good drainage, dry winters, and lots of wind protection: *Spathoglottis affinis, S. aurea, S. chrysantha, S. elmeri, S. fortunei, S. lobbii, S. ×parsonii, S. plicata, S. vanoverberghii,* and *S. vieillardii.*

Stenoglottis

Natural habitat: South Africa.

Plant form: Sympodial. Thick, fleshy, underground

roots, giving rise to a loose rosette of lance-shaped leaves, sometimes mottled or flecked with brown dots. Erect inflorescence to about 12 inches (30 centimeters). Many sequentially opening rose flowers. Deciduous in winter after flowering.

Culture: 50% to 70% shade. Put a stake in the ground to mark the spot where these species are planted because you won't see them until next spring after they lose their leaves. Keep them damp when actively growing, but give them a cool, dry rest during winter. Plant them near *Bletilla* and *Thunia* species, which like the same treatment.

Climate: Subtropical and cool climates.

Species: Only two are commonly grown, *S. fimbriata* and the larger *S. longifolia*.

Thelymitra

Natural habitat: Southern Australia and New Zealand with a single species each in New Caledonia, Papua New Guinea, and the Philippines.

Plant form: A single, erect, deciduous leaf and flower stem to 30 inches (about 75 centimeters) tall arising from a tuber. The flower stem bears few to many, often blue flowers from spring to early summer.

Culture: As for *Caladenia*, these will grow in full sun. Keep dry in hot, humid summers.

Climate: Cool temperate.

Species: *Thelymitra arenaria, T. aristata, T. crinita, T. cyanea* which needs to be grown wet year-round, *T. ixiodes, T. juncifolia, T. macmillanii,* and *T. pauciflora.*

Stenoglottis fimbriata will take very sunny conditions and is deciduous in winter.

Thelymitra Queen Adelaide would provide a highlight in temperate but frost-free gardens. (Courtesy Les Nesbitt)

Thunia

Natural habitat: Northeastern India, northern Myanmar, and northern Thailand.

Plant form: Sympodial. Tall, erect stems covered with thin, deciduous leaves. Drooping terminal inflorescences, with fragrant, large white to magenta flowers.

Culture: 30% to 50% shade. Water and fertilize frequently once growth starts in spring, but cut back watering after leaves drop. Stake newly planted canes firmly until established.

Climate: Tropical, subtropical, and cooler regions.

Species: *Thunia alba, T. bensoniae, T. marshalliana,* which is the best and most common species, and two early hybrids, *T.* Gattonensis and *T.* Veitchiana.

Many terrestrial orchid genera grow from underground tubers, which have been used for food in their habitats. In Europe and particularly in Turkey, a commercial industry grew up around the manufacture of a starchy, mucilaginous substance known as *salep* from orchid tubers. Wild-collected tubers of *Orchis, Dactylorhiza,* and other genera were used. In Australia, Aboriginal people ate the underground tubers of such genera as *Caladenia, Dipodium, Diuris, Geodorum, Glossodia, Pterostylis,* and *Thelymitra.* They also ate the pseudobulbs of *Cymbidium canaliculatum* and *C. madidum* both of which are very starchy and were eaten cooked or raw. *Cymbidium madidum,* chewed, was reputed to provide a cure for dysentery. The vanilla we use as food flavoring is prepared from the seed capsules of members of the orchid genus *Vanilla.* These vinelike plants are cultivated in several tropical countries and constitute the most important product provided by any orchid outside the cut-flower industry.

Vanda

Natural habitat: Himalayas, Sri Lanka, China through Southeast Asia and the Philippines to Papua New Guinea and Australia.

Plant form: Monopodial. Most of those suitable for growing in garden beds have erect stems and hard, semiterete leaves with thick roots. Inflorescences have many large flowers in many colors, sometimes fragrant.

Culture: 30% shade to full sun. Attach to stakes, but leave top 5 inches (12 centimeters) free. Water and fertilize regularly.

Climate: Tropical and subtropical.

Species: Most of the true *Vanda* species have strap-shaped leaves which will burn in full sun. Thus, the vandas recommended for garden beds are intergeneric hybrids (not species) between the strap-leaf types and the terete-leaved papilionanthes (although they are called vandas in horticulture). These hybrids, which have semiterete leaves, are ×*Aranda,* ×*Ascocenda,* ×*Holttumara,* ×*Mokara,* ×*Opsisanda,*1 ×*Renantanda,* ×*Trevorara,* and ×*Yusofara.*

Zygopetalum

Natural habitat: South America.

Plant form: Sympodial. Well-defined pseudobulbs with long, very broad leaves. Erect inflorescences with several good-sized flowers, usually green and brown with large purple and white lips, fragrant.

Culture: 70% shade. Protect from strong breezes and keep moist year-round. In cooler areas, grow these just as you would cymbidiums. They make sturdy, attractive additions to cool climate gardens. Their perfume is as beautiful as their dramatically colored flowers with their white and blue–purple labellums.

Climate: Subtropical and cool climates.

The best are *Z. intermedium, Z. mackaii,* and the many hybrids now available.

4

Pests

Pesticides or insecticides are designed to kill insect pests. Unfortunately, they are not very discriminating and kill or damage most creatures they contact. More creatures and insects in nature are beneficial than the few that are harmful to orchids. There is no need to use any insecticide whatsoever in the garden. Why risk harming your many friends for the dubious pleasure of hurting a few enemies? Some countries are legislating to prevent the indiscriminate use of insecticides by restricting their use to qualified, registered persons. Insecticides cause harm to the whole environment in a number of ways. A ripple effect occurs when an insect poisoned by insecticide is eaten by a predatory insect, bird, frog, lizard, or small mammal, all of which are natural predators of insect pests. Even if the insecticide ingested does not kill the natural predator, when the predator dies and forms part of the natural food chain, the poison can continue its deadly work.

The application of insecticide in the garden is similar to a shotgun blast. It covers everything in its path, not just the target insect. Unlike the shotgun, one application of insecticide can keep on killing as it falls or is washed to the ground, flows into the earth, and ends up in the water supply. A significant benefit of growing orchids naturally in your garden landscape is the ease with which predators control pests without any need for insecticides. Some insecticides in common use actually kill susceptible orchids as well as pests. The beautiful Jamaican species *Broughtonia sanguinea* is quite intolerant of malathion, the ingredient in several popular sprays. *Sarcochilus* species die if they come into contact with the slug and snail killer metaldehyde.

Orchid pests fall into two categories. The first category includes those that suck the plant's juices, such as scales, mealy bugs, mites, jassids, aphids, and thrips. Sucking pests debilitate the plant, and a weakened plant is more liable to suffer bacterial or fungal infection. Damage to the plant's surface tissue caused by sucking pests can provide a site for such an infection. An extreme infestation of sucking pests can kill a plant. No orchid gardener wants weak, sickly, damaged, or infested orchids in the garden landscape.

Pests in the second category are those that chew or bite the plant, its buds, flowers, or roots. These pests include beetles, caterpillars, cockroaches, grasshoppers, occasionally mice and rats, and slugs and snails. Damage caused by such pests is usually immediately obvious. It is an axiom of orchid growing that the orchid attacked by a chewing pest is either your best one, your rarest one, or the one whose blooms you have not yet seen, Fortunately, every pest has its own predator. Most natural predators either live in or visit our gardens. For pest-free orchid growing in your garden, simply encourage and do not discourage the predators.

Predators of the sucking pests include predatory mites, which eat harmful mites. These are available from specialist laboratories, but it is usually not necessary to import them. Harmful mites like hot, dry conditions, while orchids do not. Therefore, the simplest way to avoid mite problems is to avoid the conditions they like. Do this by hosing the host tree and all its plantings thoroughly and frequently, under and over the leaves, daily in hot, dry weather. This washes off part of any mite population and discourages the remainder. You can deter harmful mites threatening orchids in rockeries, walls, and garden beds by similar frequent hosing of plants.

Species of tiny wasps are the predators of scales and mealy bug, which are parasitized by the wasps. It pays to inspect each plant, orchid or otherwise, carefully for pests before placing it in your garden. If it has any scales, these can be scraped off with a fingernail or an old toothbrush. Scales tend to infest the underside of leaves, inside old leaf sheaths, and the junction of leaves and pseudobulbs. Destroy mealy bug, which look like a soft, squashy white scale, with a dab of methylated spirit on a fine paint brush or cotton bud. Mealy bugs sometimes infest the roots of container-grown orchids but do not last long in the open conditions of the garden landscape. Lizards

It is said that the color yellow attracts some species of thrips. Don't forego using yellow-flowered orchids in the garden, but it makes sense not to wear a yellow raincoat or yellow gardening clothes or to carry a yellow umbrella when you tend to your flowering orchids in the garden.

eat jassids with relish. Birds also catch jassids, and spiders trap these pests in their webs.

Aphids and thrips prefer hot, dry conditions to the humid, buoyant conditions loved by orchids. Frequent watering discourages both these pests. Lacewings, ladybirds, and other predatory insects devour aphids. They are very easy to remove from orchid growths and flower stems by simply hosing the infestation. Thrips do more damage to orchid flowers than plants. Remove them also with gentle use of the hose. They arrive with hot, dry winds. Discourage thrips by maintaining the humidity around your treescape, and by planting windbreaks to temper the harmful winds. Although it should not be necessary, you can make a useful, environment-friendly, topical white oil spray against scales and aphids by emulsifying vegetable oil in the food processor, adding water and a few drops of detergent. The detergent helps the white oil to spread evenly over the plant surfaces. Ultrafine spray oil is effective against most sucking pests, including mites and their eggs. If you must use it, spray only on cool days to avoid burning orchid leaves.

The second category of pests, the chewers and biters, also has predators. Spiders, lizards, birds, predatory insects such as large ants, praying mantis, and assassin bugs, and small mammals, all de-

your beetles. The so-called dendrobium beetle, an orange, black-spotted horror resembling a large ladybird, chews the leaves of some outdoor orchids, particularly dendrobiums, and has a special liking for the rock lily or king orchid, *Dendrobium speciosum*. This pest lays its eggs in immature *Dendrobium* growths and the larvae chew down into the stem, ruining it and the chance of any flowers from that growth. It favors also the long-lasting flower heads of the reedstem epidendrums or crucifix orchids.

While predatory insects, spiders, and birds will eat the dendrobium beetle, it is a fast and voracious feeder. It does the damage and lays its eggs very quickly. The best control is to inspect your orchids daily armed with a pair of pliers. The beetle's first action on discovery is to drop. If you hold your hand under the beetle you can catch it and despatch it with the pliers. This pest is active only in the warm months so beetle patrols can be suspended in the cool part of the year. Some growers report success against the beetle by using oil distilled from the Australian ti-tree or tea tree (*Melaleuca* spp.) at the rate of one teaspoon of 30% concentrated oil mixed with 12 pints (about 7 liters) of water, sprayed onto plants which are at risk of attack. This spray apparently acts as a contact killer and a repellent because of its odor. It may be necessary to re-spray frequently depending on watering frequency and natural rainfall. Perhaps adding a horticultural "sticker" or antitranspirant would make the concoction last longer.

Birds, spiders, and predatory insects including some wasps control caterpillars. Spiders, lizards, birds, frogs, and some larger species of ants hunt cockroaches. Birds, frogs, small mammals, and the larger spiders take care of grasshoppers. Insectivorous birds take an amazing number of insects

each day. Encourage them by planting bird-attracting native shrubs and allowing them plenty of densely leafed resting and nesting sites. Provide water and a birdbath to have birds working full time in your orchid garden. Keep cats away from the orchid garden. Encourage spiders by leaving their webs intact. This courtesy will be repaid when you see the number of moths, beetles, and other flying pests in their webs.

Larger predatory spiders such as the huntsman do their work at night. Frequently, they hide under loose bark on trees. If you disturb one in your garden, shriek if you must but don't kill it. Large spiders are as efficient as any pest controller is, and they do not charge for their services. The larger predatory insects include the odd-looking praying mantis and the aptly named assassin bug. Both these creatures will breed and live permanently in your garden and should be protected from disturbance. Assassin bugs live in trees but the praying mantis will wander freely over your rockery and garden-bed plants as well as your epiphytes. Frogs will make their homes in the larger vase-type bromeliads you may use as companion plants.

Orchid growers of the Victorian era knew the value of natural predators and had a keen eye for a bargain. The *Orchid Review* for September 1894, reporting an orchid sale conducted by the famous orchid auctioneers Protheroe and Morris for importers W. L. Lewis and Company of Southgate, said, "*And, by way of keeping insects in check, a case of twenty-five green tree frogs was sold for fourteen shillings.*" It would be nice if the descendants of those frogs were still keeping insects in check in some English greenhouse.

To the several qualities upon which the orchid can base its claim to recognition and value—such as rarity, exotic beauty, delicacy of coloring, wide variation in form and cultural interest—there can now be added another, thanks to the research work of scientists in a new and unusual field. A Dr. Rous of Paris, according to a recent despatch to the New York Times, *has discovered that certain essential oils obtainable from the orchid flower and injected into a person suffering from tuberculosis will aid him considerably in his fight against the disease. In other words, this erstwhile luxurious beauty of the plant world has now shown its ability to take off its coat, so to speak, roll up its sleeves, and take an active part as an effective weapon in the war against the white plague. All honor to the orchid, new-found benefactress of humanity, and to modern science, which has revealed it in this new role.*

Can it be that the orchid flower, heretofore reserved chiefly for weddings and balls, could take a place with the truly beneficial plants, if man would seriously investigate its possibilities?

—*Florists Exchange*, 9 August 1924, reported in the *Missouri Botanical Garden Bulletin* 32 (9), November 1944

Not only will they eat some of the chewing pests, but also their tadpoles thrive on any mosquito larvae that might hatch in the bromeliad vases. Some frogs like to live in the nooks, crannies, and crevices in rockeries and garden walls. Their presence as a predator in your garden is a welcome sign that nature is working for you. In the tropics and subtropics even the despised cane toad plays its part in disposing of numbers of harmful insects. The problem with the cane toad is that helpful insects are on its menu too.

Mice and rats are occasional visitors to orchid gardens. Both have a number of natural predators including hawks, owls, butcherbirds, snakes, and, in Australia, the antechinus (a tiny yet fierce carnivore) and currawongs. Domestic cats, too, sometimes earn their keep by catching rodents instead of birds and lizards. Rats will eat fleshy new orchid growths, while mice love to eat the pollen from orchid flowers, causing the flower to collapse within a day or two. The old-fashioned trap is a good standby if you suspect rodent problems. On the basis that prevention of infestation is better than having to rely on traps or friendly predators, keep your garden clear of rubbish, weeds, and overgrown grass, which provide hiding and nesting places for rodents.

Slugs and snails (gastropods) do not cause much trouble to epiphytic orchids. If your garden has a severe infestation and you can borrow some ducks, they will clean up the gastropods in a couple of days. Otherwise, you can locate any slug or snail that dares to climb your orchid host tree by making evening inspections with a flashlight. Gastropods are more likely to be found in rockeries, on garden walls, and in garden beds. Make a careful check of the garden surrounding your rockery, garden wall, and orchid bed. Gastropods love to hide in overgrown clumps of leafy plants such as iris, clivia, and agapanthus. They also crawl beneath planks and sheets of tin and into rubbish piles where conditions are cool, dark, and moist. Slugs and snails don't like tidy gardens as much as overgrown, rubbish-strewn ones.

If ducks are unavailable for ridding your garden of slugs and snails, try a beer trap. Gastropods are attracted to beer and will even forego a chew on your favorite orchid for a sip. Dispose of most of the contents of a can or bottle of beer. Tip the remainder (half an inch or a centimeter will do) into a wide-mouthed container such as an old

A predatory lizard on duty at Fairchild Tropical Garden.

paint tin. Place the tin on its side in the infested area overnight. Inspect the tin early the next morning and squash the gastropods gathered in it for their drink. If you use a little more beer, sometimes the pests will drown in it. Some would see this as a truly humane end. This treatment can be repeated until the nightly visitors are no more. Make evening inspections of your rockery, wall, and garden beds with a flashlight. As gastropods are more active at night, you can locate and deal with any that may be out and about your orchids.

Slugs but not snails are attracted to wedges of lemon in much the same way as they are to beer. A few wedges of lemon placed strategically in the rockery and garden bed will attract slugs, which you can then squash. The lemon appears to continue to work as an attractant until its dries out completely. Some of our ancestors were familiar with castle moats as constructions designed to keep enemies beyond the castle walls. Just as invaders were loath to cross the moat's water, so slugs and snails are loath to cross certain materials. These include diatomaceous earth, fine shell grits, and silicone fragments. You may be able to surround your rockery, wall, or garden bed with a gastropod moat in the form of a band of these materials to keep slugs and snails at bay. Some dealers claim that horticultural grade diatomaceous earth (not swimming pool filter grade) is very effective, although how long such a band would last in outdoor conditions is open to question.

Predators of gastropods include native carnivorous snails (distinguished by their narrow shells), frogs, cane toads, and lizards, particularly, in Australia the skinks, in the U.S. the anole lizards. The little skinks (and anoles), which are often seen

Frogs will climb trees to seek out insect pests. They are particularly sensitive to insecticides so keep your garden spray-free. (Courtesy Barry Johnson)

The subtropical terrestrial *Sarcoglottis acaulis* 'Eureka' has tender, fleshy foliage, especially attractive to slugs and snails.

sunning themselves or flitting about rockeries and walls, enjoy cockroaches, slaters (woodlice), and the smaller snails. They also munch moths and jassids, which they stalk with great cunning. The largest of the skinks is the Australian blue tongue lizard. If a blue tongue takes up residence in your rockery, you can be sure snails will not trouble your orchids. Protect all these predators and they will help to protect your orchids.

Container-grown orchids can be subject to attack by harmful fungi and bacteria. These seem to multiply when conditions are too cold, dark, damp, and airless. Such conditions are unlikely to occur in the open-air environment of your garden. Light and constant air movement in the treescape, rockery, wall, and bed ensure that these orchid enemies cannot gain a foothold. If fungi or bacteria attack any orchid in your garden landscape, it is most likely to be a terrestrial planted in shady, close conditions. Prevention is always bet-

ter than having to attempt a cure. In this case, your attention to air circulation, light, and drainage will help prevent any such attack.

If any of your plants has the misfortune to suffer a fungal infection, you may be able to obtain a fungicide from specialist orchid nurseries and suppliers. If you must use one, apply it strictly in accordance with the manufacturer's instructions. Always have regard to your own safety, that of your neighbors, and the environment in using any fungicide. Some home remedies are just as effective. The old method of treating an affected plant was to cut out the affected part down to clean tissue with a sterile razor, dust cut surfaces with flowers of sul-

Terrestrial orchids such as this hybrid *Pterostylis* Cutie 'Harold's Pride' produce leaf rosettes that rabbits and other herbivores adore. It's worth fencing off terrestrial orchid beds to keep grazing animals away. (Courtesy Les Nesbitt)

fur, and trust in this and the plant's constitution to pull it through. This method remains effective to this day, and it's much cheaper than purchasing a fungicide. Some growers of orchids in containers have discovered the fungicidal properties of powdered cinnamon used instead of flowers of sulfur. Specific applications of these home remedies do not affect the environment, nor do they harm the beneficial fungi that live in symbiosis with orchids grown the natural way.

No ready cure is available for bacterial attack. It is best to remove and burn any plant you suspect might harbor harmful bacteria or which is suffering a severe fungal infection. Allow its site to dry out before using it again. It is prudent to plant a nonrelated type or even a companion plant in a site from which you have removed a sick orchid.

Most of us aim to live in harmony with nature as far as we are able. When we develop that harmony with nature in our natural orchid gardens we find that orchid pests and diseases are no longer a problem.

5

Species or Hybrids?

Orchid growers frequently debate the respective merits of species orchids against hybrids. Each type has advantages and disadvantages. Species orchids are those which occur naturally. Many are rare. Their existence is threatened as the world's wild places shrink under the pressure of increasing populations. The wild communities of many species die when logging and land clearing destroys their habitats. The rarity of some species orchids makes them highly sought after. The only means of preserving some of these rare and threatened species may be to grow them in our gardens.

Many species orchids are markedly seasonal in their growth and flowering patterns. Those that will grow readily in your particular region will flower regularly in due season. They will be reliable also in their patterns of growth. These attributes give you something to look forward to week by week if you maintain a collection of species. You can find descriptions of species' vegetative forms and of their flowers in orchid literature. Species orchids are the blocks upon which the hybrids of the future are built. Hybridists have a limited choice of parents for future hybrids unless

they have a wide selection of cultivated species orchids to look at and consider.

For growers who enjoy reflecting on the historical aspects of orchid culture, there is no doubt that species orchids provide a link with the often-romantic past. Orchid hunters traveled over unknown, often hostile terrain, faced wild animals, deadly reptiles, insects, disease, unfriendly native populations, and difficult climates. Their endeavors resulted in the wealth of species orchids now cultivated. As Ralph Arnold (1932) put it succinctly:

> There is a romance in these old orchids, and they carry the mind back across the years to days when new species were continually reaching these shores; they serve to keep green the memories of the many intrepid collectors, and, perhaps, most of all, do they serve to illustrate the wonderful advance of orchidology, from . . . ignorance to an exact science.

As to disadvantages, some species are difficult and demanding to grow in cultivation. Some have a narrow range of growing conditions. A degree or two too cold or too hot may cause them harm. Too

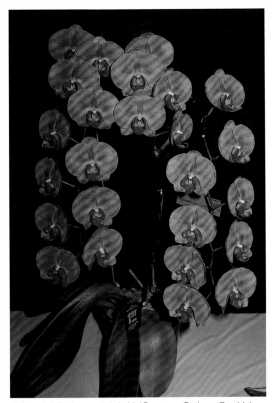

A fine pink *Phalaenopsis* hybrid. (Courtesy Graham Gamble)

To all the flowers grown in Chinese gardens, some peculiar significance or aesthetic value is attached. An orchid (Cymbidium ensifolium), called lan hwa, is regarded as the king of flowers, the modest appearance of the plant and the delicate odor of its blossoms, representing the very essence of refinement.

—E. H. "Chinese" Wilson,
A Naturalist in Western China

The last plant hunter to be employed by James Veitch and Sons, Wilson made four journeys to China collecting plants between 1899 and 1910, principally in western and southwestern China. He came to know and respect Chinese culture. Like the best of his predecessors he was observant and appreciated both the people and the countryside of the regions in which he collected.

much water in winter may not suit them. Some species are not as tolerant as hybrid orchids are of a wide range of growing conditions. Species are consistently in demand by orchid growers and some of the most popular types are not always readily available. By their very rarity, some species are expensive. Growers with limited space who want flowers year-round may not like the fact that many species flower only once a year, in a particular season.

Hybrids exhibit a trait known as hybrid vigor. In orchids this trait manifests as plants which grow strongly and are more tolerant of a wide range of growing conditions than are some species. Hybrid orchids tend to be less seasonal than species. Frequently, they flower as each new growth matures, regardless of the time of year. Their longer, less seasonal growing periods allow the landscaper more flexibility in deciding when to plant them. Hybrids in the *Cattleya* alliance often flower three or four times each year, while *Vanda* hybrids can be ever blooming in favorable conditions. Hybrids often are easier to find and purchase than are species. They tend to be cheaper, except for those with show-winning potential.

Hybridists have combined different genera to provide a vast range of intergeneric hybrids, which aim to combine the best features of each genus. For example, ×*Sophrocattleya* hybrids combine the large-flowered, showy but warmth-loving *Cattleya* with the small and shapely flowered but brilliant vermilion-red, cool-growing *Sophronitis*. The result is a medium-sized, very colorful, shapely flower borne by a small to medium-sized

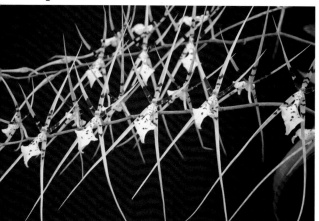

Brassia Arania Verde is larger with a more stylized form and less seasonal blooming than its parents. To some growers it is an improvement; others think the species from which it is descended have more charm.

Phalaenopsis aphrodite, a stepping stone on the path to breeding cool-tolerant, multiflowered hybrids.

Orchid hunters led adventurous lives, covering unexplored territories and facing nature in the wild. The first plant hunter sent to a foreign land by the Horticultural Society of London was a Scot, Francis Masson, who collected plants (including orchids) in South Africa towards the end of the eighteenth century. For a time he was accompanied by a Swedish botanist, Carl Per Thunberg, who had some novel ideas for dealing with African wildlife. When facing a threatening lion, said Thunberg, one only needed to stare sternly at it whereupon it would back down. If charged by a buffalo (reckoned by many of the old-time big game hunters to be the most dangerous of all African animals) Thunberg said the unfortunate plant hunter should hold his ground until the buffalo dropped its head, then simply step aside and it would miss completely. He can't have tried this trick because the buffalo lowers its head only in the last stride—too late to step aside! Fortunately for Masson, he never needed to take Thunberg's advice.

plant which is tolerant of cooler conditions than its *Cattleya* parent. The advantages to the landscaper of the myriad intergeneric hybrids now available are obvious. If you know the characteristics of each species used in an intergeneric hybrid, you have a fair idea of how the hybrid will grow and what its flowers will be like.

One disadvantage of hybrid orchids is that descriptions in the orchid literature are harder to find. While many illustrations of hybrids are published, they quickly become out-of-date as newer hybrids take their place. Fashion rules the hybrid orchid world as rigorously as it rules the world of *haute couture*. For a time miniature cattleyas are popular. As their popularity wanes the fashion swings in favor of large exhibition-type cattleyas. Dendrobiums with antelope flowers give way to the round, full-shaped flowers of another type of hardcane dendrobium. This may make it difficult to keep your garden planted with the most fashionable hybrid orchids, but it also means that those orchids temporarily out of fashion can be purchased cheaply.

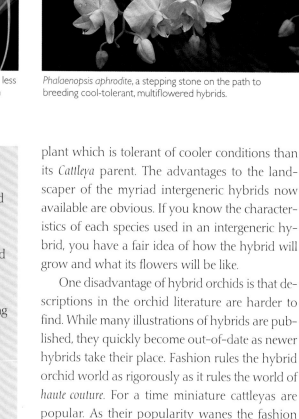

The attributes of *Miltonia* Castable include its substance, colors, and upright raceme.

Oncidium Riverwood 'Geyserland' is a hybrid of *O. tigrinum* × *O. maculatum*. While its parents are both beautiful in their own right, they are not always easy to grow. Their progeny displays large size, filled-in form and, most importantly, hybrid vigor.

There is a saying among orchid growers that it costs as much to grow a poor orchid as it does to grow a good one. Keep that in mind when selecting plants for your garden landscape. Whether you grow species, hybrids, or both types, ensure that you select healthy, well-grown plants for landscaping. If you are offered a large plant that overflows its pot, check the old stems for signs that it has already flowered. Some hybrids are notoriously shy when it comes to producing blooms. A cheap orchid is not necessarily the bargain it may appear. You will find that the colors of many orchid flowers, species and hybrids, intensify under natural conditions. Blooms on the plants in your garden landscape often outshine those on their relatives growing inside orchid houses.

William Horlacker, an orchid hunter for Sander and Sons in South America at the end of the nineteenth century, liked to tell the story of his hunt for the fabulous golden Colombian species, *Cattleya aurea*. Apparently, he met an attractive lady riding her horse and wearing several of this gorgeous cattleya's blooms. In fractured Spanish, Horlacker asked her where the orchids grew. Taking fright, no doubt at his accent, the señora screamed, bringing her husband at the gallop. Horlacker said it took every word of Spanish he knew to talk the señor out of killing him. It seems that wild husbands were more of a danger to orchid hunters than were wild animals.

PART TWO

Types of Gardens

6

The Large Garden

By an arbitrary but useful definition, a large garden comprises more than one-quarter acre (more than 1000 square meters). While few large gardens may still be found in fully urbanized areas, they are common in rural areas and special suburbs. Large gardens have both advantages and a few disadvantages over smaller gardens. The larger the garden the greater the scope for the orchid gardener. By virtue of its sheer size, a large garden is likely to contain a variety of microclimates. It may have more sheltered areas, more exposed areas, more shady areas, and more sunny areas than a smaller garden. Each one of these areas may be the perfect place to plant different orchids and their companions.

Use of Trees and Space

Most large gardens contain large, mature trees. These influence the garden climate in a number of ways. Their trunks, branches, and crowns provide shade. As the earth moves round the sun through the winter and summer solstices, these shaded areas will move. Orchid landscapers take advantage of this movement, placing most orchids so they receive some shade in midsummer and more

direct sunlight in midwinter. Large trees cool and humidify the surrounding garden through the transpiration of moisture from their foliage into the garden's atmosphere. This helps to provide the conditions under which many epiphytic orchids flourish in nature.

Large trees can act as windbreaks also, filtering hot, dry summer winds and cold winter winds to prevent their full blast reaching the large garden's orchids. Windbreaks are most effective when they are used to break up or filter damaging winds rather than to block or deflect such winds entirely. In high winds, the air current will simply flow over a solid windbreak and down its lee side with redoubled and destructive force. The same air current filtered through a living windbreak of trees and shrubs is much less likely to damage orchids growing in its lee.

Another advantage provided by large trees is the amount of food they supply to the epiphytes growing on their trunks and branches, and to the lithophytes and terrestrials below. Decaying vegetable matter, the droppings and dead bodies of insects and other animals, and substances leached by the rain from trees are all sources of orchid

A massive live oak at Marie Selby Botanical Gardens, Sarasota, Florida. You would not need many of these, even in a large garden.

food. Generally speaking, the larger the tree the greater will be the orchid food source, and the larger the garden the more large trees it will support. Orchid gardeners with large gardens have the space to emulate nature more readily than do those with smaller gardens. Large gardens can accommodate whole groves of trees and shrubs to be used specifically as orchid hosts, with room left for other garden subjects such as ornamentals, fruit trees, flower beds, and vegetables.

In a large garden, water in the form of a natural lake, pond, or dam modifies the garden's climate. Those orchid gardeners fortunate enough to have a stream or waterfall within their boundary can make this the focal point for their orchid landscape. Almost all orchids love the cool, mois-

ture-laden air currents that rise from moving water. The temperature in the immediate surrounds of a body of water is often more equable than that a short distance away.

Another advantage is that substantial, well-drained rockeries are easily sited and constructed in large gardens. The space means a large rockery can fit into the natural contours of a large garden. It allows also for appropriate plantings of trees around the rockery, and shrubs and companion plantings within it. Some large and imposing rockeries need mechanical earth-moving equipment for their construction and the large garden affords the space to make this both possible and practicable. The large garden on sloping ground lends itself to terracing. This allows you to plant

Epiphytic garden on large, leaning *Hyphaene* palm trunks.

terrestrial orchids in terraced beds and to grow lithophytic orchids on the terrace walls.

Massed Planting

Many of us have been awe-struck by the beauty of thousands of flowering plants of *Papilionanthe* Miss Joaquim all together in commercial fields in Hawaii, and by the flowering hedges of vandaceous intergeneric hybrids in Singapore. Similar effects can be obtained by massed plantings of the same orchid in large garden beds. It does not seem to matter much what type of orchid is used for a mass planting. *Papilionanthe* Miss Joaquim and the vandaceous intergeneric hybrids mentioned are great for tropical and warm subtropical beds in full sun. In more temperate areas, the reedstem epidendrums, or crucifix orchids, are equally beauti-

ful in full sun in large garden beds. Cymbidiums also lend themselves to massed plantings in large garden beds in semishade. Hybrids are available in almost every color and color combination, with flower racemes varying from totally pendulous through gracefully arching to rigidly upright.

Whether using vandas, epidendrums, cymbidiums, or any other orchids for massed plantings, consider whether they should all have approximately the same height, the same color, and the same flowering season. The Hawaiian fields of *Papilionanthe* Miss Joaquim look so marvellous in part because each plant is kept at the same height, the flowers are all identical, and all the plants are always in flower. Would a large garden bed of reedstem epidendrums look better with all the same colored flowers at the same height? Would it look better as a mix of different colored flowers all at the same height? At different heights? In several blocks of say two dozen plants each of one color per block? Would a bed of cymbidiums look better if planted in blocks of the same color, all with the same raceme habit, or would it be better to mix different raceme types and colors? These are the kinds of questions you will need to consider, and the answers will vary depending on your garden site and your particular tastes in garden design. Whatever your preferences, there will be orchids to suit.

The collector in many of us wants to have at least one of as many different types as possible. However, for large beds in large gardens there is a lot to be said for the effect provided by massed plantings of the same orchid. You might better cater for collector items in smaller separate beds or rockeries nearby. Large gardens in subtropical and temperate areas give orchid gardeners the scope to incorporate different designs and layouts. For instance, a modification of the classical walled garden would allow for plantings of terrestrial orchids in beds, lithophytes on the internal walls and in any feature rockeries, and epiphytes on suitable shrubs or trees within the walls. If your garden already contains a rocky hillside or outcrop of rocks, you have the perfect basis for a lithophytic orchid garden.

Large Orchids

Large, bold plants and massed plantings look most effective in large gardens. Fortunately, there are plenty of large, bold orchids of each of the three groups described in this book. For big plants in big trees in the tropics, it would be hard to surpass the various *Grammatophyllum* species. Complemented with large-growing vandas such as

Massed planting of *Epidendrum radicans* at RF Orchids, Florida, is effective and stays compact when grown in full sun.

But towards the summits of the mountains one discovers here and there ravines and gorges where the virgin forest persists. It is here that the plant [Cattleya labiata] is found, growing on the large trees, whose trunks are garnished with aroids, begonias, ferns, and etc. The cattleya grows chiefly on the lateral branches of the trees, in company with other orchids, bromeliads, and lichens, its roots enveloping the branches to a length of nearly 6 feet [about 2 meters], with their tips intact, and finding in the air the ingredients necessary for their existence. Here, in the shade of the evergreen foliage and in the breezy mountain air, the cattleya luxuriates. It never grows on dead trees, because the bark quickly perishes and falls off.

—Robert A. Rolfe, *Orchid Review*,
November 1907

Cattleya labiata has a long and romantic history. Rolfe used this information, supplied by Louis Forget, who was a long-time and successful orchid hunter in South America for the English firm Sander and Sons.

Vandopsis gigantea, tropical dendrobiums with antelope flowers, tropical oncidiums such as *Oncidium lanceanum*, schombburgkias with 6- to 10-foot (2- or 3-meter) flower stems, and tall-growing cattleyas such as *Cattleya amethystoglossa, C. guttata*, and their various hybrids, these would provide a framework for a grand tropical treescape.

Tropical rockeries may also include the grammatophyllums and antelope dendrobiums. Several of the large-growing *Angraecum* species from Madagascar make imposing rockery plants, notably the various forms of *A. eburneum*. Individuals of *Schomburgkia* and ×*Schombocattleya* are equally at home on trees or in well-drained rockeries in sunny positions. Tropical orchid gardeners seeking plants to grow terrestrially are well served by *Vanda* species with their myriad hybrids between the various genera. The terete- and semiterete-leaved vandas and their hybrids with *Arachnis* and *Renanthera* could form the basis for massed plantings in tropical beds. The huge and spectacular *Vandopsis lissochiloides* grows both as a lithophyte and as a terrestrial naturally. In more protected areas *Phaius tankervilliae* and *Peristeria elata* grow into very large showy specimens. A friend grew a potted plant of the former which stood over 6 feet (about 2 meters) high from pot top with huge racemes approaching 9 feet (nearly 3 meters) in length.

In subtropical and warmer temperate regions cattleyas, schomburgkias, and oncidiums could take the place of the tropical grammatophyllums and vandas in the treescape framework. *Oncidium sphacelatum* is typical of many oncidiums that grow into huge specimens capable of producing dozens of racemes with many thousands of flowers. *Oncidium leucochilum*, a Mexican species, has flower stems reaching 10 feet (3 meters) with short branches bearing hundreds of green, purple, and white flowers. Blue-flowered *Vanda* hybrids, bred from the cool-growing, high-altitude species *V. coerulea*, make excellent subjects for treescapes in these regions. The African species *Ansellia africana* grows into sturdy epiphytic clumps with canelike pseudobulbs more than 3 feet (one meter) tall, topped by branching panicles of very showy flowers in various shades of yellow and chocolate. Perhaps the showiest of the large-growing epiphytic orchids is the Australian *Dendrobium speciosum* complex. This magnificent spring-flowering species grows into huge specimens, with scores of racemes each bearing up to 60 white to golden yellow highly fragrant flowers. The pseudobulbs of *D. tarberi* and *D. rex* can reach 3 feet (one meter) in length. They make spectacular focal points on large trees in large gardens.

The names of some orchids evoke stirring and romantic memories of people or places. Consider *Oncidium carthagenense*, a beautiful species widespread in the tropical West Indies, Central and South America. It has broad, fleshy, mule-ear shaped leaves with arching, branching panicles of white, rose-purple spotted flowers. It is named after Cartagena, a port on the Caribbean coast of Colombia, having been described by a French botanist in about 1750. Cartagena was on the legendary Spanish Main, the coastline nominally ruled by Spain but ravaged by buccaneers, brigands, privateers, and men-of-war from many countries. The name *Oncidium carthagenense* invokes images of pirates, soldiers, Spanish grandees, adventurers, pieces-of-eight, doubloons, and the wrecks of treasure ships in tropical waters. These may be things of the past, but the orchid is a living treasure.

Rockeries in large subtropical and temperate gardens also call for large orchids. The *Dendrobium speciosum* complex answers the call, this time with the true *D. speciosum*, whose common name is rock lily, and with *D. rex*, called king orchid in Queensland. The former has white to cream flowers, while many clones of *D. rex* have lovely, large golden yellow flowers. Almost equally spectacular when grown as a large specimen plant in the rockery is the so-called pink rock lily, *D. kingianum*. Its flower colors vary from pure white and bicolors through the pink and mauve tones to deep purple. Nursery-raised plants of most colors are readily available from some specialist nurseries. *Dendrobium kingianum* is a smaller growing plant than *D. speciosum*, but it lends itself admirably to massed plantings in large clumps throughout the large rockery. Schomburgkias, cattleyas, and their large-growing hybrids will grow as well in well-drained rockeries as in trees. While these genera possibly are better suited to subtropical rather than temperate regions, the glorious *Schomburgkia superbiens* will grow in a sunny rockery in cool conditions.

The sobralias are excellent species for planting in big rockery pockets or garden beds in the large subtropical or cool climate garden, and they will grow into large showy specimens. Each stem bears several to many flowers in succession throughout the warmer months. *Oerstedella verrucosa*, related to the reedstem epidendrums, is another wonderful plant for a rockery or garden bed in large subtropical and warm temperate gardens. Our plant grew canelike stems 12 feet (nearly 4 meters) tall, producing four or five new growths each year. Its flower stems appeared in winter as branching panicles bearing hundreds of small white flowers. Far too big for any orchid house,

Australian botanists have elevated the named varieties of *Dendrobium speciosum* to the status of distinct species. Thus *D. speciosum* var. *capricornicum* and var. *curvicaule* are now *D. curvicaule*, *D. speciosum* var. *hillii* is now *D. tarberi*, *D. speciosum* var. *grandiflorum* is now *D. rex*, *D. speciosum* var. *pedunculatum* is now *D. pedunculatum*, and *D. speciosum* var. *speciosum* becomes *D. speciosum*. In the 1980s we walked into a valley in Australia's Great Dividing Range the floor of which was populated by river oaks *Casuarina cunninghamiana*, a natural host to *D. tarberi*. The orchids were in full and glorious bloom and the whole valley was filled with their perfume. The plants were so large that during heavy rain when their root masses were saturated, many fell to the ground. They were too large to be lifted by three men. We walked about 6 miles (10 kilometers) along the valley floor treading on the orchids, which were impossible to avoid. Such can be nature's prodigality where humans do not interfere.

Cattleya skinneri makes an excellent epiphytic specimen plant for large gardens.

Angraecum eburneum is a large-growing species, especially showy in big tropical rockeries.

A massive specimen of *Dendrobium speciosum* covering a palm trunk would make a focal point in any garden. (Courtesy Brian Pearce)

Pendulous racemes of oncidiums in epiphytic clumps look like golden rain.

A bold, imposing plant for large trees and rock gardens is the stout *Vandopsis gigantea*.

the plant looked as though clouds of small white butterflies attended it as its stems bowed and danced in the breeze in the garden.

Last but certainly not least in this short selection of large, bold plants for the large garden is the genus *Cymbidium*. Best suited to cool regions, the stately standard-sized cymbidiums provide eye-catching features in pockets in the large rockery and planted, particularly as massed plantings, in garden beds.

Maintenance

The only word of warning to be sounded in relation to large-scale orchid gardening is to ensure that the initial plantings are not too spread out. As you feed, water, and contemplate the orchids you have planted in your garden, time passes enjoyably but more rapidly than you calculate. Growing orchids the natural way is a pleasure, so keep it pleasurable. But if you plant epiphytes in trees widely separated from each other and construct rockeries and beds in different areas in your garden, you may have to drag a heavy hose a long distance across your property from site to site when watering. You may even find it necessary to install additional water outlets. Commence your orchid garden by treescaping one or more trees that are only a few yards or meters apart from each other. Construct your rockery close enough for it to be watered from the same outlet as the treescape. If possible, build the first garden bed to be planted with orchids in the same section of the garden. This kind of planning will enable you to keep a close eye on all your naturally grown orchids and to tend to them conveniently.

As you become more experienced in recognizing the microclimates in your garden and the particular requirements of the orchids you wish to

Schomburgkia superbiens is sometimes called *Laelia superbiens*, but in its native habitat of Guatemala, Honduras, and Mexico is called Saint Joseph's wand on account of its flower stalks, which can reach 12 feet (nearly 4 meters) in length. These bear up to 20 light purple flowers, each about 5.5 inches (14 centimeters) in diameter with prominent, yellow-crested veins in the lip. The pseudobulbs can grow to 20 inches (50 centimeters) and are surmounted by one or two large, stiff-textured leaves up to 14 inches (35 centimeters) long. Karl Theodor Hartweg, a plant collector for the Horticultural Society of London, introduced this species into cultivation in Europe in 1836. In a letter to his employers dated 20 August 1840 from Guatemala, Hartweg said of *Schomburgkia superbiens* which he called the "chumague": "I claim the honor of having first discovered and introduced this extraordinary plant; I mention this because I am in dispute with Mr. Skinner about it, who asserts that he sent it some years ago." Hartweg also wrote, when sending back some specimens of *S. superbiens* later that year, "This beautiful kind being from a very cold climate will succeed best if put out in the open air from May to October and afterwards to be kept in the conservatory. White frosts will not hurt it."

grow, you can extend your orchid landscape to suit your garden. In a 2-acre (8000-square-meter) property, I had an orchid garden comprising a treescape of five small casuarinas, three large turpentines (*Syncarpia glomulifera*), and a frangipani, a rockery with a 10-foot (about 3-meter) diameter, a rock wall about 16 feet (5 meters) long averaging 6 feet (nearly 2 meters) high, and several terraced

The pipes above this large wall support a sprinkler system. Damping down the plants, lawn, and gravel paths keeps the plants in a comfortably humid atmosphere.

beds. These features, which supported approximately 100 orchids, were contained in an area of no more than 65 by 50 feet (about 20 by 15 meters). I was able to water the whole area from one central point and the orchids were easy to reach with a fertilizer sprayer.

Another advantage of the large garden for orchids is that a greater variety of natural predators will live and breed in it, rather than just visit it. It can pay dividends in the field of pest control if you plant some dense thickets as nesting places for insectivorous birds. Do not clear the garden so thoroughly that you do away with hiding places for lizards, frogs, and ground–dwelling spiders. All these creatures are your allies in the natural world of the garden.

7

The Suburban Garden

For illustrating the use of orchids, any open garden of less than one-quarter acre (about 1000 square meters) can be regarded, arbitrarily, as a suburban garden. This category does not include courtyard and patio gardens. The landscaping of a suburban garden will be on a smaller scale than that of the large garden. While it may not be possible to have a grove of large trees, with their climate-modifying effect, within a suburban garden, do take notice of the gardens of surrounding properties. Trees, shrubs, and pools in adjoining gardens may have a sheltering and cooling effect on yours. Many of the advantages of the large garden can also apply to the suburban garden. There is enough scope for growing each of the three groups of orchid to satisfy the most avid orchid gardener. Each suburban garden has its sheltered side and its exposed side, its shady area and its sunny area. With a little careful planning and some imagination, any orchid gardener can transform a formerly dull suburban block into a subtropical fairyland.

Planning

One small suburban Sydney garden, which I knew, contained only three trees. At the front of the house, a permanent-barked eucalyptus covered with epiphytic bromeliads welcomed the visitor. Beside the front door a massive plant of *Dendrobium speciosum* grew and flowered in a narrow, raised brick bed. Squeezing past the house on the path to the rear garden, an amazing landscape appeared. The path was overhung with epiphytes—ferns, vines, bromeliads, and orchids. A few steps

The golden *Cattleya* hybrids provide great color accents when grown as epiphytic specimens in the garden.

131

further and another vista opened up. A green grotto planted with cymbidiums, paphiopedilums, zygopetalums, and more bromeliads took the space between two trees, another permanent-barked eucalyptus, and a tall, sprawling *Banksia*. *Coelogyne cristata* and *C.* ×*intermedia* grew into large specimens at the base and lower trunk of the *Banksia*. *Dendrobium nobile* with its hybrids and several Australian dendrobiums covered the branches

During his travels in northeastern India Sir Joseph D. Hooker visited the Teesta River in February 1849 where he was aware of dangers and discomforts not to be found in the suburban garden. He wrote that he *"walked to the skirts of the Sal forest. The great trunks of the trees were often scored by tigers' claws, this animal indulging in the cat-like propensity of rising and stretching itself against such objects."* Mentioning discomfort as well as danger Hooker continued, *"A good many plants grow along the streams, the sandy beds of which are everywhere covered with the marks of tigers' feet. The only safe way of botanizing is by pushing through the jungle on elephants; an uncomfortable method, from the quantity of ants and insects which drop from the foliage above, and from the risk of disturbing pendulous bees' and ants' nests ... The broiling heat of the elephant's black back, and the odor of its oily driver, are disagreeable accompaniments, as are its habits of snorting water from its trunk over its parched skin, and the consequences of the great bulk of green food which it consumes."* Thank heaven for our hardy forebears who bore these dangers and discomforts to bring us the wild orchids we treasure today.

—Sir Joseph D. Hooker,
Himalayan Journals, 1891

of both trees. In sunny patches among a little rockery *D. kingianum* grew and flowered prolifically.

This garden was an oasis in a street of otherwise dreary backyards. As the plants grew and filled the orchidscaped area, native birds returned to feed and nest in it. Neighborhood cats and pesky mynah birds stayed away. It was a low-cost, low-maintenance, easy-to-care-for delightful haven. If this effect was achieved with two trees, imagine how you could create an orchid garden using your existing trees and judiciously planting that extra host tree where you want it. Nor should you overlook the use of shrubs as hosts for orchids. Growers have had outstanding success with *Tibouchina* and *Lagerstroemia* (crape myrtle) as exotic host species.

Many Australian shrubs make wonderful hosts. If governed by space and height limitations, choose smaller growing species of *Callistemon*, *Callitris*, *Casuarina*, and *Melaleuca*. You may be surprised how easily and vigorously a large orchid can grow on a small host. In one garden I treescaped, hybrid cattleyas about 18 inches (45 centimeters) in height rapidly grew completely round, then up, a *Tibouchina* branch only 3 inches (about 8 centimeters) in diameter. Many of the early orchid hunters expressed astonishment at the seemingly precarious perches adopted by orchids in the wild. Do not be afraid to tie epiphytic orchids to relatively thin branches on host shrubs or trees. Those branches will grow, as will the orchids. Remember to remove the tie as soon as the orchid's roots are firmly attached or to refasten if the tie starts to cut into the host's bark.

Siting Rockeries and Beds

Even the smallest suburban gardens have room for a rockery. One of the nice features of a rockery is that it does not need to conform to any size or any formal pattern. Indeed, you could construct a small but effective rockery to accommodate just one orchid. A specimen plant of *Dendrobium speciosum* or a large *Cattleya* in its own rockery would make a wonderful focal point in a suburban garden. An excellent site for a rockery could be on the sunny side of the house close to the wall. Here, the heat trapped by the house during sunny days will be emitted at night, warming the air round the rockery. Take account of any overhanging eaves, which may prevent rain from watering the plants.

In our suburban gardens we plant color-coordinated flower beds of annuals, banks of pastel azaleas, and specimens of camellias, magnolias, and other beauties. For an exotic, colorful, and long-lasting effect why not plant a color-coordinated bed of orchids? Genera suitable for massed planting mentioned in the previous chapter are just as effective in the suburban garden. Many suburban gardens feature water, either in the form of a swimming pool or an ornamental pond. Areas around pools are very suitable for landscaping with orchids. Attach them to trees surrounding the pool and plant them in rockeries in close proximity to it. Pools increase the humidity in their vicinity and help to maintain a more even air temperature. The larger the body of water the greater this effect will be.

Orchid Types

While a suburban garden may not be able to hold as many orchids as a large garden, it has the advantage in being easier to care for. Some orchid growers concentrate on a particular genus or only a few different genera rather than subscribing to the collector's ideal of having one each of everything. For instance, some growers collect only oncidiums, others only cattleyas, dendrobiums, or cymbidiums.

This suburban gardener has started orchidscaping a stump in full sun with *Dendrobium discolor*. Note the drapes of Spanish moss.

It is hard to say what some orchids will not endure! I saw good masses of Laelia anceps *that had been growing for four years on an olive tree in a sheltered garden here. The morning I saw them there had been three degrees of frost, which had not spoilt the numerous spikes of flower that hung down in much beauty!*

—Edward H. Woodall,
Orchid Review, February 1914

Woodall lived in Nice in southern France in the early twentieth century. Although *Laelia anceps* is a native of higher and cooler elevations in Mexico, where it grows on trees and rocks with little protection from sun and wind, it is a perfect orchid for the cool garden.

Gardeners can cater to this interest by growing their favorite genus in their suburban garden. You could, for example, grow an excellent representative collection of *Oncidium* species and hybrids, with the epiphytic members on trees and shrubs, the litho-

The vibrant color and leathery texture of this *Vanda* highlight its use as a warm climate garden plant.

There is a well-authenticated story of its (the cattleya) first appearance in a Broadway, New York, flower store. A noted beau, who called in every morning for his bouton-nière, was always looking for something new. The pro-prietor had obtained a cattleya flower, and had it safely stored in the icebox awaiting his appearance. He came. Reverently the flower was placed in his buttonhole; silently he was turned towards the mirror. There was an air of mystery, the play of an artist, about the whole per-formance, and then the climax; $25 for the flower, which was paid with alacrity. It is further stated that for many days thereafter the same gentleman called regularly as usual for his orchid, but the price had dropped to $15. No wonder that some of our millionaires decided to go into the business of raising them.

—Patrick O'Mara

On 23 January 1901 O'Mara, of New York, ad-dressed the Massachusetts Horticultural Society on the place of orchid flowers in the New York market. He began his association with the florist business at the end of 1874.

Spectacular decorations for straight-trunked garden trees in good light are semiterete *Vanda* hybrids that flower year-round in warm climates.

phytic types in the rockery or on a wall, and terres-trial species in a well-drained garden bed.

The dendrobiums comprise a huge genus numbering several thousand when their hybrids are included. Old World plants, found in nature from India in the west to Samoa in the east and from Japan and Korea in the north to New Zealand in the south, dendrobiums inhabit all lev-els from hot tropical lowlands to the snowline. Their vegetative forms are as diverse as their flower shapes, sizes, and colors. The majority are epi-phytes, but a surprising number are lithophytes or terrestrials. Small wonder that dendrobiums have

The Floridian native *Encyclia cochleata*, shown here at RF Orchids, provides a talking point when grown as a garden epiphyte.

A cool subtropical Australian garden featuring orchids and companion plants in a rockery and on a rough-barked tree.

legions of enthusiastic growers. They are the orchid-landscaping genus *par excellence*. The same can be said, however, for the cattleyas and their relatives and hybrids, or for cymbidiums, or indeed many other genera. The point is that the suburban garden is an ideal place within which to grow a particular orchid genus to which you take a liking.

There is less need to concentrate on the large-growing, bold orchids to capture the visitor's attention in the suburban garden orchidscape. It is more important for you to be aware of the flowering period of each orchid in your landscape. Some gardeners enjoy a seasonal burst of color. For them,

A gorgeous flowering specimen of *Dendrobium densiflorum* adorns a live oak in the American Orchid Society garden at Delray, Florida.

Vanda tricolor gracefully displayed as an epiphyte rather than rigidly staked erect in a pot.

cymbidiums and dendrobiums, which flower from winter to spring, may be their first choice. Other gardeners prefer to have a succession of flowers throughout the year and enjoy coordinating the flowering times as well as the colors of their orchids. Some orchid growers like the bizarre and wonderful vegetative forms that many orchids adopt. Whatever your preference, there will be a place for many of your favorite orchids, growing naturally in your suburban garden landscape.

Do not allow initial orchid plantings in your suburban garden to become too spread out. This can lead to excess effort and time in caring for them, at least until the plantings are well established. It is better to concentrate the orchids and the gardener's efforts into a smaller area, making plans to expand the initial plantings as fancy strikes. Careful planning leads to even more pleasure in caring for your orchids growing the natural way.

While there is still scope for the suburban garden to provide a home for natural predators, their existence can be more threatened than in a larger area. For instance, neighborhood cats are a danger to birds, lizards, and frogs. Neighbors using insecticides can wipe out predator insects. Once you are aware of these threats, you may be able to overcome them. The bottom line is to be rigorous in your consideration of your orchids and their place in your garden.

8

The Courtyard
and Balcony Gardens

Courtyards are private open spaces for ground floor apartment and flat dwellers, while balconies are the equivalent open space for those living above ground level. Many of the factors that must be considered when growing orchids in a courtyard garden apply equally to the balcony garden.

The Courtyard Garden

The *Concise Oxford Dictionary* defines a *courtyard* as a space enclosed by walls or buildings. It defines a *patio* as an inner court open to sky, a paved usually roofless area adjoining and belonging to house. These two terms are interchangeable for the purpose of this book. Referring only to courtyards, what follows is intended to apply equally to patios. As building sites in our cities come at an ever-increasing premium, many ground-level urban dwellings take the form of apartments, condominiums, flats, or townhouses with a space enclosed by walls or buildings—a courtyard—attached. Courtyards can be excellent places for orchids.

By its very nature, the courtyard garden is likely to be quite small. The courtyard is probably a multiuse area including an outdoor living space with a table and chairs, a barbecue, perhaps an herb garden, a small pool, or even a children's play area. Orchids grown in it may have to compete with some of these uses. Orchids require and enjoy fresh air and sunlight. If part of your courtyard is roofed, save it for your living area and grow your orchids out in the open air.

Most courtyards are paved. Paving exposed to sunlight in the hot hours of the day will heat up. You may need to hose it down for your own and your plants' comfort. The heat stored in the

Dendrobium cuthbertsonii is a spectacular miniature orchid for cool, humid courtyards.

paving will be released as the temperature drops, helping to keep the courtyard a degree or two warmer than the ambient temperature.

If your courtyard already contains a tree, or if you can plant one or more host trees or shrubs, then orchids planted on the hosts will be out of the way of any other uses to which you may put your courtyard. If planting a tree or two, choose them with care, selecting types which do not grow so large as to damage structures, paving, or drains. Trees and shrubs help to modify the garden's microclimates. Orchids, as well as their growers, enjoy cool, shady surroundings in summer's heat and warm, sunny surroundings in winter. You can achieve this in the courtyard with carefully chosen and placed plantings.

Many orchids use scent to attract pollinators in nature. Orchid scents vary from those we find pleasant, such as *Cymbidium eburneum*, *Dendrobium falcorostrum*, or *Neofinetia falcata*, to those we sometimes find too heavy, such as many *Stanhopea* species whose flowers are said to smell like a chemist's shop. Then there are those which are downright revolting such as several *Bulbophyllum* and *Eria* species. *Bulbophyllum beccarii* flowers emit an odor described as similar to a long-dead herd of elephants. Needless to say, its pollinators are blowflies.

Orchid pollinators are usually insects, often bees and moths. Bees are active on warm, sunny days. Orchids pollinated by them are usually most strongly perfumed in daylight hours. Moths are active at night so orchids pollinated by them are usually perfumed at night. The flowers of such orchids frequently have a large white labellum enabling the moth to see it at a distance in low light.

If your courtyard is too small for planting trees in the ground, or if other considerations prevent this, the next chapter, "Growing Orchids on Host Trees and Shrubs in Containers Outdoors," will give you an alternative. Another alternative is to attach epiphytic orchids and companion plants to an attractive piece of dead timber. Orchids do grow on dead wood in the wild. When a host tree dies, its epiphytes continue to grow so long as the host still stands with its bark intact. Indeed, some orchids grow with astounding vigor when they get their roots into dead and rotting parts of their host. If you choose an attractive piece of weathered hardwood, for example, a driftwood branch, it should remain in good condition for many years. Fix the branch so it cannot fall or wobble about. Thoroughly soak any driftwood you collect from an ocean beach before use to rid it of salts. Orchids are very sensitive to salts, and contact with salt water is usually fatal to them. Fix the base of the hardwood to a metal ground peg rather than burying it in the ground. If covered by soil the wood is likely to rot quite quickly. Orchids growing on a bare piece of driftwood in the courtyard garden will not receive the natural food they would get on a living tree, so maintain a regular fertilizing program, even after the plants are well established.

The average courtyard is probably too small for any but a small feature rockery. However, the walls enclosing courtyards are sometimes of masonry construction. Some masonry walls are suitable for growing lithophytic orchids, especially bare concrete walls, either solid or in block form. If you want to grow some lithophytes but have no room for a rockery and no masonry walls, you may be able to line an existing wall with thin concrete or aggregate blocks, or even concrete-based pavers. If you build your own wall in this fashion, you can

A courtyard vertical garden planted on two tall queen palms (*Syagrus romanzoffiana*). *Dendrobium discolor* and *D. moschatum* as well as *Cattleya* intergeneric hybrids and numerous bromeliads are among many plants which thrive in this small, enclosed space.

leave occasional gaps in the masonry for greater ease in attaching plants. You might insert the odd block or paver as a small horizontal shelf to which you can tie a lithophyte securely. Remember to provide adequate drainage at the foot of the wall to cope with the runoff from watering. Water lithophytes growing on courtyard walls frequently.

You can also grow lithophytic orchids on free-standing rocks. Of course, the size of the rock is limited by the space available and the ease with which you can move it. *Laelia endsfeldzii*, a yellow-flowered Brazilian species that grows naturally on rocks, grew for us for many years on a football-sized granite boulder. Tied on with nylon strips, which soon weathered, the plant grew well and flowered in the garden. We carried it to occasional orchid displays when it was in bloom. Experiment with *Dendrobium kingianum* on free-standing rocks. This species is easy to obtain from the nursery trade, easy to attach to a rock, and easy to grow in all but tropical climates. Experiment with waterproof, nontoxic glue for ease of attachment of this and other lightweight plants to nonporous surfaces.

For terrestrial orchids in a courtyard, a raised garden bed is preferable to one at ground level.

In days gone by the famous Hawaiian orchid growers and hybridists Goodale and May Moir had a massive specimen of *Oncidium sphacelatum* growing in a huge masonry planter in their garden. At flowering time it bore hundreds of flower stems with almost-incalculable numbers of its golden, chestnut-barred flowers. The Moirs are said to have given a dinner party each year so their friends could enjoy this amazing floral bounty. A specimen such as this could look dramatic as the focal point in a courtyard garden.

A *Vanda* flowering on a courtyard palm.

Cattleya skinneri var. *alba*, a beautiful species for courtyards, growing at RF Orchids, Florida, on a dwarf date palm, *Phoenix roebelenii.*

You will improve both drainage and air circulation greatly by raising the bed. Orchids are likely to suffer from excess water, which rots their roots and is usually a fatal condition, if you plant them at ground level in a courtyard. Besides, a raised bed lifts the orchid flowers closer to eye level. It's easier to work, too. Add an extra dimension in decoration to the courtyard garden by growing epiphytes on trees in moveable containers and lithophytes on free-standing rocks. The small area of the courtyard allows you, the orchid gardener, to concentrate on particular facets which you may overlook if growing on a bigger scale. Arranging the courtyard garden can be more akin to interior decorating.

Paying attention to flowering seasons and colors can pay dividends. Many courtyard orchid gardeners aim to have one or more orchids in flower on every day of the year. Fragrant orchids, of which there are thousands, are delightful in the outdoor living area. Try some of the *Brassavola* species that are perfumed at night and the Australian native dendrobiums that perfume the air on warm spring mornings.

Small-growing and miniature orchids are charming in the confined space of the courtyard garden. Orchids with bizarre vegetative shapes, such as leaves like rat tails or saw teeth, become even more interesting when you can examine them close at hand.

The only equipment you need in the courtyard orchid garden is a lightweight hose with an adjustable nozzle capable of emitting a fine spray to increase humidity on hot, dry days, and a sprayer capable of holding 2 to 9 pints (1 to 5 liters) of fertilizer in solution. Courtyard gardens do not offer much encouragement to natural predators, so make frequent careful inspections of your orchids to ensure they remain pest-free.

The Balcony Garden

Balconies usually have tiled, paved, or concrete floors and two, sometimes three, masonry walls. Balconies also have particular conditions which growers must take into account. They tend to be windy, dry, and not very humid. Depending on its aspect, a balcony may be sunny or shady. You can use these conditions to enable you to grow some epiphytic and lithophytic orchids on your balcony in the natural way.

How can you make your balcony suitable for orchids? If your balcony is windy, you may need to screen it. The best and probably the easiest material to use is shadecloth, which is available in a variety of colors and mesh sizes. The advantage of shadecloth over a solid material is that it filters and reduces the wind speed rather than blocking it entirely. It allows the plants some air movement. You could use other materials as a windbreak, but it is important that any material used admits light. You may find one of the modern plastics, carbon fiber, or glass suitable. If you

The hardiest epiphytes are the so-called atmospheric epiphytes, or air plants. Their nutrients come from minute amounts of dust dissolved in rain along with scant material that is leached by rain from bark surfaces. Some common groups of air plants include lichens, bromeliads, and orchids. Air plants are the first to colonize bare limbs and the hardiest of them are found high in a tree's crown, the hottest and driest of canopy locations. It is essential that these plants be able to obtain water from humid air.
—Donald Perry,
Life Above the Jungle Floor, 1988

Balcony conditions bear some resemblance to conditions in rainforest canopies, particularly those in emergent trees' crowns.

use wind-excluding material, make some provision for ventilation.

Air movement is most important to all orchids. One of its important functions in the balcony garden is to help keep the plants from overheating. Of course, a constant airflow over the balcony garden will dry both it and the atmosphere out more rapidly than a ground level garden. Thus, you need to provide for keeping humidity at a reasonable level. Simply place trays of moist gravel on the balcony floor. Have the trays a convenient size to handle—not so large that they are too heavy or unwieldy, nor so small that they do not retain much moisture. They need not exceed 1.5 inches (about 3 centimeters) in depth. Keeping them constantly moist will benefit your orchids. You may be able to purchase a structure resembling a small shadehouse designed specifically for balconies. You could make or have such a structure made to your own requirements quite simply. Consider using shadecloth over a frame of rigid plastic tubing with a built-in floor containing gravel trays.

Rhyncholaelias are excellent species for balconies. *Rhyncholaelia glauca* is almost a xerophyte, growing well on a live host, driftwood, or cork plaque.

Rhyncholaelia digbyana likes good light and humidity. Its fringed flowers are perfumed.

Reedstem epidendrums and their intergeneric cousins such as this ✕*Epicattleya* Matutina are good, tough, sun-loving balcony plants.

Carefully consider the use of companion plants for your balcony orchid garden. Ferns and large-leafed aroids are good if they are adequately shaded. If they thrive, you will know conditions are amply humid for most orchids. Bromeliads are wonderful companion plants for balcony gardens, adding significantly to the ambience through their water-storing vases as well as their exotic appearance.

You will need to grow host trees in containers for epiphytic orchids in your balcony garden. The points raised in relation to container-grown trees apply. You cannot let host trees on the balcony grow too high, so choose one which either will not grow too tall for your balcony or which is amenable to pruning. You can also grow epiphytic orchids on your balcony on attractive pieces of hardwood as outlined under the previous heading. Secure the wood particularly well so there is no possibility of it wobbling or even falling. You will need to check your orchids grown in this way carefully each day to ensure they do not remain too dry.

Because of its elevation, the balcony will have more air movement and an atmosphere that is naturally drier than that at ground level. This means you may need to give your plants a thorough drenching every day, subject of course to prevailing weather conditions. As balconies, perforce, are roofed, you can discount the possibility of the balcony garden receiving any natural rainfall. Any rain the orchids might receive is a bonus.

There are really only two methods of growing lithophytic orchids in the balcony garden. Attach them to free-standing rocks or to the balcony's masonry walls. If you can't drill holes in the walls to affix the plants, use glue to attach lightweight plants. Drape orchids attached to the balcony wall with Spanish moss to enhance their immediate microclimate. Place free-standing rocks with orchids attached directly on the gravel surface of the humidifying trays. Unless you have well-drained planter boxes built in to your balcony, you will need to grow terrestrial orchids in pots.

Consider your balcony's aspect when choosing orchids to grow on it. In which direction does it face? Is it sunny in the morning? In the afternoon? Is it sunny at all? Do cold winter winds blow directly into it or does it face a milder breeze from the sea? If your balcony does not face the sun and does face the direction from which cold winter winds blow, select cooler-growing orchids which do not require high light levels. Protect them from wintery wind blasts by enclosing your balcony or using a structure with walls of windproof materials such as plastic or glass.

Genera suitable for shady balconies may include *Bulbophyllum*, *Coelogyne*, *Eria*, *Maxillaria*, some oncidiums, *Sarcochilus* hybrids, *Sophronitis*, and *Cattleya* hybrids involving *Sophronitis* in their makeup. Provided their large folded leaves are protected from strong winds, anguloas, lycastes, and their

hybrids should take shady balcony conditions. Sunny balcony gardens, protected from the full force of cold winds, offer a wider range of orchids. With space even more circumscribed on a balcony than in the courtyard garden, the gardener could concentrate on small, tough, fragrant orchids that bloom several times each year.

In warmer regions choose the smaller growing monopodial hybrids such as ×*Ascocenda*, ×*Christieara*, ×*Rhynchocentrum*, and ×*Vascostylis*, brassavolas, broughtonias, cattleyas, encyclias, and the myriad intergeneric hybrids between them which are all suitable for tropical and subtropical balconies. Many of these are fragrant and most of the hybrids bloom more than once each year. In cooler regions bifrenarias, brassias, summer- and autumn-flowering cattleyas and their hybrids especially with sophronitis, dendrobiums, the coolgrowing encyclias, laelias, holcoglossums, miltonias, and oncidiums are just a few of the genera from which you can make suitable selections.

You need some equipment to care for your balcony garden including a means of applying water, preferably as a drenching spray, and of applying fertilizer. Use a hand-held sprayer and a watering can with a fine rose if you can't attach a hose to a fitting inside the apartment. If you use a hand-held sprayer to water orchids, make sure you give the plants and their roots a thorough soaking at each watering, not just a superficial spray. Orchids in hot, dry areas really appreciate a misting from a hand-held sprayer several times on a hot day. Keep your sprayer nearby so you can treat your orchids as you look at them.

There is little possibility for natural predators to visit the balcony garden with the possible exception of skinks and geckos. A number of insect pests do fly so keep up a regime of checks and inspections for pests.

9

Growing Orchids on Host Trees and Shrubs in Containers Outdoors

Gardeners restricted to courtyards, patios, and balconies, or just with difficult gardens, who wish to grow epiphytes the natural way can provide themselves with a veritable orchid jungle by using host trees and shrubs in containers. A good number of suitable hosts grow well in pots or tubs, some outside and some even as indoor plants. Growing their hosts in containers adds a whole new dimension to the concept of growing orchids the way they grow in nature.

Select a host that is suitable for container growing. If space is not an issue, then you will find many palms make excellent tub specimens as well as excellent hosts for epiphytes. Some trees that grow to large sizes if planted out will stay at a manageable size in a pot or tub. Choose a species that will grow in your climate. For instance, maple (*Acer*) and some rhododendron species will grow in containers, like cool climates, and make good hosts, although they do not thrive in the tropics and warm subtropics. *Pandanus* and *Plumeria* grow well in containers in warmer regions but struggle in cold conditions. *Citrus*, especially lemons, grow well in containers in most climates if protected from winter freezes. Here are some shrub and tree

genera and species to consider, not exhaustive but simply comprising some hosts which have been tried successfully: *Acer, Banksia, Callistemon, Citrus, Cordyline terminalis, Erythrina, Dracaena marginata* and *D. umbraculifera, Eugenia, Gordonia anomala, Grevillea, Melaleuca, Pandanus, Plumeria, Prunus, Rhododendron, Tibouchina,* and *Yucca elephantipes.* The best small-growing host palm, which is easy to handle both horticulturally and physically, is *Phoenix roebelenii.*

Use a container for your host tree large enough to accommodate several years' growth. Be prepared to pot-on the tree, ultimately to the largest container you are able to handle. Make sure your container is heavy enough or so well-secured that it does not tip over in windy weather or as the tree grows taller. It is fine to choose a decorative container which pleases you and suits its surroundings. Refresh the tree every few years by removing as much old, tired potting mix as possible and replacing it with fresh medium. While your container-grown tree will benefit from the water and fertilizer you will apply to the epiphytes growing on it, once a month give it a thorough drenching watering to help wash out any harmful salts and deposits which may have accumulated in the potting medium. Be prepared to prune the tree to keep it the appropriate size and to remove any cluttering or excessively shading branches. Prune branching trees and shrubs to an open framework with no inward-growing branches for easier access to attach and maintain epiphytes.

Attach and care for epiphytes in just the same way as you would if using a garden tree, as described in chapter 1, "The Epiphytes: Growing Orchids on Trees." You will enjoy selecting orchids and companion plants that suit your tree in your particular conditions. Remember that some orchids, particularly hardcane, antelope-flowered dendrobiums and some of the vandaceous genera, grow quite tall, maybe too tall for your container-grown tree. Keep your plantings in proportion. Planting one or more vase-type bromeliads at the base of your tree will help proportionately to tie the tree in to its container as well as to provide beneficial humidity for the epiphytes attached above.

If you grow your own orchid jungle on container-grown host trees you may even have an advantage over the gardener whose trees are in the ground. You can move your containers where you like, perhaps to take advantage of the changing seasons or maybe to enjoy an orchid flowering at a particular time. Better still, your ready-made jungle can provide a stunning focal point in an orchid society exhibit.

10
Orchids in Marginal Areas

Growers can and do grow orchids in some inland regions where the climate is more extreme than in the coastal regions. Problems in these regions include cold, wet winters, very hot summers, and lack of humidity. Growers may be able counter these problems by taking steps to modify the garden climate. The single criterion for planting orchids in the garden is that your garden must be frost-free. (This criterion does not apply if you are planting temperate orchids.) In general, if your garden is subject to regular frosts, then growing orchids, other than the temperate ones, naturally in it is not for you. In such areas you will require an orchid house, probably with some form of heating in the coldest period. If, however, you live in an area subject to only occasional frosts, say three or four each winter, you can grow many orchids in your garden. Sometimes a little ingenuity can make the difference between success and failure.

To modify your garden climate you need to break down cold winds which can blow with such force that the chill factor they generate kills leaves and branches on the sides of trees and shrubs, even natives, which are exposed to the wind. In North America the cold winds come down from the Arctic as northerlies. In Australia they blow from the Antarctic in the southwest. Modify these chill winds by growing windbreaks on the northern boundary of your garden in the Northern Hemisphere and on the southern and southwestern boundary in the Southern Hemisphere. As mentioned in chapter 6, "The Large Garden," windbreaks are most effective when they break up or filter damaging winds. Triple-staggered rows of trees with the hardiest planted closest to the cold wind direction, that is the north in the Northern Hemisphere, the southwest in the Southern Hemisphere, make efficient windbreaks. The innermost row can be reasonably tall, bushy shrubs planted quite closely.

While on the subject of damaging winds we should acknowledge the occurrence of hurricanes particularly in Florida, its neighboring states, and the Caribbean Islands. There is little growers can do to protect orchids naturalized in their gardens from the ravages of a hurricane other than to use densely planted windbreaks. Perhaps palms with their single trunks, able to bend before the wind, survive as hosts better than other trees. Established epiphytic orchids are tremendously tenacious and the older well-rooted parts of tough orchids like schomburgkias and oncidiums are more likely to stay attached to their host than new growths and inflorescences. So, if part of the plant survives, it provides the basis for a new garden after the hurricane. If trees bearing orchids are knocked over rather than smashed by the hurricane, growers may be able to stand them up afterwards. As well as being tenacious, some orchids are swift to colonize areas devastated by natural disasters. *Spathoglottis* species from nearby Java and Sumatra were among the first green plants to establish on the ash-strewn slopes of Krakatoa Island after the immense volcanic eruption in 1883. In any event, the human spirit has proved to be even more tenacious than orchids, and most orchid growers are able to meet and rise above Nature's occasional challenges.

Epiphytic orchids will often survive in a marginal frost area where other orchids would perish. Even if frost is on the ground, the temperature in a tree 6 to 10 feet (2 or 3 meters) above ground level is probably a few degrees above freezing. This may be enough to enable cool-growing orchids to prosper. When cold spells are forecast, do not water orchids in your garden. They are better able to survive very low temperatures if they are dry.

If you have only a few orchids in your landscape, you may be able to cover them with some layers of newspaper when a frosty night is forecast. Newspaper is cheap and effective insulation. Four or five sheets can prevent frost forming on the

Some orchid hunters remained tight-lipped about the habitats and conditions in which orchids they found grew. Wilhelm Micholitz took such an interest in the orchids he collected that he went into detail describing habitats and conditions. Writing to Sander and Sons, his employer, from Rangoon in 1906, Micholitz described the conditions under which *Dendrobium wardianum*, one of the most beautiful of all softcane dendrobiums, grew: *You will never be able to grow them with much success either in England or Belgium. The south of France or Italy might do better. Dendrobium wardianum grows chiefly on trees but also often on rocks, mostly in positions where it gets the full benefit of the sun specially during the winter months. . . . The finest [plants] are found above the frost line, that is where the hoarfrost is frequent from November until February and where in exposed positions even water gets a thin covering of ice. Strange to say the plants do not suffer from the cold. Perhaps, since there is always bright sunshine during the day though the nights are bitterly cold, the plants store up sufficient latent heat to carry them through the night. . . . You would easily give them the cold, you cannot give them the bright sunshine. However I think you may safely try to give them a more substantial fare than the time-honored mixture of sphagnum and rubbish.*

I have noticed two years ago and now also, since Dendrobium wardianum is getting scarce, many of the natives take the small plants I reject back to their villages and plant them. Some tie them on trees, others seem to fix them on rocks and again others simply plant them in the ground like cabbages. And the result is not by any means discouraging specially in the first two methods where the men plaster the roots over with mud or cow dung. The plants do well and make good growths and I always found the mud and specially the rotten cow dung full of roots!

This seems an excellent endorsement for growing orchids the natural way in what might be considered at first thought a marginal area.

plants. Fix it in place with clothespins, adhesive tape, or garden twine. You can use plastic also to keep off rain and frost. A layer of bubble wrap under a tough plastic sheet can be effective. Ensure you anchor newspaper and plastic well to keep them in place if covering terrestrials. Remove plastic covers as soon as the frost danger has passed as sun on the plastic the following morning may generate enough heat to burn and kill the orchids. In cold climate regions some hardware and nursery suppliers stock frost cloth which you can use as a blanket to cover or wrap orchids in your garden.

Place extra mulch on garden beds with terrestrial orchids as a protection against frost. If you cover dormant terrestrials, remember to thin out the extra mulch when the cold has passed so that their new growths can reach the surface. In addition to covering your orchids, you can give them a protective coating of an antitranspirant. Widely used in the nursery industry, these come in liquid form and are usually diluted with water before being sprayed on. If using an antitranspirant for cold protection, read and understand the instructions. Ascertain how long the antitranspirant will last under your conditions, apply it at close to the maximum recommended strength, and be prepared to renew it as required. Antitranspirants gradually wash off and new growth arising after application will not be covered.

As another temporary measure, you could build a portable screen from shadecloth and plastic to place over your landscaped orchids during the coldest periods. Of course, such a measure could be used only to protect rockeries or garden beds. However, as frosts form at ground level, orchids in trees are likely to be further from the danger zone. Commercially produced plastic sleeves and wraps to protect young trees from cold are available. Gardeners in marginal areas have used

them for orchids. Gardeners could also use a portable, plastic-roofed screen, like a cold frame, in regions with dry summers and wet winters to protect orchids in the landscape from unwanted winter rain. Do not be in a hurry to keep all rain off. Like all plants, orchids thrive on rainfall. You can water, feed, and pamper your orchids to the utmost. They will grow well, but as soon as they are exposed to natural rainfall, they become green and turgid, bursting with vitality in a way artificial means cannot reproduce. Monitor your orchids carefully in rainy periods. You might put up the plastic-roofed screen only in winter when your rockery and garden-bed plants are in danger of being overwatered. Rain is never a problem for orchids growing epiphytically.

You may be able to adopt an updated version of the old Floridian smudge pot to ward off the worst cold nights that threaten subzero temperatures. Citrus growers used, and some may still use, oil-burning smudge pots in their orchards. The smoke given off by the burning fuel reduced the heat loss from radiation, preventing freezing in the orchard. However, environmental protection laws in most countries would not allow gardeners to use these devices, especially in urban areas. These days fruit and vegetable growers threatened with occasional severe frosts use huge fans over their crops to mix warm air from lower layers with the freezing air and keep it from settling. Keen gardeners could adopt a similar idea to protect orchids in their gardens in marginal areas.

You can heat gardens simply by using solar energy. The landscape itself can store the sun's warmth. Just think how rocks heat up in sunlight. As they cool down at night, rocks emit the heat stored during the day. While this heat may not be as noticeable as that from an electric radiator, an increase of a degree or two above the ambient

Cool-growing oncidiums and cyrtochilums thriving on water-filled pipes at Everglades Orchids.

ters) away. Some gardeners use solar heat stored in water as a passive heat source in cold weather. Black plastic containers of water, the larger the better, heated by the sun during the day slowly give out the heat as they cool. You could partially bury such containers in the garden and disguise them so the natural look is maintained. Some growers heat their orchid houses by circulating water heated by the sun through black polythene pipes. Gardeners could use this system in the garden provided they take some care to preserve the natural appearance. You would only need the system during the cold months. You would remove and store it for the balance of the year.

If heat is your climatic problem, increase the orchids' shade covering by extra tree planting, companion planting, and use of shadecloth in the garden. Make a temporary shadecloth roof to install over the orchids in summer. This would increase humidity levels around the orchids. Temper hot winds by creating effective windbreaks with additional plantings of shrubs and trees and using shadecloth or lattice screens. If you can exclude or temper drying winds you will raise humidity levels in your garden. Counter heat and low humidity by using water as a cooling and humidifying agent. Notice the change in temperature from walking on the sunny pavement to sitting under a shady tree in the nearby park. Notice an even-greater change if there is a fountain close to the tree with a gentle breeze blowing through it. Feel how cool and pleasant it is beside a waterfall on a warm day in the forest.

Many orchid growers are familiar with what in Australia is called the Coolgardie safe method of maintaining a cool environment to store food. The temperature of the air circulating through a hessian cover, standing in water and kept damp by capillary action, is reduced noticeably. This

temperature may be all a particular orchid requires to flourish in the garden. So, if you place some rocks strategically to act as heat sinks in your garden, they could be assets during cold winters. Solid brick or stone paths and walls can also act as heat storers.

A bed of vandas thrived for me in a marginal climate planted about 20 inches (50 centimeters) from a brick house wall which faced the sun. At 9 p.m. in winter the wall, heated by the sun during the day, was still warm to the touch. Heat radiating from it protected the vandas from ground temperatures as low as 38°F (4°C) a few feet (me-

principal, cooling by water evaporation, has been used for cooling greenhouses with fans pulling outside air into the house through a wall of wet pads. You can obtain this effect in your garden by using a sprinkler system delivering the finest mist-like droplets of water possible. Direct the sprinklers under shade trees and onto shrubs planted as windbreaks. Used in this way, sprinklers allow cool air from the evaporation of the droplets to flow around the landscaping whenever breezes blow. You can fit timers to the system to allow it to operate in the hottest part of each day. Observation and experimentation will tell you when and for how long it needs to operate. You can make such a system as simple (with hand taps and manual timers) or as expensive (with automatic controllers, solenoids, thermostats, humidistats, and the like) as you wish. You may even be able to rig up a hessian screen in the garden to use on the Coolgardie safe principle. Have regard to the direction of the hot winds if you try a screen. Mon-

The *Orchid Review* for May 1913 mentioned orchids growing on trees in what we might call a marginal area, the gardens of La Mortola between Mentone and Ventimiglia on the Italian Riviera. The orchids comprised *Coelogyne cristata*, *Laelia albida*, *L. anceps* (in bud), *Oncidium brevifolium* (in flower with a branching panicle of more than 50 flowers), *O. crispum*, *O. dasystyle*, *O. forbesii*, *O. incurvum*, *O. maculatum*, *Odontoglossum crispum*, *O. triumphans*, and (of all things) *Dendrobium superbiens*, a tropical species. Experimentation and innovation have always been the order of the day among orchid growers.

itor its water supply and remove it as soon as the worst of summer's heat has passed.

Some warm-climate gardeners use much the same principle to grow cool epiphytic and lithophytic genera in temperatures that would be too high otherwise. They block and seal one end of a hollow unglazed earthenware or concrete pipe so it is watertight, drill a couple of holes in the other end to insert a wire to hang the pipe, affix their cool-growing orchids firmly to the exterior surface, and keep the pipe filled with water. The water gradually percolates through the porous earthenware or concrete. Its evaporation ensures cool, moist conditions at the orchids' roots, which attach readily. The surface never becomes waterlogged as air circulates freely round the hanging pipe. Genera such as *Dendrobium* and *Oncidium* from high altitudes grow well under this method in warm low altitude climates. Experiment with different genera in your particular conditions. You may be surprised to find a number of formerly difficult species will thrive for you.

Orchid growers in Europe and North America have for years moved indoor- or greenhouse-grown orchids out into the garden during the warmer months, returning them to winter quarters as soon as frost threatens. This routine allows the orchids to benefit from increased light, fresh air, and natural rain during their growing season. Growers in marginal areas who have suitable winter quarters such as a sunroom, glassed-in veranda, or even bay windows in the house might try this practice. Orchid growers generally are inventive and ingenious. No doubt, some are already using other simple effective methods of growing orchids the natural way in gardens in marginal areas.

PART THREE

Containers
in the Garden

11

Growing Orchids in Pots and Other Containers

While this book is intended for those who wish to grow orchids as they grow in nature (and no orchid has yet been found in the wild growing in a pot), some growers may need to keep their orchids in pots or other containers. You may not be in a permanent location, for example, or you may wish to move your plants to various parts of your garden. Nevertheless, do consider growing orchids the natural way wherever possible. The late Hermon Slade, a doyen among garden orchid growers, said that the only one thing worse than a potted orchid is a potted mind. For those who must keep their orchids in pots, here are some suggestions about growing them in the garden, without any special form of housing.

Container Types

Growers use three types of pots, each provided with a drainage hole or holes, for the culture of orchids: terracotta, plastic, and ceramic. Do not use any pot that does not have at least one generous drainage hole in the bottom. It is not suitable for orchids.

Terracotta pots are made of fired, glazed or unglazed clay. They are available in many different sizes, from 1.5 inches (3 centimeters) up to tubs capable of holding specimen-sized cymbidiums, and in several different designs. Those designed specifically for epiphytic orchids are unglazed and have slots in the sides to admit more air to the orchid's roots. Another type of terracotta pot has a squat design with the diameter greater than the vertical height. This type is often called an azalea pot and is suitable for all orchids except the most strongly rooted terrestrial genera such as *Cymbidium* and *Sobralia*. Not too much potting medium is needed to fill the pot, saving on wastage.

The standard terracotta flowerpot is deeper than its diameter and usually tapers a little from a narrower base to a broader top. It is suitable for the strongly rooted terrestrial genera, but too deep for fine- or shallow-rooted orchids as it holds too much potting medium, which such orchids do not and cannot utilize. Other designs of terracotta pots are sometimes available, ranging from saucers to tubs to fancy types. Soak unglazed terracotta pots overnight before use to ensure the pot is damp. If pots are used bone dry, osmosis can cause moisture to be drawn from the potting medium to the pot, and even from the newly potted orchid, with consequent harm to the plant.

A white terete *Vanda* grows in a big terracotta pot.

breeze, particularly so with the larger sizes of azalea pots and tubs. Similarly, the smaller sizes of slotted pots are not too heavy for hanging in the garden. When potting orchids in terracotta, growers usually place broken pieces of pot, broken bricks, or stones over the drainage hole to stop the potting medium from clogging it. This material also acts as ballast, adding weight to the bottom of the pot. Plastic pots are very light and prone to blowing over and rolling around in any breeze. Plants in plastic pots in the garden become top heavy. Ceramic pots are heavy but usually too expensive to risk being broken.

Because of their porosity and color, terracotta pots remain cooler than the thin-walled, usually black, plastic pots in hot weather and warmer in cold weather. Warmer-growing orchids such as many of the vandas and the tropical dendrobiums appreciate equable temperatures about their roots. Many gardeners prefer the look of unglazed terracotta in the garden. Its nonshiny finish and natural color seem to complement plants better than do the ubiquitous shiny black plastic pots. To reuse both plastic and terracotta pots, soak them in a solution of bleach to kill any harmful pathogens, then scrub to remove dirt, salts, and old roots, and finally soak them in clean water. Unglazed terracotta pots dry out more quickly than plastic, ceramic, or glazed terracotta pots, necessitating more frequent watering. This is an advantage to the orchid because it assists in maintaining the rhythm of the wet/dry cycle.

The best plastic pots are designed specifically for orchids. The manufacturers of these either are orchid growers themselves or consult with experienced orchid growers. Your orchids are special feature plants in your garden, so if you must use plastic pots, only use those specifically designed

Being porous, unglazed terracotta lets air in through the pot walls and lets water evaporate out through the walls. This suits epiphytic and lithophytic orchids as they need air round roots, taking in oxygen through those organs. Evaporation through the pot sides helps remove excess water from the potting medium and prevents rotting roots. Plastic and ceramic pots do not breathe. The only way water can escape from them and oxygen can enter is through the bottom drainage holes or from the surface of the potting medium. Unglazed terracotta is preferable for orchids.

Terracotta is heavy, therefore pots are less inclined to tip over or to be blown over in the

English novelist H. Rider Haggard, best known for his romantic adventure story *She*, was a committed gardener and orchid lover. He maintained three orchid houses, growing a wide range of genera. In 1904 he published *A Gardener's Year* which was a diary of the year 1903 describing his garden and his activities in it month by month.

for orchids. Plastic pots are much cheaper than the other types. You can use those designed specifically for orchids with confidence that they will do the job. Plastic pots are much lighter to handle than terracotta pots. They do not need to be soaked before use.

It is easy to punch additional holes for drainage or aeration in plastic pots but nearly impossible to do this with terracotta pots. The impervious walls of plastic pots do not retain salts, which build up from hard water and chemicals in potting media and fertilizers, to anywhere near the same degree as unglazed terracotta. The potting medium in plastic pots stays more damp than that in unglazed terracotta as there is no evaporation through the plastic pot walls. Water orchids in plastic pots a little less frequently. However, plastic pots do dry out quite quickly in the garden, exposed to constant air movement and sunlight. By virtue of their impervious finish, plastic pots seldom attract growths of algae or moss on the exterior surface. Terracotta pots sometimes harbor such growths, which some gardeners find unattractive, and need to be scrubbed clean. Plastic pots are easy to wipe with a damp cloth if they become dirty and you wish to bring orchids into the house or display them.

It is quite easy to remove the roots of potted orchids without damage from properly designed plastic pots. Because they are slightly flexible, give a gentle squeeze around the pot walls. This is often all that is needed to loosen the orchid's roots. If the pot is overgrown cut it up with a pair of garden scissors and remove the orchid. Roots do tend to stick more firmly to terracotta, but you can remove them by running a thin blade round the inside wall, by letting the orchid dry out for a few days or, for species such as *Vanda* with thick, fleshy roots, by soaking them thoroughly. Simply break a root-bound terracotta pot with a rap or two with a hammer, pick out the loose pieces, clean up any dead or broken roots, and repot the orchid, broken pieces of pot and all, into a larger pot.

Very few ceramic pots are designed or suitable for orchids. Many are wider in the middle than at the top. This makes it extremely difficult to extract a well-rooted plant at repotting time if the rootball has expanded to fill the widest space. Many ceramic pots are top heavy, designed for indoor rather than garden use. Use them for indoor decoration, slipping pots of flowering orchids into them, then returning the orchid pot to the garden when flowering is done.

Never leave a potted orchid standing in a saucer of water no matter whether planted in a plastic, terracotta, or ceramic pot. To do so is to invite rotting roots and stagnant potting medium. If you must grow orchids in pots in your garden, the advantages of unglazed terracotta pots, especially in the larger sizes, outweigh the disadvantages of the other types.

Growers often use baskets made of wire, plastic, or wood for growing orchids in the garden. These are designed for hanging and are generally sold complete with wire or chain hangers. Most

Cymbidium erythrostylum in a plastic pot.

epiphytic orchids enjoy the additional light and air movement gained by hanging their containers. Experiment with different heights for hanging and with the differing amounts of light and shade in your garden until you find the microclimate that suits each of your orchids in baskets.

Many sympodial orchids such as bulbophyllums and coelogynes have elongated rhizomes, which scramble across their containers with quite a distance between pseudobulbs. When they reach the edge of their pot they have nowhere to go but out beyond the pot rim into the air. Potted in a basket, such types are able to extend their rhizomes down and round the basket's exterior surface. This they do with much gusto, assuming a much more natural and charming appearance than they have in the rigid confines of a pot. Bas-

kets allow more air to reach the roots of orchids growing in them. As the basket is suspended, the orchid has space for its roots to dangle freely in the air, just as those of many species do in nature.

Some orchid genera, including acinetas, some houlletias, and the very popular stanhopeas, send their flower scapes straight down. Grown in pots the scapes are trapped, but in baskets they are able to drill through both potting media and lining to display their fabulous and fascinating flowers below.

Wire baskets need to be lined with material to prevent the potting medium from falling through. Growers use materials such as coconut fiber, paperbark sheets (the bark of *Melaleuca* species), sphagnum moss, shade cloth, and even several thicknesses of newspaper for lining. Plastic baskets

Hardwood baskets, such as this one containing *Cattleya luteola* from Brazil, can be suspended or placed on a surface.

Lycaste balsamae 'Everglades' grows well in a squat, rigid plastic pot.

are usually made specifically for orchids. They look somewhat like a rigid mesh pot. Lining is not usually required, as the holes in the mesh are small enough to prevent all but very fine potting media from falling through. Some of the early plastic baskets became brittle and prone to split-

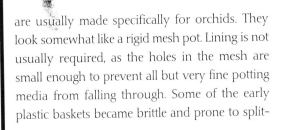

Sir Joseph Banks, probably the pre-eminent scientist of his day, was no armchair traveler. He made his first botanizing trip in 1766 to Newfoundland, where he may have been the first plant collector to lose his collection under the threat of the elements. His collection was jettisoned to help save the ship in a storm. His subsequent journey with Captain James Cook on the *Endeavour* is famous. As well as being a hands-on traveler, Banks was a hands-on orchid grower, cultivating several tropical epiphytes successfully in woven wicker baskets in the early nineteenth century. He is recorded as being the first in England to flower, in 1819, the lovely *Vanda tessellata*, then known as *V. roxburghii*.

ting, dumping their contents on the ground. Make sure any plastic basket you use has been ultraviolet stabilized.

Orchid growers often employ wooden baskets made from teakwood slats, but any hardwood will do. They are usually square, sometimes rectangular, or even octagonal. They are constructed on the pigsty design, secured by wire inserted through holes drilled through each slat at the corners. Growers commonly use them to cultivate vandaceous genera, which generally resent having their roots buried in potting medium. They secure the orchid to the slats with wire and allow it to grow with no potting medium whatsoever. In good conditions orchid roots quickly attach to the wood, hanging vertically once they grow beyond their basket. However, growers often use a coarse potting medium in wooden baskets.

Enthusiasts make other basketlike containers to cultivate various orchid genera. Hanging cylinders made from the heavy plastic mesh used to exclude leaves from roof gutters are particularly useful for some of the smaller epiphytes. Fill the

Like many vandaceous orchids *Rhynchostylis gigantea* 'Olympia Starfire' grows well in a wooden basket.

The showy *Trichopilia hennisiana* displayed at its best in a basket.

cylinder with a potting medium that retains some moisture and tie the orchid to the exterior surface. Some growers make "socks" from shadecloth or similar flexible but inert material, sewing it onto a wire rim. These are a combination of the wire basket and the plastic basket. Their advantage is that the grower can tailor make them to the particular orchid.

You must suspend wire baskets, hanging cylinders, and "socks." They will not sit comfortably on a surface. You can either suspend plastic and wooden baskets or place them on a surface, although it rather defeats the purpose of using a basket if you don't hang it. Baskets of all types dry

out more quickly than pots, particularly when hanging in the garden exposed to free air movement. Water orchids in wire and plastic baskets every two or three days, depending on the weather conditions and the density of the potting medium. Water orchids hanging in the garden in wooden baskets with no potting medium every day except perhaps for cold, overcast wintry days, even more frequently on hot, windy days.

Many epiphytic orchids grow well on slabs of various materials including cork from the cork oak (*Quercus suber*), fiber from various tree fern species, or well-weathered hardwood. Growers often designate these as mounts for orchids rather than containers, as the plants are grown on them, not in them. Some growers use coconut husks and coconut shells where they are readily available. Tie orchids to mounts in the same fashion as you would attach them to trees. Fix them so firmly that they cannot move and damage new roots. Provide wire hooks near the tops of mounts to hang them. Orchids on mounts will dry out very quickly in garden conditions so you should water

Cattleya Kew × *C. labiata* growing in a hollow log which can be moved in the courtyard to take advantage of the blooms.

Many orchids grow better on mounts than in containers. This lovely *Encyclia alata* enjoys the air round its roots on a large hardwood mount.

Large growers like these individuals of *Cymbidium finlaysonianum* look great and grow well in tall hollow logs.

them every day, more frequently in warm, windy weather. Fertilize them carefully, as mounts are not a great food source for orchids. Some orchids, particularly some of the smaller-growing vandaceous genera, do not like tree fern mounts and prefer cork or hardwood slabs.

Several epiphytic species, notably cymbidiums, grow naturally in hollow branches, knotholes, and concavities in host trees. You might obtain hollow logs from firewood suppliers, timber mills, and sites recently cleared for development or road widening. Do not collect hollow logs from natural bush or forest, as they are probably the home of native animals or reptiles. In particular, do not cut standing dead trees or hollow branches. In many countries they, too, are homes for wild animals and are important nesting sites for several endangered bird species. The interior of a hollow log usually stays quite damp after a thorough watering. The walls do not breathe like unglazed terracotta pots. Once they are established, orchids in logs will not need as much water at the roots as those potted in terracotta, although they appreciate a spray over their foliage on warm days. Fertilize them as you do your other orchids.

Repotting Orchids

Orchids need a new home when they have outgrown their container. Even the most casual inspection will tell you when your orchid is rootbound, straining the pot walls with growths spilling over the rim. Just as humans feel uncomfortable crammed into clothes too small for them, so orchids look uncomfortable in containers that have become too small. Isn't this the perfect time to free them forever from container-bound constraints and plant them in your garden to grow the natural way?

Donald Beaton was one of the first growers to practice coolhouse culture for orchids coming from cool climates. Sir William Hooker described him as "one of the ablest and most scientific gardeners of this country." In Paxton's *Magazine of Botany* for 1836, Beaton described how he grew newly imported epiphytic orchids. He tied them onto firm, damp balls of moss and kept the moss, but not the plants, damp. When root growth started, he placed the ball into a forked stick comprising three twigs arising from the same point, then suspended the stick. When the plant was well established, he potted it, stick and all, so that the ball of moss was just above the surface of the potting medium. John Gibson, sent to India in 1836 to collect orchids for the Duke of Devonshire, used a similar technique when packing the thousands of plants he found in the Khasia Hills. It was successful because his shipments arrived in good condition. There is no reason why this idea would not be successful in the present day.

Orchid growers who keep their plants in pots generally aim at repotting each orchid after three years. The orchid should have filled its pot after this time, and its potting medium will have deteriorated almost to the useless stage. Potting media, apart from inert materials like sand, gravel, or pumice, start to break down from the moment they are put into the pot. The most common ingredient in potting media is pine bark. In garden conditions nitrogen-consuming bacteria and minute fungi inhabit the bark and gradually break it down. As the bark breaks down it provides sustenance for the orchid's roots. If you leave it much longer, there is a danger that the bark will break down to mud, which will smother the orchid's roots, keeping them too wet and eventually killing the plant.

The best time to repot any orchid is just as it is about to start into growth. Repotting at this time causes the least disturbance to the plant, enabling it to send its new roots into the potting medium and its new growths across the surface. Many orchids commence growing in the period from the end of winter to the end of spring. Some commence growing in autumn. Some grow year-round, but not many start growths in the heat of midsummer or the cold of midwinter. The initial signs that a sympodial orchid is about to start into growth include a swelling at or near the base of the youngest pseudobulb, often called the lead

bulb, and the appearance of new root tips on visible roots and from the base of the youngest pseudobulb. Monopodial orchids signal their season of growth by producing new roots from their stems and new root tips on existing roots. The newest leaf starts to emerge from the apex of the plant. Monopodials often start new growth in the warmer months. As a rule of thumb, spring is the safest period in which to repot orchids. However, if you acquire an overgrown, root-bound orchid, tackle it without delay, avoiding only the respective hottest and the coldest times of year. The sooner you split up, clean up, and repot such an orchid—or better yet, plant it out in your garden in the natural way—the sooner it will start to grow.

Certain orchids have fetched fabulous prices over the years. They reached their high watermark in England in the early twentieth century when there was a mania for heavily colored forms of *Odontoglossum crispum*, called solid-blotched crispums. Good growers could divide plants regularly and put them up for sale when established, thus recouping their initial outlay and often making a substantial profit. In the *Orchid Review* for November 1937 the late A. A. McBean, orchid nurseyman, reminisced about *O. crispum* var. *pittianum* which received a First Class Certificate (the highest possible award) from the Royal Horticultural Society and a Gold Medal from the Manchester and North of England Orchid Society. In 1906 Protheroe and Morris, the famous orchid auctioneers, put up for sale a duplicate comprising just three pseudobulbs. All the notable growers of the day, English and continental, were present. McBean takes up the story:

However, the late Mr. F. Sander, founder of the present famous Saint Albans and Bruges firm, was commissioned to purchase this plant; we could not accept the commission as we were hoping to purchase the plant at round about 700 guineas, so imagine the tension when the price soared to 1000 guineas, and the bidding still going strong! My last bid was 1125 guineas, followed by 1150 guineas in the baron's interest. The auctioneer remarked, "It is against you, McBean," to which I replied, "Thank God for it, sir." Following that sale, we sold a neat duplicate, one bulb and growth, at 800 guineas, and two small duplicates at 1100 guineas the pair, so that within five years of Mr. Pitt's purchase of the original plant, he had obtained 3000 guineas for duplicates, and still retained the leading and best portion of this distinguished and lucrative orchid.

This was at the time the highest price paid for an orchid sold by auction and, as far as was known, privately.

Potting media for orchids vary from those containing many ingredients, made to complicated formulas, to very simple ones containing just one ingredient such as pine bark, gravel, sphagnum moss, or charcoal. All successful potting media have one factor in common—they are well drained. As your potted orchids will be growing outdoors in your garden, subject to all the vagaries of the weather, the single most important requirement of their potting medium is that it be very free draining. You can obtain bags of potting media specially prepared for specific types of orchid from general plant nurseries as well as from specialist orchid nurseries. Using such a medium will save time in making up your own potting medium. As you become more experienced in growing orchids in your own conditions, if you intend to stick with containers you can decide on media that suit you. However, many very experienced orchid growers use commercially prepared media exclusively.

Take the orchid to be repotted out of its old container. To avoid a wrestle with a tightly rootbound plant, try bumping the pot on the ground or potting bench. Thump the sides of a plastic pot with your fist. Even if that doesn't work it's good therapy! If that does not loosen it, run a thinbladed knife round the pot wall between the pot and the root mass. If the orchid still won't budge, turn the pot on its side and hose out all old potting medium. If all else fails to dislodge the plant, break the pot if terracotta or cut it if plastic. It's cheaper to sacrifice a pot than to damage a valuable plant.

Once the orchid is out of its pot, gently separate its roots using your fingers like a comb, and shake the plant to help untangle the root mass. Trim off any dead or broken roots and old bulbs or canes. If the plant is large, old, and in dire need of repotting, its roots may appear as a big potshaped mass. To make this manageable, simply cut off the bottom half of the root mass. Sterilize the cutting tool before and after use to prevent the spread of disease. To divide any sympodial orchid, simply cut the rhizome connecting the pseudobulbs or stems with a sterile cutter, leaving at least four pseudobulbs or stems connected. You can discard the oldest bulbs or retain them for propagation. As large to specimen-sized orchid plants look better in the garden than small ones, you may care to plant several divisions of the orchid you are handling in the same pot. Place them so that their leads face outwards to produce an even, balanced specimen as they grow.

You can obtain specimen-sized plants reasonably quickly by cutting the rhizomes early in the third year while leaving the orchid in its pot. It will produce a new growth from the older bulbs near the cut. Pot the whole orchid, including the divisions you have created, into a bigger container at the end of the year rather than pulling it apart. Choose a pot that will accommodate three years' growth but no more. Orchids do not like to be overpotted as the unused portion of the potting medium will stay too wet, become sour, and harm the orchid. Besides, it is a costly waste of potting medium. Yet another reason for growing orchids the natural way in your garden is that it's cheaper—no cost for pots and potting media.

Check the plant to be potted, removing any dead leaves or leaf husks. These can provide hiding places for pests. Split old *Cymbidium* husks vertically, then peel them off sideways taking particular care of any new growths or growth buds, often called eyes, at the base of the bulbs. If using a terracotta pot, place some pieces of broken pot, tiles, crocks, brick, or even burnt bones on edge across the bottom to provide free drainage and retain the potting medium without blocking the drainage hole. If using a plastic pot,

For some years I have cultivated at Nice Cypripedium insigne *[now properly known as* Paphiopedilum insigne*] and some of its best varieties in pots, to adorn the porch of my villa during the winter. Save that there is overhead protection from rain there is no special protection of any kind given them in winter, though there are several degrees of frost in severe winters.*

—Edward H. Woodall, *Orchid Review*, 1909

Woodall also grew the supposedly delicate *Paphiopedilum fairrieanum* "in pots under the shelter and shade of a fine olive tree where Cypripedium insigne *passes the summer . . . in the full draught of the summer sea breezes . . . [It] has become thoroughly established, and its vigor and growth exceed anything I have seen elsewhere."* Five years later Woodall wrote again to say how well his plants had continued to grow *"at the foot of an olive tree with some sheltering shrubs to screen the plants from summer suns and winter frosts . . . having endured lately, without apparent injury, three nights below freezing and a snowstorm that for a short time threatened to fill their pouches with snow."*

you don't need to use such material for drainage, but you may need to add it simply as ballast to keep the pot from blowing over. Spread the orchid's roots in the new pot holding the plant so the bases of its bulbs are about three-quarters of an inch (2 centimeters) below the pot rim. Pour in the potting medium, tapping the pot several times on the ground or potting bench to settle the medium around the orchid's roots, until it reaches a level just below the pot rim. Settle a newly potted orchid firmly in the pot to prevent it wobbling and damaging newly growing roots or falling over. Tie cattleyas and dendrobiums with heavy pseudobulbs to stakes inserted in the pot to ensure stability.

Use a similar technique to repot orchids in baskets. As these containers are often too shallow to allow stakes to be used effectively, try tying top-heavy pseudobulbs to the basket's wire hangers. At their initial watering, soak newly potted orchids thoroughly to ensure the potting medium is wet throughout, then water sparingly for about a month to encourage new root activity. Place the orchids in a slightly more shady spot than their final growing position for two or three weeks to enable them to recuperate from repotting, then move each to its permanent growing place in the garden.

12

Container-grown Orchids
in the Garden

*A*void placing container-grown orchids in positions that are exposed to excessive wind, subject to heavy traffic, or in the way of garden implements. One of the drawbacks of orchids in pots is that they are not anchored to the terrain in the same way as they are fixed when grown in the natural way. Pots will blow over in strong wind, damaging their precious contents. Similarly, romping children or dogs can knock over pots, damage plants, and break flower stems. Select positions out of their reach in the garden. Avoid positions where pots will be threatened by mowers or other garden implements. Ensure hoses are not left lying where pots will be knocked over when the hose is moved.

If you place orchid pots directly on the ground in the garden, their drainage is likely to be blocked so the potting medium will stay too wet. Worms, which block drainage, and harmful insects can enter the pots through the drainage holes. Tree or shrub roots are invasive. Pots placed near or over them on the ground provide a ready source of water and food and will be invaded with surprising rapidity. Water and garden soil carry some pathogens that can be harmful to orchids. These

may find their way into pots placed directly on the ground. To keep your potted orchids off the ground use low benches made from heavy gauge wire mesh such as that manufactured as fencing mesh, galvanized pipes, hardwood strips, or similar materials. Sheets of corrugated iron will do the job but could look unsightly in the garden. You can place pots and hollow logs individually on bricks, flat stones, or pavers to keep their bases above ground level. Slugs and snails love the cool, damp shelter provided by orchid pots and logs on the ground. Make sure you inspect all containers, benches, and supports placed near ground level to catch any pests which may damage your plants. Located under trees in the garden, your orchids in containers will catch much of the detritus falling from above, including leaves and twigs. Do not let this detritus build up to bury the orchid's bulbs. It may cut down the amount of light and air available to the orchid and can form a comfortable home for orchid pests.

Attach basket hangers and other suspended orchid containers carefully, ensuring they are slip-proof at their points of suspension. If you hang them from trees, choose a branch stout enough to support their weight. If you hang them under a garden structure, such as a pergola, trellis, or gazebo, ensure it too is strong enough to support them. Baskets and containers may look effective hung from walls or fences. Make certain the means of attachment is really secure. Hanging baskets become surprisingly heavy when soaked through in heavy rain. Do not hang containers, however light they may be, from dead limbs. They will fall when least expected. It is almost axiomatic that in so doing the flowers that you might have waited a year or more to see will be smashed.

Use wire, either galvanised, stainless steel, or heavy copper, to hang the basket or other container. Ensure the hangers are securely attached to the basket. All wires exposed to the elements will corrode eventually. Check them at reasonable intervals and be sure to replace any that show signs of corrosion. Otherwise, that axiom about containers falling when least expected will be proved again. Plastic-coated wire corrodes under the plastic where you can't see it. Hanging containers can swing about in strong breezes, so it is sensible to suspend them where they cannot crash against anything solid which might damage them. If you hang them above head height, take containers down occasionally to check their contents at close range. Ill-directed hosing or boisterous weather conditions can wash out potting medium, while birds can take a liking to basket lining such as coconut fiber, which makes fine nesting material.

Orchids mounted on slabs of cork, tree fern, or weathered hardwood grow well in the garden if you take some care in their positioning, subsequent watering and fertilizing. It's best to hang mounted orchids at a slight angle from vertical. If you hang them vertically, raindrops and water applied overhead can glance off the mount's surface before wetting the attached orchid's roots. If you fix them at an angle of up to say 45° from the vertical, rain and applied water will drench the mount and orchid and will penetrate the fibers of tree fern mounts. An easy way of fixing the angle at which you intend to hang mounts is to hook them onto an A-frame made of two sheets of heavy gauge galvanized wire mesh. Attach a single sheet of wire mesh at the appropriate angle to a garden wall or fence.

Certain epiphytic species grow in such tangles or in such a scrambling manner as to be impossible to accommodate in a pot. Species such as *Rodriguezia decora*, pendant *Scuticaria hadwenii*, the pencil-leafed *Dockrillia teretifolia* (formerly *Dendrobium teretifolium*) and its allies, the true miltonias, and many oncidiums grow much better on mounts with their roots exposed to the air than they do in pots.

Cork and weathered hardwood slabs have very little moisture-retaining capacity. You may need to water orchids mounted on these materials every day, and twice a day in hot summers. Tree fern slabs retain more moisture once soaked, but dry out rapidly in garden conditions. Water them daily in hot weather, too. Water orchids in pots

Ralph E. Arnold writing in the *Orchid Review* in 1949 advocated growing several species of *Calanthe* as hardy plants outdoors in protected parts of England. He suggested placing them in "moist and sheltered nooks in the rock garden." He recommended especially *C. discolor* and *C. tricarinata* and thought possibly *C. alpina* and *C. nipponica* would be worth trying.

and baskets so heavily that you see water escaping from the pot's drainage holes, and then water for a few seconds longer. Apply the same principal to orchids in baskets. Thoroughly drench mounted orchids, don't just give them a casual spray with the hose.

Orchids in hanging baskets and containers and on mounts are often exposed to higher levels of light than are those in pots at ground level. Orchids growing in high light require more frequent applications of fertilizer than those in shadier conditions. Fertilizing actively growing orchids weekly with a weak solution of fertilizer will keep them in good condition, promoting strong growths and good flowerings. You can add slow-release fertilizers to containers of orchids in the garden. Use these fertilizers sparingly and cover the granules with a shallow layer of potting medium to prevent them from breaking down in strong light. Solid organic fertilizers are not good in pots. We cannot determine precisely what elements are contained in some manures. It is possible that they contain substances that could be harmful to orchids. A solid organic fertilizer can break down the potting medium more rapidly than what it should.

When you inspect container-grown orchids in your garden, have a good look at your plants' appearance. Patches of sunburn on leaves and bulbs mean the orchid is receiving too much direct sunlight. Move it to a slightly shadier location. Lush growths of a deep green color accompanied by no or few flowers mean the orchid is growing in too much shade. Give it more light but not so much that it burns. Brown roots, leaf drop, and a constantly wet potting medium mean something is amiss with the pot's drainage system. Repot immediately into a better-drained pot and potting medium.

Bring your orchids indoors when they are in flower. Place them in a cool place out of drafts and out of direct sunlight. Enjoy the flowers on the plant for a couple of weeks, then cut the flower stems, put them in a vase and return the orchid to its garden home.

Courtyards and balconies are clearly delineated and perhaps more formal in appearance than the open garden. They lend themselves more readily than does the garden to growing orchids in pots. You can even use decorative ceramic containers where there is no danger of their being broken. Place orchid pots on decorative plant stands and plinths where they are not in danger of being knocked or blown over. In a pinch, you can place containers directly on hard, flat, paved, or concrete courtyard floors where there is no soil and no worms to block their drainage. Finding adequate shade for some orchids in the courtyard or sunny balcony can be a problem if there are no sheltering trees or shrubs. You can overcome this problem by using simple overhead shadecloth screens, either free-standing or fixed horizontally to walls.

Orchids placed against a western wall facing east need shelter from direct sunlight from say 9 a.m. in midsummer. Protect those against a west-facing courtyard or balcony wall until the sun starts to lose its power at say 5 p.m. in midsummer. Shade orchids facing the sun's midsummer path (facing north in the Southern Hemisphere, south in the Northern Hemisphere) from about 9 a.m. till 5 p.m. Shade those already facing the shady side away from the sun's path (facing south in the Southern Hemisphere, north in the Northern Hemisphere) only if the midsummer sun shines directly on them during the hottest eight hours of the day. Orchids suspended in baskets in the courtyard or balcony or mounted on slabs

Cymbidium Girrawheen 'Enid' was the best-known orchid in Australia immediately after World War II. It was the first cymbidium to be granted a First Class Certificate in Australia. In 1947 a Dr. A. C. Burstal won Grand Champion of the New South Wales Orchid Society Spring Show with *C.* Girrawheen 'Enid' which was then worth about £800 per green bulb. This period marked the start of what became known as the Westonbirt boom. Thousands of *Cymbidium* hybrids were exported from England by the pre-eminent hybridist H. G. Alexander, who had formed a commercial nursery to take over the fabulous orchid collection of Lieutenant Colonel Sir George Holford at Westonbirt after the latter's death. These plants, mostly bearing well-shaped pastel blooms, formed the basis for Australia's lucrative *Cymbidium* cut-flower export trade. They were bred from the legendary *C. alexanderi* 'Westonbirt'. *Cymbidium* back-bulbs were valued at one-quarter the price of the same plant's green bulbs. I remember being shown a propagating tray with a dozen or so *C.* Girrawheen 'Enid' back-bulbs just starting to shoot. The nurseryman said they were worth £200 each, an unimaginable amount to a schoolboy with two shillings a week pocket money.

hooked onto wire frames need shade too. Indeed, mounted orchids on wire frames attached to courtyard or balcony walls add an exotic, subtropical air to the outdoor living space. It's easy to care for them once you establish a watering and fertilizing regime. They take up little space and provide a source of intrigue and interest for visitors.

Place shade-loving genera such as paphiopedilums where they receive extra protection from taller, leafy genera such as cymbidiums. If you group orchids together in the courtyard, they are easier to inspect and care for. Grouping assists in creating a humid, sheltered microclimate that orchids appreciate. Adding container-grown companion plants, especially ferns and bromeliads, in the courtyard garden gives a bonus to both the orchids and the gardener. On the balcony, place orchids and companion plants on damp gravel trays to keep humidity levels up.

Have a neighbor, friend, or relative water your orchids, including those in your garden, if you go away for more than a few days. Give them explicit written instructions so there can be no mistakes. One trick worth mentioning can assist in growing high-elevation, cool-growing species in marginal areas. In periods of hot, dry weather slip the potted species inside a bigger pot lined with damp sphagnum moss. This creates a cool, damp environment which can help to pull more delicate species through difficult weather conditions.

13

Growing Orchids Indoors

*O*rchids are much more adaptable than many would-be growers realize. Orchids have been grown indoors for many years in countries and regions with temperate to cold climates. Positions for orchids in the home vary from a simple gravel tray on a sunny windowsill to a conservatory-type garden room or sunroom to a special orchid room complete with temperature and humidity controls and banks of artificial lights. In general, orchids are comfortable in the same conditions as humans are. If conditions in your home are comfortable for you, then they will suit a number of orchids. You do not enjoy having wet feet, sitting in a drafty or stuffy room, excessive heat, near-freezing temperature, too much direct sunlight, permanently dark conditions, extreme humidity, or aridity. Neither do most orchids.

You do enjoy fresh air with gentle air circulation, temperatures averaging 60°F to 70°F (about 15°C to 20°C) with a drop of a few degrees in the evening, moderate sunlight, and a humidity level of about 60%. So do most orchids. As all these beneficial conditions are available in your home, it follows that some orchids will grow there with

Phalaenopsis, commonly known as moth orchid, is among the most popular houseplants in the world.

Phalaenopsis Brother Lanuer 'F K'.

Paphiopedilum St. Swithin, a candidate for indoor growing in similar conditions to *Phalaenopsis*.

A nice white *Phalaenopsis* with the raceme trained to arch decoratively.

you. Why not give them a try? They make wonderful house companions. The best place to try orchids is on a windowsill that incorporates as many of these conditions as possible. Bay windows and picture windows provide light and either generous sill space or generous floor space for a piece of furniture on which to accommodate orchids.

The most suitable windowsill is probably in your living room, dining room, or bedroom rather than your bathroom or kitchen. You probably spend more time in the living room and bedroom so you will have made these rooms as comfortable as you can. Orchids appreciate this comfort too. If your plants are growing in your favorite room, you will spend more time enjoying them and they will benefit from your extra attention. What about the bathroom, with all that humidity and warmth from the shower? Well, this warmth and humidity is only present for the short time you actually use the bathroom. When you leave, the temperature drops, the light goes out, and the moisture in the air condenses. Orchids don't like to be cold and wet, so the average bathroom is not a good room for growing orchids indoors.

The ideal windowsill for orchids faces the sun for the longest period each day. In the Southern Hemisphere, such a window would face north. In the Northern Hemisphere, it would face south. Direct sunlight through a glass window is usually too intense for orchids in the home. Provide shade by curtaining windows with filmy material to filter the sun. The exact amount of sunlight to admit is one of those variables to be determined according to your own conditions and to the type of orchids you wish to grow. The sun will be close to perpendicular for several weeks at the hottest time in midsummer. It may not shine directly in the window at that time. At its lowest in midwinter the sun will shine directly in. With the curtain drawn at the brightest time of day, hold your hand between the sun and your indoor orchid. If you can just see a hazy shadow of your hand on the orchid, it is receiving the right amount of light.

If your window faces west, it may receive so much afternoon sun that it becomes uncomfortably hot for both you and your orchids. Use shade, ventilation, and air movement to ameliorate hot, stuffy conditions. Air conditioning in summer and any form of heating in winter will dry the air in your home as well as cool or heat it. If you place your orchid pots on trays of gravel, kept damp, the extra humidity provided will suit your plants. Mist their leaves with a fine spray from a hand-held sprayer once or twice each day when your air conditioner or heater is in use. Place gravel trays on the windowsill or on a table or cart that can be rolled next to the window or moved away as weather conditions dictate.

Orchids growing indoors will not dry out as quickly as those outside. In summer you may need to water them two or three times each week depending on the amount of light and air movement

The first man-made orchid hybrid, *Calanthe Dominyi*, was made in the nursery of James Veitch and Sons in 1853 and flowered in 1856. If the firm was fortunate in having John Dominy as its first hybridist, it was doubly so in having the able John Seden as Dominy's successor. The skill, imagination, and dedication of these two hybridists ensured that Veitch had a virtual mortgage on the field of hybrid orchids for nearly twenty-five years. Until 1880, if the orchid grower wanted to purchase a hybrid he had to get it from James Veitch and Sons. Fortunately, many of the early hybridists kept full records of the orchid crosses they made. The orchid is unique among plant families in that a system of registration of hybrids was instituted and lists of the registrations were prepared and printed since the early twentieth century by Sander and Sons. This task was taken over subsequently by the Royal Horticultural Society. Unlike other plant families, a record of all orchid hybrids accepted for registration is available. The record includes the hybrid's name, its parents, the hybridist, and the year of registration.

they receive. Reduce this in winter to a weekly watering unless your heater dries them out more quickly. Water your orchids in the kitchen sink using a fine-rosed watering can and lukewarm water. Like all orchids, those growing indoors need fertilizer while they are in active growth. Err on the side of caution and use half-strength fertilizer at perhaps fortnightly intervals until you gain experience of your particular conditions.

Some orchid genera do not take kindly to indoor culture. Cymbidiums for one are real children

Paphiopedilum malipoense, another beautiful slipper orchid that enjoys warmth and humidity but not stuffy indoor conditions.

of the fresh air and resent being cooped up indoors. Vandas and dendrobiums of the hardcane or antelope type generally require longer hours of sunlight than they will receive in the home. Obviously, some of the bigger growing tropical genera are unsuitable for indoor growing. Many of the smaller-growing genera with lower light requirements are quite suitable for indoor culture. Paphiopedilums can make good indoor orchids as they have a lower light requirement than many other genera. They tend to be small to medium-sized plants, so they do not occupy too much space. They do not like to dry out completely. Periodically, wipe the leaves of all indoor orchids gently with a damp cloth to remove dust that cuts down the leaves' light intake.

The best genus for indoor culture, and indeed by now just about the most popular house plant in the world, is the fabulous *Phalaenopsis* commonly known as the moth orchid and affectionately called the phal or phalie. This is a tropical genus, principally from Southeast Asia and the Philippines, with odd species in India, southern China, Papua New Guinea, and northern Australia. The plants are monopodials, with no discernible stem and with broad, soft, fleshy leaves which indicate their liking for warm, shady, humid positions. *Phalaenopsis* hybrids are produced by the thousand and are available in all colors and combinations but blue. Their flowers, which bear a fanciful resemblance to moths, will last in good condition for many weeks. Arching sprays of the large-flowered white and pink forms are a decorator's dream, and one spray will remain in good condition on the plant in the home for three or four months. Phalaenopsis enjoy broadly the same conditions we do and make wonderful plants for the indoor gardener. They are only suitable as garden plants in the tropics and perhaps the warmest subtropics. Being tropical, *Phalaenopsis* plants do not like cold water. Water them with tepid or room-temperature water. If your town water supply is heavily chlorinated or hard, use filtered water for your phals. Of all orchids, phals are almost gross feeders. In good conditions they grow actively through the year, carrying flowers for months. They need a lot of fuel to keep them going. Many growers use an inorganic soluble fertilizer alternately with an organic one, feeding their phals at every watering with a weak fertilizer solution. Use fertilizers at say 10% or no more than 20% of the manufacturer's recommended strength, simply adding them to the watering can when the water is at the right temperature. Phals like their roots to be damp at all times. Don't let them dry out.

After watering, lift an indoor orchid pot to get an idea of how heavy it feels when wet. Lift it again in a day or two. When it become appreciably lighter, it needs water again. With practice you can use this method to determine whether or not any container-grown plant needs water. If you live where outside temperatures plunge in cold weather, be ready to move your phals back from their window positions on cold nights. Similarly, keep them back from the glass in sunny windows because their broad, soft leaves burn easily, usually with fatal results. Phals initiate flower stems in autumn as day length shortens and temperatures drop a little. Once the flower stem has grown to about 4 inches (10 centimeters), do not turn the plant. Tropism influences the flower stem to follow the strongest light source and if you keep turning the plant every few days, the stem will twist or zigzag instead of growing up and arching attractively. When the flowers open, move your phal out of bright light to get the maximum life and color out of the flowers. Do try growing a gorgeous *Phalaenopsis* in your home. It's hard to imagine a more beautiful or longer-lasting easy-to-grow indoor flowering plant.

Growing Orchids on Trees and Shrubs Indoors

The good news for would-be orchid growers in temperate and cold climates is that you too can grow epiphytes on a host tree—inside your house. If you have a sunroom, plant room, or conservatory you have the perfect set-up to grow epiphytic orchids and companion plants on trees or shrubs in your home. Even if you live in an apartment, all you need is a reasonably well-lit position with room for a 15- to 20-inch (35- to 50-centimeter) diameter container with a correspondingly large gravel-filled drip tray under it. Then you can locate the best position for the potted host tree inside your home.

Some host trees that will grow indoors include *Cordyline terminalis*, which has red foliage, *Dracaena marginata*, *D. umbraculifera*, *Phoenix roebelenii*, and *Yucca elephantipes*. Because you, not natural rainfall, will be watering the epiphytes in your indoor jungle, you can use *Ficus* species and the umbrella tree (*Schefflera actinophylla*), both of which make excellent, hardy indoor plants. Prune any dense or awkwardly placed foliage to give clear access to the trunk and main branches. Attach epiphytes to your indoor host just the same as you would to a garden tree, as described in chapter 1, "The Epiphytes: Growing Orchids on Trees."

How about light for your indoor garden? By their very nature, sunrooms, plant rooms, and conservatories are usually placed on the sunny side of the house. In the Northern Hemisphere,

A clear-stemmed *Ficus* in a tub, ready for orchidscaping.

The *Ficus* with *Dendrobium lituiflorum* (top) and *D. draconis* tied on with nylon strips. The green tie on the trunk keeps the stems of *D. lituiflorum* from wobbling.

this is the south side, in the Southern, the north side. The sunny side is the best aspect for growing host trees and their attached epiphytes indoors. Dwellings, including apartments, without a special plant room usually have a veranda, lanai, patio, or balcony on the sunny side. The room adjoining this feature will provide the best conditions for an indoor orchidscape. In the warmer months both your host tree and its epiphytic planting will benefit from a spell outdoors in the fresh air. What better place for this interlude than your veranda, lanai, patio, or balcony?

Orchids need air movement, but in the winter you won't be opening windows to let in fresh air because you might freeze. Probably, you will use some form of heating in the house, perhaps central heating, maybe reverse cycle air conditioning. While this may provide your indoor jungle with the temperature its denizens need, it is unlikely to provide them with enough air movement. Supplement your heating system by using a small, gently blowing fan to direct warm air onto the host tree with just sufficient force to move its leaves, as though it was in a jungle zephyr. Turn

The *Ficus* trimmed and dressed with Spanish moss. The tree has several other orchid species attached, including orange *Polystachya bella* and the fragrant *Dendrobium scabrilingue* near its crown.

the fan off at night when you go to bed, and start it again in the morning.

Use a pressure sprayer to water your orchidscape, applying water to your epiphytes until you see a stream running down the host's branches and trunk. You may need to do this daily if your home is heated, as central heating and especially air conditioning dry out both the atmosphere and plants within their ambit. To ensure your host tree stays healthy, keep it damp. You may need to water it thoroughly, perhaps once a month or more frequently depending on your conditions. Wet its leaves several times each week with a fine spray from your sprayer or an atomizer kept for that purpose. This helps to keep up the humidity level your orchids need. During the warm months, while your epiphytes are growing actively, feed them with a soluble fertilizer mixed at half the manufacturer's recommended strength once a fortnight. If your host tree grows in a conservatory or a well-lit location, fertilize your epiphytes every seven to ten days. The more light orchids have the more food they can use.

Indoor trees or shrubs planted with orchids and companions provide a fabulous decorative effect. Try brightly colored miniature *Cattleya* hybrids, particularly those with *Sophronitis* in their bloodlines, for red, yellow, and orange tones. The small, cool-growing *Dendrobium moniliforme* and its hybrids have fragrant white- and pastel-toned flowers. Attached carefully and kept well watered, *Phalaenopsis* makes a superb indoor epiphyte. Because its flowers last for months, it looks spectacular as part of the orchidscape in your living room. The attractively mottled leaves some pink phals sport add to their effect. Even when the orchids are out of bloom, colorful bromeliads and lush ferns in your indoor treescape look stunning. Amaze your friends and visitors with your own indoor orchid jungle.

Conclusion

I sometimes hear a committed orchid grower say, "I just love my orchids." As incredible as this sounds, I can vouch for the truthfulness of the statement that if you do love your orchids they will grow better for you. Some growers believe their plants grow better when they talk to them, though not necessarily within earshot of neighbors or visitors. The more intense your interest in your plants, the more you will discover about them and the better they will grow, leading in turn to your increased pleasure. Enthusiasm is infectious.

Orchids growing well in your garden landscape are a joy to behold. Your friends and visitors will admire them and ask you for pieces. You can remove divisions of well-grown plants for your friends without harming the original specimen. Use a sharp blade, and cut off any roots damaged in the removal. You can propagate pieces of your landscaped plants to add to your own garden plantings. Do this by cutting the rhizome of sympodial orchids between every third and fourth bulb. Count back from the leading bulb and allow three more bulbs behind it. Most orchids respond to this treatment by producing new growths from the bulbs closest to the cuts. Remove these newly growing sections to extend your plantings or leave them to allow the original plant to build up to specimen size.

When we consider the vast range of conditions in which orchids grow throughout the world, the astounding numbers of different species and hybrids and their diversity of form and growth habit, we can see there is truly a place for every orchid. I hope your interest in this wonderful plant family has been piqued if you are not yet an orchid grower. Grow your first orchids the natural way. If you are an orchid grower, add some of your plants to your garden landscape. You will add another dimension to your enjoyment of both your orchids and your garden. As you landscape your garden with orchids, you will learn that not only is there a place for every orchid, there is an orchid for every place in your garden. Better yet, if you grow them the natural way, you will know that you will never have to repot another orchid.

Table of Recommended Orchids

The following table summarizes in an easily accessible format a few of the many orchid species suitable for use in the garden landscape. It is not exhaustive. Imaginative growers in all regions will add scores, if not hundreds, of other species to it. Nor does the list include many hybrids, inter-generic or otherwise, of which there are thousands suitable for landscaping.

Please refer to the orchid literature for specific information about these species. The table will, however, give you a quick and easy means to assess any orchids you are considering purchasing to see whether they will fare well in your garden.

Plant name	Tree (T) Rockery (R) Bed (GB)	Monopodial (M) Sympodial (S)	Tropical (TR) Subtropical (ST) Cooler (C) Temperate (CT)	Main color	Flowering	Fragrant (F)	Comments
Acampe							
longifolia	T,R	M	TR	Yellow	Summer	F	Small flowers, long thick leaves
Ada							
aurantiaca	T	S	C	Orange	Winter	—	Small plant, brilliant flowers
Aerides							
crispa	T	M	ST,C	Pastel pink	Summer	F	Erect grower, warm C areas only
falcata	T	M	TR	White/pink	Summer	F	Var. *houlletiana* has yellow/pink flowers
kraibiensis	R	M	TR,ST	Rose	Summer	F	Dwarf species, good on walls
lawrenceae	T	M	TR,ST	White/purple	Autumn	F	Large species, warm ST only
leeana	T	M	TR,ST	Purple/red	Late spring	—	Small plant, very bright color
maculosa	T	M	ST	Purple spots	Autumn	F	Thick leaves, branching sprays
multiflora	T	M	ST,C	Rose pink	Summer	F	Grow high to enjoy pendant flower stems
odorata	T	M	TR,ST,C	White/purple	Summer	F	Makes a large specimen
quinquevulnera	T	M	TR	White/purple	Autumn	F	Warm ST
rosea	T	M	ST,C	Amethyst	Summer	F	Cool grower, long inflorescences
Angraecum							
bicallosum	T	M	ST	Green/white	Summer	F	Small grower, most elegant
comorense	T	M	ST	Green/white	Autumn	F	Strong grower, long racemes
compactum	T	M	ST	White	Summer	F	Small grower, branches readily
didieri	T	M	ST	White	Spring	F	Small grower, forms clumps
eburneum	T,R	M	TR,ST	Green/white	Winter	F	Very large grower, warm ST only
eichlerianum	T	M	TR	Green/white	Summer	F	Large vining type
elephantinum	T	M	TR,ST	Cream/white	Spring	F	Large flowers, small plant
humbertii	R	M	TR,ST	Cream/white	Autumn	F	Long racemes, small grower
infundibulare	T	M	TR	White	Summer	F	Long, branching, vining type
leonis	T	M	TR,ST	White	Spring	F	Fleshy leaves, short grower
longicalcar	R	M	TR,ST	Green/white	Autumn	F	Long racemes. Makes a good specimen
scottianum	T	M	TR,ST	White	Winter	F	Terete leaves, flowers when small

				Color	Season		Notes
sesquipedale	T, R	M	TR, ST	White	Winter/spring	F	A must for its magnificent huge flowers
sororium	R	M	ST, C	White	Spring	F	Stately plant, large flat flowers
vigueri	T	M	TR, ST	Brown/white	Spring	F	Neat plant, fabulous flowers
Anguloa							
clowesii	R	S	ST, C	Golden	Spring	F	Large bulb, plicate leaves, single showy bloom. Shade, wind protection, damp when warm, dry in winter
ruckeri	R	S	ST, C	Red	Spring	F	As for *A. clowesii*
uniflora	R	S	ST, C	Pale pink	Spring	F	As for *A. clowesii*
Ansellia							
africana	T	S	TR, ST	Yellow/brown	Spring	F	Imposing grower. Panicles of showy blooms
Arachnis							
flos-aëris	GB	M	TR, ST	Yellow/purple	All year	F	Full sun; water and fertilize regularly. Warm ST only. Everblooming in TR
hookeriana	GB	M	TR, ST	Cream/white	Summer	F	As for *A. flos-aëris*
xmaingayi	GB	M	TR, ST	Pinkish white	Summer	F	As for *A. flos-aëris*
Arpophyllum							
alpinum	T, R	S	ST, C	Pink	Spring	—	Makes a good specimen
spicatum	T, R	S	ST, C	Purple	Spring	—	Grow into a large clump
Arundina							
graminifolia	R, GB	S	TR, ST	Rose/pink	All year	F	Warm ST only
Ascocentrum							
ampullaceum	T, R	M	ST, C	Rose	Spring	—	Try in warm C regions
aurantiacum	T, R	M	TR, ST	Orange	Spring	—	Very small but bright flowers
curvifolium	T	M	TR, ST	Red	Summer	—	Warm ST only
garayi	T, R	M	TR, ST	Yellow	Spring	—	Quickly clumping. Try on walls—a small plant
Barkeria							
cyclotella	T	S	ST	Magenta	Winter	—	Deciduous, scandent, with showy blooms. Moist when growing, cool and dry in winter. Roots mostly in the air. Under 12 inches (30 cm) tall
elegans	T	S	ST	Lilac	Winter	—	As for *B. cyclotella*
lindleyana	T	S	ST	Rose	Autumn	—	As for *B. cyclotella*
skinneri	T	S	ST	Cerise	Winter	—	As for *B. cyclotella*

Plant name	Tree (T) Rockery (R) Bed (GB)	Monopodial (M) Sympodial (S)	Tropical (TR) Subtropical (ST) Cooler (C) Temperate (CT)	Main color	Flowering	Fragrant (F)	Comments
Bifrenaria							
harrisoniae	T,R	S	ST,C	Cream/purple	Spring	F	Very hardy, with very fragrant long-lasting blooms. Moist when growing, dry in winter
inodora	T,R	S	ST,C	Green/rose	Spring	F	As for B. harrisoniae
tetragona	T,R	S	ST,C	Green/brown	Summer	F	As for B. harrisoniae
tyrianthina	T,R	S	ST,C	Purple	Summer	F	As for B. harrisoniae
Bletilla							
striata	R, GB	S	C, CT	Purple	Summer	—	A hardy orchid
Brassavola							
acaulis	T	S	TR, ST	Green/white	Autumn	F	A large pendulous plant
cordata	T,R	S	TR, ST	Green/white	Autumn	F	Good on trees and on walls
cucullata	T	S	TR, ST	White/pink	Winter	F	Long pendant leaves, huge flower
flagellaris	T	S	TR, ST	White	Spring	F	Terete leaves, lovely fragrance
nodosa	T,R	S	TR, ST	White	All year	F	Tropical courtyards and balconies
perrinii	T	S	TR, ST	Green/white	Spring	F	Makes a good specimen
Brassia							
arcuigera	T	S	ST	Yellow/brown	Spring	F	Spidery flowers to 14 inches (40 cm) long
caudata	T	S	ST,C	Yellow	Autumn	F	Warmer parts of cool regions
gireoudiana	T	S	ST,C	Yellow/brown	Summer	F	Try in warm areas of C regions
maculata	T	S	ST	Green/purple	Spring	F	Long lasting and very fragrant
verrucosa	T	S	ST,C	Green/spots	Summer	F	Vigorous and quite cool growing
Bulbophyllum							
amesianum	T,R	S	TR, ST	Red	Summer	F	Small, creeping grower
baileyi	T,R	S	TR, ST	Cream/yellow	Spring	F	Australian species. Warm ST only
barbigerum	T	S	TR	Rose	Summer	F	Strange long-haired labellum
biflorum	T	S	TR	Rose spots	Summer	F	Creeper, long-tailed flowers
blumei	T	S	TR	Red	Winter	—	Creeper, grows low down on trees
collettii	T,R	S	TR, ST	Red stripes	Spring	F	Rambler, attractive heads of flower

Species				Color	Season		Notes
dayanum	T,R	S	TR,ST	Purple	Spring	F	Clusters, lovely flowers, bad smell
dearei	T	S	TR,ST	Yellow/red	Summer	F	Very nice, grow shady
fascinator	T,R	S	TR,ST,C	Brown/red	Autumn	—	Long blooms, warm C regions only
gracillimum	T	S	TR,ST	Crimson	Summer	F	Slender creeping type
leopardinum	T,R	S	ST,C	Yellow/red	Summer	—	Creeping type, try shady walls
lobbii	T	S	TR	Yellow	Summer	F	Large flowers, clustering type
longiflorum	T	S	TR,ST	Yellow/purple	Summer	F	Creeping type, Australian species
macranthum	T	S	TR	Purple spots	Spring	F	Creeping type, likes shade
makoyanum	T,R	S	TR,ST	Yellow	Winter	F	Small, creeping type
medusae	T,R	S	TR,ST	Cream	Autumn	F	Fantastic "mopheads" of blooms
ornatissimum	T,R	S	ST	Yellow/red	Autumn	F	Long-tailed blooms, creeper
rothschildianum	T,R	S	ST,C	Red/brown	Autumn	F	Warm C regions
Caladenia							
carnea	GB	Tubers	C,CT	Pink	Spring	F	Variable species
catenata	GB	Tubers	C,CT	White	Winter	—	Grow in semishade
dilatata	GB	Tubers	C,CT	Green/red	Spring	—	Widespread. Tall flower stems
flava	GB	Tubers	C,CT	Yellow	Spring	—	Prefers low humidity
latifolia	GB	Tubers	C,CT	Pink	Spring	—	Sandy soil, grows cool
menziesii	GB	Tubers	C,CT	White/red	Spring	F	Flowering stimulated by fire
tentaculata	GB	Tubers	C,CT	Green	Spring	—	Large, spectacular spidery flowers
Calanthe							
brevicornu	R,GB	S	C,CT	Brown	Spring	—	Protect from wind, grow shady
cardioglossa	R,GB	S	ST	Rose	Autumn	—	Deciduous, keep dry in winter
caudatilabella	R,GB	S	C,CT	Pink	Spring	—	Temperate gardens, protect from wind
ceciliae	R,GB	S	TR,ST	White/blue	Autumn	—	Protect from wind, grow shady
discolor	R,GB	S	C,CT	Violet	Spring	—	Protect from wind, grow shady
fimbriata	R,GB	S	C,CT	Violet	Spring	—	Protect from wind, grow shady
hizen	R,GB	S	C,CT	Red	Spring	—	Cool grower, protect from wind
madagascariensis	R,GB	S	TR,ST	Rose/purple	Autumn	—	Small grower, grow very shady
masuca	R,GB	S	C,CT	Violet/magenta	Summer	—	Protect from wind, grow shady
rosea	R,GB	S	ST	Rose	Winter	—	Deciduous, keep dry in winter
rubens	R,GB	S	ST	Pink	Winter	—	Deciduous, keep dry in winter
sieboldii	R,GB	S	C,CT	Yellow	Spring	—	Protect from wind, grow shady

Plant name	Tree (T) Rockery (R) Bed (GB)	Monopodial (M) Sympodial (S)	Tropical (TR) Subtropical (ST) Cooler (C) Temperate (CT)	Main color	Flowering	Fragrant (F)	Comments
Calanthe, (continued)							
sylvatica	R, GB	S	TR, ST	Purple	Spring	—	Small grower, grow very shady
tricarinata	R, GB	S	C, CT	Yellow/red	Spring	—	Protect from wind, grow shady
triplicata	R, GB	S	TR, ST, C	White	Summer	—	Protect from wind, grow shady, warm C region
vestita	R, GB	S	ST	White/rose	Winter	—	Deciduous, keep dry in winter
Cattleya							
aclandiae	T, R	S	TR, ST	Olive/purple	Spring	F	Small grower for trees and walls
amethystoglossa	T, R	S	TR, ST	Amethyst	Spring	F	Very tall. Clusters of flowers
aurantiaca	T, R	S	ST	Orange	Summer	—	Many bright small blooms, clusters
aurea	T	S	TR, ST	Gold/crimson	Autumn	F	Warm ST only
bicolor	T, R	S	TR, ST	Olive/rose	Autumn	F	Tall plant, keep drier in winter
bowringiana	T, R	S	TR, ST	Rose	Autumn	—	Tall and strong, good rockery plant
dowiana	T	S	TR, ST	Gold/crimson	Autumn	F	Warm ST only
eldorado	T	S	TR	White/rose	Summer	F	Likes tropical conditions
forbesii	T, R	S	ST, C	Pale green	Summer	F	Small grower, warm C regions
gaskelliana	T, R	S	ST, C	Lilac/purple	Summer	F	Huge blooms, warm C regions
intermedia	T, R	S	ST, C	White/crimson	Spring	F	Small plant, try in warm C regions
labiata	T, R	S	TR, ST	Rose	Autumn	F	Lovely large flowers
loddigesii	T, R	S	ST, C	Lilac	Autumn	F	Good on trees and walls
lueddemanniana	T, R	S	TR	Rose	Spring	F	Likes open, airy, warm conditions
mossiae	T, R	S	ST	Purple	Spring	F	Beautiful large-flowered species
percivaliana	T, R	S	ST	Purple	Winter	F	Small grower, keep shady
rex	T	S	TR	Cream/rose	Summer	F	Keep cool and dry in winter
skinneri	T, R	S	TR, ST	Rose	Spring	—	Easy grower, blooms in clusters
trianaei	T, R	S	TR, ST, C	Rose	Winter	—	Large, lovely blooms
violacea	T, R	S	TR	Rose/purple	Summer	F	Must have warm conditions
walkeriana	T, R	S	TR, ST	Rose/purple	Spring	F	Good on garden walls
warneri	T, R	S	TR, ST, C	Amethyst	Summer	F	Sturdy grower, large flowers
warscewiczii	T, R	S	ST, C	Mauve/purple	Summer	F	Warm C regions only

Caularthron							
bicornutum	T,R	S	TR,ST	White	Spring	F	Warm ST only
Chysis							
aurea	T	S	TR,ST	Yellow	Summer	F	Deciduous, pendulous bulb, large flowers with new growth. Water heavily when growing, less in winter
bractescens	T	S	TR,ST	White	Spring	F	As for C. aurea
laevis	T	S	TR,ST	Yellow/orange	Spring	F	As for C. aurea
lemminghei	T	S	TR,ST	White/purple	Summer	F	As for C. aurea
Cochlioda							
noezliana	T	S	C	Scarlet	Autumn	—	Small and graceful. Cool, moist, shady
rosea	T	S	C	Rose	Spring	—	Small and graceful. Cool, moist, shady
vulcanica	T	S	C	Rose	Autumn	—	Small and graceful. Cool, moist, shady
Coelogyne							
amoena	T,R	S	C	White	Spring	F	Clumps readily, likes shade
asperata	T,R	S	ST	White	Summer	F	Pendulous racemes
barbata	T,R	S	C	White/sepia	Winter	F	Protect flowers from winter rain
cristata	T,R	S	C	White/yellow	Winter	F	Likes cool shade and moisture
cumingii	T,R	S	TR,ST	White/orange	Summer	F	Small grower, rambling type
dayana	T	S	TR,ST	Yellow/tan	Spring	F	Very long, pendulous racemes
elata	T,R	S	C	White	Spring	F	Stout rambling type, large bulbs
fimbriata	T,R	S	ST,C	Green/yellow	Autumn	F	Small scrambler, good on walls
flaccida	T,R	S	ST,C	Cream	Spring	F	Makes excellent specimens
fragrans	T,R	S	TR,ST	Green	All year	F	Likes nearly full sun to flower
fuliginosa	R	S	ST,C	Brown	Winter	—	Rambles well in rockeries
graminifolia	T,R	S	TR,ST	White	Summer	F	Clustered bulbs, thin leaves
huettneriana	T,R	S	ST,C	White	Spring	F	Small rambler
mooreana	T,R	S	ST,C	White	Spring	F	Robust, lovely large flowers
nervosa	R	S	ST,C	White	Summer	F	Erect racemes, crinkly bulbs
nitida	T,R	S	C	White	Spring	F	Small, clustered bulbs. Neat plant
ochracea	T,R	S	C	White	Summer	F	Small grower, keep damp and shady
ovalis	T,R	S	ST,C	Green	Summer	F	Scrambling species on rocks

Plant name	Tree (T) Rockery (R) Bed (GB)	Monopodial (M) Sympodial (S)	Tropical (TR) Subtropical (ST) Cooler (C) Temperate (CT)	Main color	Flowering	Fragrant (F)	Comments
Coelogyne, (continued)							
pandurata	T,R	S	TR,ST	Green/black	Autumn	F	Large rambling grower. Lovely
primulina	T,R	S	ST	Green	Summer	F	Small rambling type
rossiana	T,R	S	ST	White/brown	Autumn	F	Clustered bulbs, compact grower
speciosa	T,R	S	TR,ST	Green/tan	Spring	F	Large bulbs in clusters
tomentosa	T,R	S	TR,ST,C	Yellow/brown	Summer	F	Long, pendulous racemes, large grower, warm C regions only
Cuitlauzina							
pendula	T,R	S	C	White/pink	Summer	F	Clustered bulbs, pendulous racemes
Cymbidium							
aloifolium	T	S	TR,ST	Cream/red	Spring	F	Thick leaves, pendulous racemes
atropurpureum	T	S	TR,ST	Maroon	Spring	F	Long, pendulous racemes
chloranthum	T	S	TR	Green/yellow	Summer	—	Grow in moist, shady locales
dayanum	T,R	S	ST,C	Cream/red	Autumn	—	Small grower, scape arches down
devonianum	T,R	S	C	Purple/brown	Spring	F	Broad leaves, pendulous scapes
eburneum	T,R	S	ST,C	White	Winter	F	Tufted growth, keep shady
ensifolium	R,GB	S	ST,C	Green/brown	Autumn	F	Grow in light shade, keep damp
erythraeum	T,R,GB	S	ST,C	Green/red	Spring	F	Narrow leaves, arching racemes
erythrostylum	T,R,GB	S	ST,C	White/red	Spring	—	Neat medium-size plant
finlaysonianum	T,R	S	TR,ST	Yellow/green	Autumn	F	Large plant, very long racemes
floribundum	T,R	S	C	Red/brown	Spring	—	Miniature, grow on walls and trees
goeringii	R,GB	S	C,CT	Green	Spring	F	Grows in temperate gardens
hookerianum	T,R,GB	S	C	Green	Spring	F	Large plant, likes cool conditions
insigne	R,GB	S	ST,C	White/pink	Spring	—	Lovely terrestrial, erect racemes
iridioides	T,R,GB	S	ST,C	Yellow/red	Autumn	F	Robust grower, likes shade
lowianum	T,R,GB	S	ST,C	Green/red	Spring	—	Long scapes
madidum	T	S	TR,ST,C	Green	Spring	F	Grow in tree hollow or staghorn fern

sanderae	T, R, GB	S	ST, C	White/purple	Spring	F	Long, arching racemes
sinense	R, GB	S	ST, C	Purple/brown	Winter	F	Upright raceme, medium size, semishade
Cypripedium							
tracyanum	T, R, GB	S	ST, C	Brown/red	Winter	F	Grow in semishade, very nice
acaule	GB	S	CT	Brown/pink	Spring/summer	—	Shady, moist while growing
arietinum	GB	S	CT	Brown/pink	Spring	—	Shady, moist while growing
californicum	GB	S	CT	Brown/yellow	Spring/summer	—	Semishade
formosanum	GB	S	CT	White/purple	Spring/summer	—	Shady, moist while growing
japonicum	GB	S	CT	Green/pink	Spring/summer	—	Shady, moist while growing
macranthum	GB	S	CT	Rose pink	Spring/summer	—	Shady, moist while growing
montanum	GB	S	CT	Brown/purple	Spring/summer	—	Shady, moist while growing
parviflorum	GB	S	CT	Yellow	Spring/summer	—	Shady, moist while growing
reginae	GB	S	CT	White/pink	Spring/summer	—	Semishade, grow in a bog garden
Dactylorhiza							
aristata	GB	Tuberous	CT	Purple	Spring/summer	—	Moist, semishade
elata	GB	Tuberous	CT	Magenta	Spring/summer	—	Moist, semishade
foliosa	GB	Tuberous	CT	Purple	Spring/summer	—	Moist, semishade
fuchsii	GB	Tuberous	CT	Pink	Spring/summer	—	Semishade, likes limestone soils
majalis	GB	Tuberous	CT	Purple	Spring/summer	—	Moist
praetermissa	GB	Tuberous	CT	Pale purple	Spring/summer	—	Semishade near water
purpurea	GB	Tuberous	CT	Purple	Spring/summer	—	Moist, semishade
Dendrobium							
adae	T, R	S	TR, ST, C	White	Spring	—	Slim clumping type, cool and humid
aemulum	T, R	S	ST, C	White	Spring	—	Small and slim, grow into a big clump
affine	T, R	S	TR	White	Autumn	—	Grows hot, loves paperbarks
anosmum	T	S	TR, ST	Mauve	Spring	F	Pendulous stems, deciduous. Attach high in tree
aphrodite	T, R	S	TR, ST	Cream/maroon	Spring	F	Thick, deciduous 30-cm stems
atroviolaceum	T, R	S	TR, ST	Cream/ purple	Spring	F	Very long-lasting blooms
bellatulum	T, R	S	ST, C	White/red	Spring	F	Miniature species, lovely blooms
bensoniae	T, R	S	TR, ST	White/purple	Spring	F	Dry winter, keep wet while growing
bigibbum	T, R	S	TR, ST	Rose	Autumn	—	Warm ST, water daily when growing, dry after flowering,

Plant name	Tree (T) Rockery (R) Bed (GB)	Monopodial (M) Sympodial (S)	Tropical (TR) Subtropical (ST) Cooler (C) Temperate (CT)	Main color	Flowering	Fragrant (F)	Comments
Dendrobium , (continued)							
canaliculatum	T,R	S	TR,ST	Yellow/brown	Spring	F	Small clumping, good on paperbarks and walls. Dry winter: Warm ST
chrysanthum	T	S	TR,ST,C	Gold/purple	Autumn	F	Long, pendulous, deciduous
chryseum	T,R	S	ST,C	Gold/maroon	Spring	F	Slim canes, flowers have fringed labellums
chrysotoxum	T,R	S	ST,C	Gold	Spring	F	Stout stems, lovely arching scapes
conanthum	T,R,GB	S	TR	Yellow/purple	Winter	—	Tall hardcane type
crumenatum	T,R	S	TR,ST	White	All year	F	Blooms short-lived, very fragrant
curvicaule	T,R	S	ST,C	White	Spring	F	Stout grower, long sprays
dearei	T,R	S	TR,ST	White/green	Summer	—	Strong stems, lovely large blooms
×delicatum	R	S	ST,C	White/pink	Spring	F	Very good in rockeries and walls
densiflorum	T,R	S	ST,C	Yellow	Spring	F	Trusses of gorgeous blooms
discolor	T,R,GB	S	TR,ST	Bronze	Spring	F	Tall hardcane, long-lasting flowers, takes full sun
falcorostrum	T,R	S	C	White	Spring	F	Gorgeous cool-growing species
farmeri	T,R	S	ST,C	Lilac/yellow	Spring	—	Attractive drooping sprays
fimbriatum	T,R	S	ST,C	Gold/maroon	Spring	F	Tall canes, sprays of large blooms
fleckeri	T,R	S	ST,C	Apricot	Spring	F	Slim stems, grow cool and humid
formosum	T,R	S	TR,ST	White/yellow	Winter	—	Large, beautiful flowers
gibsonii	T,R	S	TR,ST,C	Yellow/brown	Autumn	F	Tall canes, lovely drooping sprays
gouldii	T,R,GB	S	TR	White/purple	Autumn	—	Tall hardcane, antelope flowers
×gracillimum	T,R	S	ST,C	Cream	Spring	F	Tall stems, good in rockeries
helix	T,R,GB	S	TR	Yellow	Winter	—	Tall hardcane, very twisty blooms
johannis	T,R	S	TR,ST	Brown	Autumn	F	Small hardcane, antelope flowers
johnsoniae	T,R	S	ST	White	Autumn	F	Small plant, huge lovely flowers

jonesii	T,R	S	ST,C	White	Spring	F	Good plant for rocks and walls
kingianum	R	S	ST,C	Pink	Spring	F	Wonderful in rockeries and walls
lasianthera	T,R,GB	S	TR	Red/mauve	Summer	—	Tall hardcane needs heat and humidity
lindleyi	T,R	S	ST,C	Yellow	Spring	F	Small creeper, charming sprays
lineale	T,R,GB	S	TR	Cream/mauve	Autumn	F	Tall hardcane, antelope flowers
lithocola	R	S	TR,ST	Rose	Autumn	—	Compact hardcane, full-shaped blooms, full sun
macrophyllum	T,R	S	TR,ST	Yellow/purple	Spring	F	Stout plant, long-lasting blooms
macropus	T,R	S	ST,C	Yellow/red	Spring	F	Slim stems, grow cool and humid
moniliforme	T,R	S	ST,C	White	Spring	F	Charming, small, cool species
monophyllum	T,R	S	ST,C	Yellow	Spring	F	Rambler, grows well on damp rocks and trees
moschatum	T,R	S	TR,ST,C	Buff	Spring	F	Tall canes, large fringed blooms
nindii	T,R	S	TR	Mauve/lilac	Spring	F	Tall hardcane. Heat and humidity. Try leaves in sun, roots in shade
nobile	T,R	S	ST,C	White/rose	Spring	F	Good for trees, rockeries, and walls
parishii	T,R	S	ST,C	Rose/purple	Spring	F	Stout plant, fuzzy hairy labellum
pendulum	T,R	S	ST,C	White/magenta	Winter	F	Swollen stem nodes, looks different. Beautiful
polysema	T,R	S	ST,C	Green/maroon	Summer	F	Warm C only, keep drier in winter
primulinum	T,R	S	ST,C	Pink/yellow	Spring	F	Thick, pendulous stems
pulchellum	T,R	S	ST,C	Cream/maroon	Spring	F	Long, sturdy 6-ft. (2-m) canes, large flowers
rennellii	T,R	S	TR	White/purple	Summer	F	Medium hardcane, antelope flowers
rex	T,R	S	ST,C	Yellow	Spring	F	Sturdy bulbs
speciosum	R	S	ST,C	Cream	Spring	F	Sturdy specimen, grows on walls, bright light
spectabile	T,R	S	TR,ST	Yellow/purple	Winter	—	Large, spectacular flowers
stratiotes	T,R,GB	S	TR	White/green	Summer	—	Medium hardcane, antelope flowers
strebloceras	T,R	S	TR	Brown	Autumn	F	Larger hardcane, antelope flowers
striaenopsis	T,R	S	TR	Rose	Autumn	—	Long racemes, full-shaped bloom. Dry in winter

Plant name	Tree (T) Rockery (R) Bed (GB)	Monopodial (M) Sympodial (S)	Tropical (TR) Subtropical (ST) Cooler (C) Temperate (CT)	Main color	Flowering	Fragrant (F)	Comments
Dendrobium, (continued)							
superbiens	T,R	S	TR	Rose	Autumn	—	Medium hardcane, fuller blooms
tangerinum	T,R	S	TR	Orange	Winter	—	Medium hardcane, antelope flowers
tarberi	T,R	S	ST,C	Cream/white	Spring	F	Stout, tall canes; a good specimen in shade
taurinum	T,R,GB	S	TR	Purple	Autumn	—	Tall hardcane, bull's head blooms
tetragonum	T,R	S	ST,C	Green/brown	Spring	F	Wiry, pendulous stems. Trees, walls, and rocks
thyrsiflorum	T,R	S	ST,C	White/gold	Spring	F	Lovely flowers in large bunches
tokai	T,R	S	TR,ST	Green/yellow	Spring	—	Medium hardcane, antelope flowers
victoria-reginae	T	S	ST,C	Blue/white	All year	—	Keep shady and moist. Beautiful
violaceoflavens	T,R,GB	S	TR	Yellow/violet	Autumn	—	Huge hardcane, full-shaped large blooms
wardianum	T,R	S	ST,C	White/magenta	Spring	F	Stout deciduous type, lovely
Diuris							
alba	GB	Tubers	C,CT	White/purple	Winter/spring	—	Light shade
aurea	GB	Tubers	ST,C,CT	Golden	Spring	—	Keep moist from late summer
corymbosa	GB	Tubers	C,CT	Yellow	Winter/spring	—	Water well in autumn and winter
cuneata	GB	Tubers	C,CT	Lilac	Spring	—	Light shade
maculata	GB	Tubers	C,CT	Yellow/purple	Spring	—	Light shade
punctata	GB	Tubers	C,CT	Purple	Spring	F	Light shade. Moist in autumn
sulphurea	GB	Tubers	C,CT	Yellow/brown	Spring	—	Light shade. Dry in summer
Dockrillia							
bowmanii	T,R	S	ST,C	Green/white	Spring	—	Straggly grower, keep humid
calamiformis	T,R	S	TR,ST,C	Cream/yellow	Spring	F	Great for trees and high walls
cucumerina	T	S	C	Cream/purple	Summer	—	Creeper; keep shady. Knobby leaf
fairfaxii	T,R	S	C	Yellow	Spring	F	Good on shady walls or high, shady branches
fuliginosa	T	S	TR,ST,C	Black/brown	Spring	F	Pendulous pencil-leaf species. Warm C regions

linguiformis	T,R	S	ST,C	White	Spring	F	Flat, creeping type. Full sun if watered regularly
pugioniformis	T,R	S	C	Green	Spring	F	Likes cool, humid, shade. Try on shady trees
rigida	T,R	S	TR,ST,C	Cream/red	All year	F	Small clumping species
striolata	R	S	C	Yellow/brown	Spring	F	Short pencil type, rocks and walls
teretifolia	T,R	S	ST,C	White	Spring	F	Trees and high walls in good light
Encyclia							
alata	T,R	S	ST	Brown	Summer	F	Bulbs cluster, branching scapes
altissima	R	S	TR,ST	Yellow/brown	Winter	F	Tall panicles, xerophytic on rocks
aromatica	T,R	S	ST	Cream/brown	Summer	F	Clustered bulbs, paniculate scape
baculus	T,R	S	ST,C	Cream/purple	Spring	F	Keep a little shady and damp, drier if cold
boothiana	T,R	S	ST	Yellow/brown	Winter	F	Small grower, erect scape
bractescens	T,R	S	ST	Tan/pink	Spring	F	Small, wiry leaves, erect scape
brassavolae	T,R	S	ST,C	Green/violet	Autumn	F	Clumps, keep a little shaded
chacaoensis	T,R	S	ST,C	Cream/green	Spring	F	Clusters, short upright racemes
citrina	T	S	C	Yellow	Spring	F	Pendant. Needs cool dry winter. Trees or walls. Beautiful
cochleata	T,R	S	ST,C	Cream/purple	All year	—	Tall scape, flowers open sequentially
cordigera	T,R	S	TR,ST	Brown/purple	Spring	F	Clustered bulbs, arching scape, large flowers
dichroma	T,R	S	TR,ST	Rose/purple	Autumn	F	Many lovely blooms, erect scapes
fragrans	T,R	S	ST	Cream	Spring	F	Slim bulbs, highly fragrant
gracilis	R	S	TR,ST	Tan/white	Summer	F	Tall bulbs, tall panicles. Handsome
guatemalensis	T,R	S	ST	Brown/yellow	Summer	—	Ovoid bulbs, tall branched scape
longifolia	T,R	S	TR,ST	Green/white	All year	F	Clustered bulbs, tall scapes
mariae	T,R	S	C	Lime/white	Summer	—	Spectacular. Keep drier in winter
michuacana	R	S	ST,C	Brown	Spring	—	Large plant, tall branched scapes
nematocaulon	T,R	S	TR,ST	Brown/yellow	Spring	—	Small plant, erect racemes. Neat on small trees

Plant name	Tree (T) Rockery (R) Bed (GB)	Monopodial (M) Sympodial (S)	Tropical (TR) Subtropical (ST) Cooler (C) Temperate (CT)	Main color	Flowering	Fragrant (F)	Comments
Encyclia, (continued)							
osmantha	T,R	S	TR, ST	Yellow/cream	Autumn	F	Robust, branching inflorescence
patens	T,R	S	TR, ST	Bronze	Summer	F	Clustered bulbs, short branching scapes. Try on walls
phoenicea	T,R	S	TR, ST	Purple	Summer	F	Keep dry in winter. Very fragrant
plicata	T,R	S	TR, ST	Green/purple	Summer	F	Robust plant, tall inflorescence
polybulbon	T,R	S	TR, ST	Brown/white	Spring	F	Small creeper, a good filler on trees and damp walls
prismatocarpa	R	S,	ST, C	Yellow/magenta	Autumn	F	Robust, erect scape; rockeries
radiata	T,R	S	ST, C	Cream/violet	Summer	F	Slim bulbs, erect racemes
selligera	T,R	S	TR, ST	Yellow/pink	Summer	F	Robust, blooms on tall panicle
tampensis	T,R	S	ST	Green/white	Spring	F	Small plant, makes big specimens
vespa	T,R	S	ST, C	Green/brown	Spring	F	Tall bulbs, erect, densely flowered scapes
vitellina	T,R	S	C	Scarlet	Autumn	—	Clustered bulbs, erect scapes, dry in winter
Epidendrum							
anceps	T,R	S	ST, C	Tan/pink	All year	F	Tall leafy stems, keep shaded
ciliare	T,R	S	TR, ST, C	Green/white	Winter	F	Stout plant, large fringed blooms
cinnabarinum	R, GB	S	TR, ST, C	Orange	All year	—	Reedstem "crucifix" type. Full sun
coriifolium	T,R	S	ST, C	Green	Autumn	—	Thick stems, medium shade
evectum	R, GB	S	TR, ST, C	Purple	Summer	—	Reedstem "crucifix" type. Full sun
falcatum	T,R	S	ST, C	White/green	Summer	F	Pendant leaves, large blooms
ibaguense	R, GB	S	TR, ST, C	Orange/red	All year	—	Reedstem "crucifix" type. Full sun
magnoliae	T	S	ST, C	Green	All year	—	Small grower, tolerates cold. Grow with resurrection fern
nocturnum	T,R	S	TR, ST	Green/white	Summer	F	Tall leafy stems, humid and shady
pseudepidendrum	T,R	S	TR, ST	Green/orange	Autumn	—	Spectacular. Grow warm and humid

radicans	R, GB	S	TR, ST, C	Orange	All year	—	Straggly reedstem. Full sun
stamfordianum	T, R	S	TR, ST	Yellow/pink	Winter	F	Tall bulbs, long panicle from base
Epipactis							
gigantea	R, GB	S	C, CT	Yellow/purple	Spring/summer	—	Grow in moist soil or bog garden
palustris	R, GB	S	C, CT	Purple/white	Summer	—	Moist soil with limestone
Eria							
albido-tomentosa	T, R	S	ST, C	Green	Autumn	F	Rambler for trees and walls
barbata	T, R	S	ST, C	Tan	Autumn	F	Tall branched scapes, ovoid bulbs
bractescens	T, R	S	ST	Cream	Summer	—	Cylindrical bulbs, erect scapes
coronaria	T, R	S	C	White/yellow	Winter	F	Slim stems, lovely large blooms
floribunda	T, R	S	TR, ST	Pink	Spring	—	Slim; masses of tiny flowers. Neat
hyacinthoides	T, R	S	ST	White/violet	Spring	F	Flowers like hyacinth stems
javanica	T, R	S	TR, ST	White	Summer	—	Robust rambler; lovely starlike blooms
rhynchostyloides	T, R	S	ST, C	White/red	Spring	F	Ovoid bulbs, short dense scapes
spicata	T, R	S	ST, C	White	Spring	F	Thick, oblong bulbs; short, densely flowered raceme. Lovely perfume
Gastrorchis							
francoisii	R, GB	S	ST, C	Pink/yellow	Spring	—	Gorgeous. Heavy shade, moist. Try in warm C or in a special bed in a shady courtyard
humblotii	R, GB	S	ST, C	Carmine	Spring	—	As for *G. francoisii*
schlecterii	R, GB	S	ST, C	White/red	Summer	—	As for *G. francoisii*
Gongora							
armeniaca	T	S	ST	Orange	Summer	F	Shade. Water and fertilize regularly. Protect leaves from wind. Hang at head height to enjoy fragrant blooms
atropurpurea	T	S	TR, ST	Red	Summer	F	As for *G. armeniaca*
bufonia	T	S	TR, ST	Rose/brown	Autumn	F	As for *G. armeniaca*
galeata	T	S	ST, C	Brown	Summer	F	As for *G. armeniaca*
maculata	T	S	TR, ST	Yellow/red	All year	F	As for *G. armeniaca*
quinquenervis	T	S	TR, ST	Yellow/red	Autumn	F	As for *G. armeniaca*
portentosa	T	S	ST	Tan	Spring	F	As for *G. armeniaca*
truncata	T	S	TR, ST	Cream/red	Summer	F	As for *G. armeniaca*

Plant name	Tree (T) Rockery (R) Bed (GB)	Monopodial (M) Sympodial (S)	Tropical (TR) Subtropical (ST) Cooler (C) Temperate (CT)	Main color	Flowering	Fragrant (F)	Comments
Grammatophyllum							
elegans	T,R	S	TR,ST	Chocolate	Spring	—	Large plant, arching scape. Warm ST only
measuresianum	T,R	S	TR,ST	Yellow/brown	Summer	F	Stout bulbs, very long racemes
scriptum	T,R	S	TR,ST	Yellow/brown	Summer	—	Robust, long scape, more than 50 blooms
speciosum	T,R,GB	S	TR	Yellow/red	Autumn	F	Massive plant, needs huge tree or its own rockery or garden bed
stapeliaeflorum	T,R	S	TR,ST	Brown/violet	Summer	—	Medium size; pendulous scapes
Himantoglossum							
hircinum	GB	Tubers	C,CT	Green/red	Spring/summer	F	Dry gravelly soil with limestone
longibracteatum	GB	Tubers	C,CT	Purple/brown	Spring	—	Dry gravelly soil, low humidity
Holcoglossum							
amesianum	T,R	M	C	White/pink	Summer	F	Semiterete lithophyte, lovely broad flowers
flavescens	T,R	M	C	White/yellow	Spring	F	Small, cool grower. Needs good light, moisture
kimballianum	T,R	M	C	White/amethyst	Autumn	F	Gorgeous showy cool species. Needs good light
subulifolium	T,R	M	C	White	Autumn	F	Pendant. For damp walls, mossy trees, good light
Laelia							
albida	T,R	S	C	Pink	Winter	F	Needs dry winter
anceps	T,R	S	ST,C	Rose/purple	Autumn	F	Grow on rocks, walls, and trees
autumnalis	T,R	S	ST,C	Pink/purple	Autumn	F	Long scapes, dry winter
blumenscheinii	R	S	ST,C	Yellow	Spring	—	Rock grower; tall erect racemes
cinnabarina	R	S	ST,C	Cinnabar	Spring	—	Robust rock grower; tall scapes
crispa	T,R	S	ST	White	Summer	F	Sturdy *Cattleya*-like plant and bloom
crispata	R	S	ST,C	Magenta	Spring	—	Clustered rock dweller; good light, dry winters
fidelensis	T,R	S	ST,C	Pink	Summer	—	Small grower; lovely large blooms
flava	R	S	ST,C	Gold	Spring	—	Stout, leathery rock grower
gouldiana	T,R	S	ST,C	Red/rose	Winter	F	Lovely blooms on erect scapes

grandis	T,R	S	TR, ST	Yellow	Summer	—	Another *Cattleya*-like species
harpophylla	T	S	ST,C	Orange	Spring	—	Slim, cool, shady, and damp
jongheana	T,R	S	ST,C	Rose	Spring	—	Huge blooms, cool, slightly drier in winter
lobata	R	S	ST	Rose/violet	Spring	F	*Cattleya*-like, grow on rocks and walls
lundii	T,R	S	ST,C	White/purple	Autumn	—	Small creeping type
milleri	R	S	ST,C	Red	Summer	—	Sturdy beautiful rock dweller
perrinii	T,R	S	ST,C	Pink/rose	Autumn	—	Flat-flowered *Cattleya*-like species
pumila	T,R	S	ST,C	Rose	Autumn	F	Large flowers, dwarf plant. Cool, humid, shady
purpurata	T,R	S	ST,C	Purple	Summer	F	Large and lovely *Cattleya*-like type
rubescens	T,R	S	ST,C	Pink	Winter	—	Dwarf, long scapes, cool in winter
sincorana	T,R	S	C	Rose/purple	Summer	—	Lovely large blooms, dwarf plant
speciosa	T,R	S	C	Lilac/rose	Spring	F	Tough oval bulbs, dry winter
tenebrosa	T,R	S	ST	Brown/purple	Spring	F	Large dark, *Cattleya*-like
xanthina	T,R	S	ST	Yellow	Summer	—	Smaller growing, *Cattleya*-like
Lanium							
avicula	T,R	S	TR, ST	Cream	Autumn	—	Tiny creeper; erect scapes, keep moist and shady. Warm ST only
Lemboglossum							
bictoniense	T,R	S	ST,C	Tan/pink	Spring	F	Strong plant, long erect scape
cervantesii	T,R	S	C	White/brown	Winter	F	Dwarf, keep moist, lovely blooms
cordatum	T,R	S	C	White/brown	Autumn	—	Medium size; long-tailed blooms
nebulosum	T,R	S	C	White/red	Spring	—	Clustered bulbs; keep moist
rossii	T,R	S	C	Pink/brown	Spring	—	Small, flat bulbs; keep moist
Lycaste							
aromatica	T,R	S	ST,C	Yellow	Spring	F	Deciduous. Protect from wind. Moist while growing, dry in winter. Warm C regions. 50% shade
consobrina	T,R	S	ST,C	Yellow	Spring	F	As for *L. aromatica*
cruenta	T,R	S	ST,C	Yellow	Spring	F	As for *L. aromatica*
deppei	T,R	S	ST,C	Green/red spots	Summer	F	As for *L. aromatica*

Plant name	Tree (T) Rockery (R) Bed (GB)	Monopodial (M) Sympodial (S)	Tropical (TR) Subtropical (ST) Cooler (C) Temperate (CT)	Main color	Flowering	Fragrant (F)	Comments
Lycaste , (continued)							
macrophylla	T,R	S	ST	Olive/red	Summer	F	Evergreen. Protect from wind. Moist year-round, 70% shade
skinneri	T,R	S	ST,C	Pink	Winter	F	As for *L. macrophylla*
Lyperanthus							
serratus	GB	Tubers	C,CT	Red/brown	Spring	—	Dry summer; water well in autumn
suaveolens	GB	Tubers	C,CT	Yellow/brown	Spring	F	Light shade, water well in autumn
Maxillaria							
cucullata	T,R	S	ST,C	Buff/red	Autumn	—	Clustered bulbs, many flowers
eburnea	T,R	S	C	Cream	Summer	F	Large blooms, keep shaded, damp
elatior	T,R	S	ST,C	Orange/red	Spring	—	Strong, base of walls or tree trunks
grandiflora	T,R	S	C	White	Summer	F	Flat bulbs, grow shady and moist
houtteana	T,R	S	ST,C	Brown/yellow	Spring	—	Scrambler, good on damp walls
luteoalba	T,R	S	ST,C	Yellow	Spring	F	Large flowers, likes shade
marginata	T,R	S	ST,C	Yellow/red	Summer	—	Creeper for trees and rockeries
meleagris	T,R	S	ST,C	Red/maroon	Summer	—	Clusters, makes good filler on tree
nigrescens	T,R	S	ST,C	Purple/brown	Summer	—	Likes humid, shady sites
notylioglossa	T,R	S	ST,C	Green/white	Spring	—	Small creeper; charming blooms, moist, shady
ochroleuca	T,R	S	ST,C	Cream	Summer	—	Keep cool, shady, and moist
picta	T,R	S	ST,C	Yellow/red	Spring	F	Clustered bulbs, good in rockeries
porphyrostele	T,R	S	ST,C	Yellow/purple	Spring	—	Many blooms, trees and rockeries
rufescens	T,R	S	ST,C	Yellow/brown	All year	F	Small plant, keep shaded and humid
sanderiana	T	S	C	White/red	Autumn	F	Cool, humid, and shady. Spectacular
seidelii	T,R	S	ST,C	Yellow	Spring	—	Tiny plant. Cool, shady and damp

tenuifolia	T, R	S	ST, C	Red/yellow	Autumn	F	Scrambler for trees and walls
variabilis	T, R	S	ST, C	Yellow/red	All year	—	Good as a filler on trees or walls
Miltonia							
Bluntii	T, R	S	ST, C	Cream/purple	Autumn	F	Regular watering when growing, drier in winter. Naturally turns yellow in summer. Try in warm C
candida	T, R	S	ST, C	Chestnut/white	Autumn	—	As for M. Bluntii
citrina	T, R	S	ST, C	Yellow/purple	Summer	—	As for M. Bluntii
clowesii	T, R	S	ST, C	Chestnut/white	Autumn	—	As for M. Bluntii
cuneata	T, R	S	ST, C	Brown/white	Spring	—	As for M. Bluntii
flavescens	T, R	S	ST, C	Cream/yellow	Autumn	F	As for M. Bluntii
regnellii	T, R	S	ST, C	White/rose	Autumn	—	As for M. Bluntii
spectabilis	T, R	S	ST, C	Cream/purple	Summer	—	As for M. Bluntii
Neobenthamia							
gracilis	R, GB	S	TR, ST	White	All year	F	Tall, slim stems, full sun, keep damp
Neofinetia							
falcata	T, R	M	ST, C	White	Summer	F	Small grower, makes clumps. Semishade and damp in trees. In bloom it looks like a rocket-burst. Beautiful
Oerstedella							
centradenia	T, R	S	TR, ST	Pink	Winter	—	Tufts, semishade, keep moist
schumanniana	T, R	S	ST	Blue/brown	Summer	F	Tall, warty stems. Semishade, moist. Lovely panicles of blooms
verrucosa	T, R, GB	S	ST	White	Winter	F	Very tall, semishade, keep moist
wallisii	T, R	S	ST	Yellow/red	Autumn	F	Fine species, semishade, keep damp
Oncidium							
ampliatum	T, R	S	TR, ST	Yellow	Spring	—	Flat bulbs. Huge panicles
baueri	T, R	S	TR, ST	Yellow/brown	Spring	—	Robust. Scapes to 10 ft (3 m) tall
carthagenense	T, R	S	TR, ST	White/rose	Summer	—	"Mule ear," best in trees
cebolleta	T, R	S	TR, ST	Yellow/red	Spring	—	"Rat tail" leaves, trees or walls
cheirophorum	T, R	S	ST, C	Yellow	Winter	F	Dwarf, lovely sprays, trees or walls
concolor	T, R	S	ST, C	Yellow	Spring	—	Small plant, beautiful clear color
crispum	T, R	S	ST, C	Chestnut/yellow	Spring	—	Clustered bulbs, trees or walls

Plant name	Tree (T) Rockery (R) Bed (GB)	Monopodial (M) Sympodial (S)	Tropical (TR) Subtropical (ST) Cooler (C) Temperate (CT)	Main color	Flowering	Fragrant (F)	Comments
Oncidium, (continued)							
ensatum	R	S	TR, ST	Olive/yellow	Autumn	—	Rockery or bed, scapes can rebloom
flexuosum	T,R	S	TR, ST, C	Yellow	Autumn	—	Scandent, good on trees and walls
forbesii	T,R	S	ST, C	Chestnut/gold	Autumn	—	Showy species for trees or walls
gardneri	T,R	S	ST, C	Gold/brown	Summer	—	Clustered bulbs. Keep humid
lanceanum	T,R	S	TR, ST	Chocolate/rose	Summer	F	Beautiful "mule ear," semishade
luridum	T,R	S	TR, ST	Yellow/brown	Summer	—	Robust "mule ear," trees and walls. Well drained
marshallianum	T,R	S	C	Yellow/brown	Spring	—	Lovely large flowers in panicles
ornithorhynchum	T,R	S	ST, C	Pink	Autumn	F	Clustered bulbs; clouds of flowers
panamense	T,R	S	TR, ST	Yellow/olive	Winter	—	Robust; very long panicles to 3 m
sarcodes	T,R	S	ST, C	Chestnut/yellow	Spring	—	Semishade, humid, drier winter
sphacelatum	T,R	S	ST	Yellow/brown	Spring	—	Robust, makes great specimens
splendidum	R	S	TR, ST	Yellow/brown	Spring	—	Stout. Xerophyte. Dry in winter. Try on walls
stipitatum	T,R	S	TR, ST	Yellow/brown	Summer	—	"Rat tail" for warm trees and walls
stramineum	T,R	S	TR, ST	White/red	Summer	—	Charming dwarf "mule ear"
tigrinum	T,R	S	ST, C	Yellow/brown	Winter	F	Erect panicle, beautiful large blooms
varicosum	T,R	S	ST, C	Yellow	Autumn	—	Spectacular panicles, walls and trees
Orchis							
aristata	GB	Tubers	C, CT	Magenta	Summer	—	Well-drained soil in sunny beds
coriophora	GB	Tubers	C, CT	Green/red	Summer	F	Well-drained soil in sunny beds
latifolia	GB	Tubers	C, CT	Pink	Spring/summer	—	Rich, well-drained soil in sunny bed
laxiflora	GB	Tubers	C, CT	Red/purple	Summer	—	Gravelly, well-drained soil
maculata	GB	Tubers	C, CT	Lilac/red	Spring	—	Rich, well-drained soil in sunny bed
mascula	GB	Tubers	C, CT	Purple	Spring	F	Any well-drained soil

Species				Flower	Season		Notes
morio	GB	Tubers	C, CT	Pink/purple	Spring	—	Dry, gravelly, alkaline soils
palustris	GB	Tubers	C, CT	Purple	Summer	—	Prefers damp soils
Ornithophora							
radicans	T	S	ST	White/red	Autumn	—	Small creeper, long rhizomes. Moist, bright light
Osmoglossum							
pulchellum	T, R	S	ST, C	White	Autumn	F	Compact plant, erect scape. Semishade, moist while growing
Papilionanthe							
hookeriana	R, GB	M	TR	Mauve/purple	All year	—	Terete leaf, full sun in beds
teres	R, GB	M	TR, ST	Rose/pink	Spring	F	Terete, full sun. Warm ST only
tricuspidata	R, GB	M	TR	Mauve/pink	All year	—	Terete, needs full tropical sun
vandara	T, R	M	ST, C	White	Spring	F	Semishade, grows well cool
Peristeria							
elata	R, GB	S	TR, ST	White	Summer	F	Large bulbs and leaves. Protect from wind. Warm ST regions only. Damp while growing, dry in winter
Phaius							
amboinensis	R, GB	S	TR, ST	White/yellow	Autumn	F	Stemlike bulbs, protect from wind
flavus	R, GB	S	ST, C	Yellow	Spring	F	Tall racemes, protect from wind
luteus	R, GB	S	ST	Yellow	Summer	—	Keep protected, shady, and damp
mishmensis	R, GB	S	ST	Pink	Autumn	—	Stemlike bulbs, shady, sheltered
pulchellus	R, GB	S	TR, ST	Cream/red	Spring	—	Grow shady, sheltered, and damp
tankervilliae	R, GB	S	TR, ST	Brown/purple	Spring	F	Robust plant. Protect from wind. Wet summer, drier winter
Platanthera							
bifolia	GB	Tubers	C, CT	White	Spring	—	Well-drained loamy soils. Moist year-round but not hot and wet
blephariglottis	GB	Tubers	C, CT	White	Summer	F	As for *P. bifolia*
ciliaris	GB	Tubers	C, CT	Orange	Summer/autumn	—	As for *P. bifolia*
dilatata	GB	Tubers	C, CT	White	Summer/autumn	F	As for *P. bifolia*
fimbriata	GB	Tubers	C, CT	Lilac/pink	Summer	F	As for *P. bifolia*
integra	GB	Tubers	C, CT	Yellow/orange	Autumn	F	As for *P. bifolia*
montana	GB	Tubers	C, CT	White/green	Spring/summer	F	As for *P. bifolia*
nivea	GB	Tubers	C, CT	White	Summer	F	As for *P. bifolia*

Plant name	Tree (T) Rockery (R) Bed (GB)	Monopodial (M) Sympodial (S)	Tropical (TR) Subtropical (ST) Cooler (C) Temperate (CT)	Main color	Flowering	Fragrant (F)	Comments
Pleione							
bulbocodioides	R, GB	S	C, CT	Rose/pink	Spring	—	Shady. Dry after leaves fall, water again when buds appear. Good near top of wall or rockery, in a special bed, or in a cool courtyard
formosana	R, GB	S	C, CT	Blush pink	Autumn	F	As for *P. bulbocodioides*
limprichtii	R, GB	S	C, CT	Rose/lilac	Autumn	F	As for *P. bulbocodioides*
speciosa	R, GB	S	C, CT	Purple/yellow	Autumn	F	As for *P. bulbocodioides*
Polystachya							
adansoniae	T, R	S	TR, ST	White/mauve	Spring	—	Small clusters, keep moist and warm
bella	T, R	S	ST	Golden	Summer	—	Very pretty species, moist on trees
ottonis	T, R	S	ST	White/yellow	Autumn	—	Small clusters for trees or walls
pubescens	T, R	S	ST, C	Yellow	Summer	F	Lovely, small, fragrant species
Psychopsis							
krameriana	T, R	S	TR, ST	Brown/orange	Autumn	—	A fabulous "butterfly" orchid. Warm, humid, semishade. Scape persists for years. Warm ST only
papilio	T, R	S	TR, ST	Red/brown	All year	—	As for *P. krameriana*
Pterostylis							
abrupta	GB	Tubers	C, CT	Green/white	Summer/autumn	—	Semishade in moist areas
baptistii	GB	Tubers	ST, C, CT	White/green/brown	Spring	—	Largest flowers. Shade, damp year-round
curta	GB	Tubers	C, CT	Green/brown	Winter/spring	—	Grow semishady and damp
nutans	GB.	Tubers	C, CT	Green	Winter	—	Semishade, forms colonies
pedunculata	GB	Tubers	C, CT	White/brown	Spring	—	Damp, shady beds
stricta	GB	Tubers	ST, C, CT	White/green	Winter	—	Grow in semishade
Renanthera							
coccinea	R, GB	M	TR, ST	Red/yellow	Spring	—	Tall grower, sunny beds, brilliant blooms
imschootiana	T, R	M	TR, ST	Scarlet	Summer	—	Grows to 3 ft. (1 m). Bright light, warm

matutina	T,R	M	TR,ST	Red/crimson	Autumn	—	Medium height, bright light. Plant at base of wall
monachica	T,R	M	TR,ST	Orange/red	Spring	—	Sturdy smaller plant, arching scape
philippinensis	T,R	M	TR,ST	Red	All year	—	Up to 3 ft. (1 m). Panicles of red blooms
pulchella	T,R	M	TR,ST	Yellow/red	Autumn	—	Small, sturdy grower
storiei	R, GB	M	TR,ST	Scarlet/red	Summer	—	Tall, robust plant for sunny beds
Rhyncholaelia							
digbyana	T,R	S	TR,ST	Cream/green	Summer	F	*Cattleya*-like, fabulous fringed lip
glauca	T,R	S	ST	Green/white	Spring	F	Smaller grower, drier winter
Rhynchostylis							
coelestis	T,R	M	TR,ST	White/blue	Summer	F	Forms clumps, erect stems. Warm ST only
gigantea	T,R	M	TR,ST	White/amethyst	Autumn	F	Short grower, arching sprays
retusa	T,R	M	TR,ST	Amethyst	Spring	F	Stout plant, pendulous raceme. Very showy
Rodriguezia							
decora	T	S	ST	White/brown	Winter	—	Scandent plant, semishade, water well
lanceolata	T	S	ST	Red	All year	—	Semishade on ascending branch. Keep damp
venusta	T	S	ST	White	Autumn	F	Creeping rhizome, small bulb, fan leaves. Moist, 70% shade
Sarcochilus							
falcatus	T	M	C	White	Spring	F	Attach to shady trees, keep moist all year
hartmannii	R	M	ST,C	White/red	Spring	—	Use rockery pockets, semishade
Schomburgkia							
crispa	T,R	S	TR,ST	Tan/pink	Summer	—	Robust plant, many large flowers. Warm ST only. Sun. Water and fertilize regularly when growing, slightly drier in winter
elata	T,R	S	TR,ST	Brown/magenta	Summer	—	As for *S. crispa*
exaltata	T,R	S	TR,ST	Magenta/white	Spring	—	As for *S. crispa*
fimbriata	T,R	S	TR,ST	Brown/purple	Spring	—	As for *S. crispa*
lyonsii	T,R	S	TR,ST	White/purple	Summer	—	As for *S. crispa*
moyobambae	T,R	S	TR,ST	Purple/rose	Summer	—	Smaller growing species

Plant name	Tree (T) Rockery (R) Bed (GB)	Monopodial (M) Sympodial (S)	Tropical (TR) Subtropical (ST) Cooler (C) Temperate (CT)	Main color	Flowering	Fragrant (F)	Comments
Schomburgkia, (continued)							
rosea	T,R	S	ST	Rose/pink	Spring	—	As for S. crispa
splendida	T,R	S	TR,ST	Dark purple	Summer	—	As for S. crispa
superbiens	T,R	S	ST,C	Rose/purple	Autumn	—	Very long stems, large flowers. Cool regions
thomsoniana	T,R	S	TR,ST	Yellow/maroon	Summer	—	A small grower
tibicinis	T,R	S	TR,ST	Pale purple	Spring	—	Hollow pseudobulbs
undulata	T,R	S	TR,ST	Brown/violet	Spring	—	As for S. crispa
Scuticaria							
hadwenii	T,R	S	ST	Yellow/white	Summer	F	Short slim stems, whiplike leaves, single 3-in. (7-cm) flowers
steelii	T,R	S	TR,ST	Yellow/red	Autumn	F	Even longer pendant leaves
Sobralia							
callosa	R,GB	S	TR,ST	Blue/purple	Summer	F	Charming miniature
decora	R,GB	S	ST,C	Pink/rose	Summer	F	Tall clustered stems, thick roots. Large blooms sequentially during the warm months. Perfect for large rockery pockets and sunny beds. Moist year-round, fertilize regularly, do not disturb roots. Will grow cool to at least south of Sydney and north to San Francisco
leucoxantha	R,GB	S	ST,C	White/yellow	Summer	F	As for S. decora
macrantha	R,GB	S	ST,C	Rose/purple	Summer	F	As for S. decora
violacea	R,GB	S	ST,C	Lilac/purple	Summer	F	As for S. decora
xantholeuca	R,GB	S	ST,C	Golden	Summer	F	As for S. decora
Sophronitis							
brevipedunculata	T,R	S	C	Red	Spring	—	Small bulb, huge flower. Cool, humid, bright light
cernua	T,R	S	ST,C	Cinnabar	Summer	—	Tiny plant, short scape, 5 to 6 bright blooms. Moist, 70% shade
coccinea	T,R	S	C	Red	Spring	—	Small bulb, huge flower. Cool, moist, semishade

				Color	Season		Notes
mantiqueirae	T,R	S	C	Red	Summer	—	Small plant for mossy trees and walls
rosea	T,R	S	C	Rose	Winter	—	Small plant. Cool, humid, moist, 70% shade
Spathoglottis							
affinis	R,GB	S	TR,ST	Yellow/purple	Summer	—	Protect from wind. Fertilize regularly while growing.
aurea	R,GB	S	TR,ST	Golden	Spring	—	As for *S. affinis*
chrysantha	R,GB	S	TR,ST	Yellow/red	Spring	—	As for *S. affinis*
elmeri	R,GB	S	ST	Yellow	Spring	—	As for *S. affinis*
fortunei	R,GB	S	ST	Gold/red	Winter	—	As for *S. affinis*
lobbii	R,GB	S	TR,ST	Yellow	Autumn	—	As for *S. affinis*
xparsonii	R,GB	S	TR,ST	Orange	All year	—	As for *S. affinis*
plicata	R,GB	S	TR,ST	Purple	All year	—	As for *S. affinis*
vanoverberghii	R,GB	S	TR,ST	Lemon	Spring	—	As for *S. affinis*
vieillardii	R,GB	S	TR,ST	Purple	Autumn	—	As for *S. affinis*
Stanhopea							
candida	T	S	TR	White	Summer	F	Showy flowers for semishady trees or high walls
connata	T	S	TR,ST	Yellow	Summer	F	Showy flowers for semishady trees or high walls
devoniensis	T,R	S	TR,ST,C	Yellow/purple	Summer	F	Showy flowers for semishady trees or high walls
ecornuta	T,R	S	TR,ST	Cream/yellow	Summer	F	Showy flowers for semishady trees or high walls
grandiflora	T,R	S	TR,ST	Cream/red	Autumn	F	Showy flowers for semishady trees or high walls
graveolens	T,R	S	TR,ST,C	Pale yellow	Summer	F	Showy flowers for semishady trees or high walls
hernandezii	T,R	S	TR,ST,C	Yellow/purple	Summer	F	Showy flowers for semishady trees or high walls
insignis	T,R	S	TR,ST,C	Cream/violet	Autumn	F	Showy flowers for semishady trees or high walls
nigroviolacea	T,R	S	TR,ST,C	Yellow/maroon	Summer	F	Try in C regions
oculata	T,R	S	TR,ST,C	Yellow/red	Summer	F	Try in C regions
reichenbachiana	T	S	TR	White	Summer	F	Showy flowers for semishady trees or high walls
saccata	T,R	S	ST,C	Cream/brown	Summer	F	Showy flowers for semishady trees or high walls
tigrina	T,R	S	TR,ST,C	Yellow/maroon	Summer	F	Showy flowers for semishady trees or high walls

Plant name	Tree (T) Rockery (R) Bed (GB)	Monopodial (M) Sympodial (S)	Tropical (TR) Subtropical (ST) Cooler (C) Temperate (CT)	Main color	Flowering	Fragrant (F)	Comments
Stanhopea, (continued)							
wardii	T,R	S	TR,ST,C	Yellow/purple	Autumn	F	Showy flowers for semishady trees or high walls
Stenoglottis							
fimbriata	R,GB	S	ST,C	Rose	Autumn	—	Deciduous. Dry in winter, 50% shade
longifolia	R,GB	S	ST,C	Rose	Autumn	—	Deciduous. Dry in winter, 50% shade
Thelymitra							
arenaria	GB	Tubers	C,CT	Blue	Spring	—	Full sun, dry summer, water well new fall growth
aristata	GB	Tubers	C,CT	Blue	Spring	—	Full sun, dry summer, water well new fall growth
crinita	GB	Tubers	C,CT	Blue	Spring	—	Full sun, dry summer, water well new fall growth
cyanea	GB	Tubers	C,CT	Blue	Spring/summer	—	Grow wet. Try it in the bog garden
ixiodes	GB	Tubers	C,CT	Blue	Spring	—	As for *T. arenaria*. Flowers open better in dry conditions than in humid weather
juncifolia	GB	Tubers	C,CT	Mauve	Spring	—	As for *T. ixiodes*
macmillanii	GB	Tubers	C,CT	Salmon/red	Spring	—	As for *T. ixiodes*
Thunia							
alba	T,R	S	TR,ST,C	White/purple	Summer	—	Showy blooms, dry in winter
bensoniae	T,R	S	TR,ST,C	Magenta/gold	Summer	F	Showy blooms, dry in winter
marshalliana	T,R	S	TR,ST,C	White/orange	Summer	F	Showy blooms, dry in winter
Trichopilia							
fragrans	T,R	S	ST	Cream/white	Winter	F	Shady and damp. Try in warm C regions
hennisiana	T,R	S	ST	White	Spring	F	Shady and damp. Try in warm C regions
laxa	T,R	S	ST	Olive/white	Autumn	F	Shady and damp. Try in warm C regions
marginata	T,R	S	ST	Olive/red	Spring	F	Shady and damp. Try in warm C regions
suavis	T,R	S	ST	White/pink	Spring	F	Shady and damp. Try in warm C regions

tortilis	T,R	S	ST	Lavender/white	Winter	F	Shady and damp. Try in warm C regions

Trudelia

alpina	T,R	M	ST,C	Lime/maroon	Spring	F	Short stem. Cool, moist, dry in winter in C regions
cristata	T,R	M	ST,C	Green/red	Spring	F	As for T. alpina
pumila	T,R	M	ST,C	White/purple	Summer	F	As for T. alpina

Vanda

bensonii	T,R	M	ST	Chestnut/pink	Autumn	F	Medium size; long racemes
brunnea	T	M	TR, ST	Brown	Spring	F	Larger grower, good on trees
coerulea	T,R	M	ST,C	Blue	Autumn	—	Grow cool and moist, dry winter
coerulescens	T,R	M	ST,C	Blue	Summer	F	Long sprays, keep cool and moist
dearei	T	M	TR	Cream	Summer	F	Robust, too big for rockeries
denisoniana	T,R	M	TR, ST	Yellow	Spring	F	Stout plant, short arching scapes
hindsii	T,R	M	TR	Brown/white	Summer	F	Tall, robust Australian species
insignis	T	M	TR	Brown/mauve	Autumn	F	Robust, too sprawling for rockeries and walls
javierae	T,R	M	ST, C	White	Autumn	—	New species, beautiful blooms
lilacina	T,R	M	ST	White/lilac	Spring	—	Small clumping plant
limbata	T,R	M	TR	Cinnamon/rose	Summer	F	Medium size; erect racemes
liouvillei	T	M	TR	Brown	Spring	F	Another robust grower
luzonica	T,R	M	TR, ST	White/magenta	Spring	F	Medium size; branches readily
roeblingiana	T,R	M	ST,C	Brown/yellow	Winter	—	Long racemes, cool grower
sanderiana	T	M	TR	Pink/yellow	Autumn	F	The biggest blooms. Needs warmth and humidity
tricolor	T,R	M	TR, ST	White/purple	Autumn	F	Good robust grower

Vandopsis

gigantea	T,R	M	TR, ST	Yellow/brown	Summer	F	Short stems, long thick leaves. 30% shade
lissochiloides	T,R	M	TR	Yellow/magenta	Summer	F	Robust, tall. Leathery leaves, long-lasting blooms

Zygopetalum

crinitum	R, GB	S	ST, C	Green/red	Autumn	F	Medium bulbs, broad leaves, erect scapes, good-sized blooms
intermedium	R, GB	S	ST,C	Green/violet	Autumn	F	More robust, keep damp
mackaii	R, GB	S	ST,C	Green/blue	Autumn	F	Robust, easy growing

Glossary

column the central organ of the orchid flower bearing its sexual parts. Most orchids bear perfect flowers combining both sexes in the same flower

inflorescence that part of a plant bearing its flowers

labellum the lip of the orchid flower, the modified third petal

monopodial having a stem with a single axis which grows from the apex

node the point on a stem at which a leaf is attached or from which flower shoots or growth shoots emanate

panicle a branched inflorescence

pathogen a specific disease-causing organism such as a bacterium, a fungus, or a virus

plicate folded and pleated lengthwise

pseudobulb the thick, often bulblike stem of a sympodial orchid

raceme an unbranched inflorescence

rhizome the stem connecting pseudobulbs, usually having nodes and roots and giving rise to shoots

scape the basal part of an inflorescence and the part bearing flowers

semiterete of a thickened leaf grooved lengthwise, intermediate between a terete leaf and a strap-shaped leaf, usually referring to *Vanda* hybrids

shoot a horticultural term for a new growth, which may or may not give rise to flowers

sympodial a type of growth with successive stems or pseudobulbs either joined by an obvious rhizome or with each new stem or pseudobulb arising from the base of the previous one

terete of a tapered leaf that is round in cross-section like a pencil

vandaceous like a *Vanda*; said of all monopodial orchids

xerophyte a plant able to grow in dry conditions

Bibliography

In addition to the books and papers listed below, I have consulted various periodicals which will provide all orchid growers with on-going valuable information. Among these are *American Orchid Society Bulletin* (now titled *Orchids*), *Australian Orchid Review*, *Awards Quarterly*, *Gardener's Chronicle*, *Orchids Australia*, *Orchid Digest*, and *Orchid Review*.

Arnold, Ralph E. 1932. "Some Old Epidendrums." *Orchid Review* (November) 40 (473): 330.

Arnold, Ralph E. 1949. "Some Hardy Calanthes." *Orchid Review* (March) 57 (669): 45.

Bechtel, Helmut, Phillip Cribb, and Edmund Launert. 1992. *The Manual of Cultivated Orchid Species.* 3rd ed. London: Blandford Press.

Burbidge, F. W. 1890. *Gardens of the Sun.* London: J. Murray.

Cox, J. M. 1946. *A Cultural Table of Orchidaceous Plants.* Sydney: Shepherd Press.

Cribb, A. B., and J. W. Cribb. 1975. *Wild Food in Australia.* Sydney: William Collins.

Ellis, W. 1858. *Three Visits to Madagascar.* London: J. Murray.

Fennell, T. A., Jr. 1959. *Orchids for Home and Garden.* New York: Rinehart.

Fowlie, J. A., M.D. 1970. *The Genus* Lycaste. California: Day Printing.

Fowlie, J. A., M.D. 1977. *The Brazilian Bifoliate Cattleyas and Their Color Varieties.* California: Day Printing.

Grant, B. 1895. *Orchids of Burma.* Dehera Dun: M/S Bishen Singh and Mahendera Pal Singh.

Hartweg, Karl Theodor. Unpublished letters to the Horticultural Society.

Hawkes, A. D. 1961. *Orchids: Their Botany and Culture.* London: Peter Owen.

Hawkes, A. D. 1965. *Encyclopaedia of Cultivated Orchids.* London: Faber.

Hooker, J. D. 1891. *Himalayan Journals.* 2nd ed. London: Ward, Lock, Bowden, and Company.

Millican, A. 1891. *Travels and Adventures of an Orchid Hunter.* London: Cassell and Company.

Micholitz, Wilhelm. Unpublished letters to H. F. C. Sander.

Mulder, D., T. Mulder-Roelfsema, and A. Schuiteman. 1990. *Orchids Travel by Air.* Wageningen: Het Houten Hert.

Neal, J. 1994. *Growing Phalaenopsis at Home.* Sydney: Earth Productions.

Northen, R. T. 1970. *Home Growing Orchids.* 3rd ed. New York: Van Nostrand Reinhold.

Perry, D. R. 1988. *Life Above the Jungle Floor.* New York: Simon and Schuster.

Pridgeon, Alec., ed. 1992. *What Orchid Is That?* Sydney: Weldon Publishing.

Rentoul, J. N. 1980. *Growing Orchids: Book One, Cymbidiums and Slippers*. Melbourne: Lothian Publishing.

Rentoul, J. N. 1982. *Growing Orchids: Book Two, The Cattleyas and Other Epiphytes*. Melbourne: Lothian Publishing.

Rentoul, J. N. 1982. *Growing Orchids: Book Three, Vandas, Dendrobiums and Others*. Melbourne: Lothian Publishing.

Rentoul, J. N. 1985. *Growing Orchids: Book Four, The Australasian Families*. Melbourne: Lothian Publishing.

Royal Horticultural Society. 1946–1998. *Sanders' List of Orchid Hybrids*. London: Royal Horticultural Society.

Sanders, St. Albans. 1927. *Sanders' Orchid Guide*. Antwerp: Kohler.

Sanders, St. Albans. 1946. *Sanders' Complete List of Orchid Hybrids*. Reprint. American Orchid Society.

Veitch, James. 1906. *Hortus Veitchii*. London.

Veitch, James and Sons. 1963. *A Manual of Orchidaceous Plants*. Chelsea, 1887–1894. Reprint. Amsterdam: A. Asher and Company.

Williams, B. S., and H. Williams. 1961. *The Orchid Grower's Manual*. 7th ed. Reprint. Weldon and Wesley and Hanford Publishing.

Wilson, Ernest Henry. 1977. *A Naturalist in Western China*. Theophrastus.

Subject Index

Plant Names Index

Italicized numbers indicate photo pages.

Acacia, 26
Acer, 144
Acineta, 155
Acoelorrhaphe wrightii, 25
Ada, 40
    aurantiaca, 40
Aechmea, 33,
    Little Mary, *65*
Aerides, 14, 16, 40, 54
    crassifolia, 41
    crispa, 41
    falcata, 41
    falcata var. *houlletiana*, 41
    fieldingii, see *A. rosea*
    Hermon Slade, *40*, 41
    lawrenceae, 41
    jarckiana, see *A. leeana*
    leeana, 41
    maculosa, 41
    multiflora, 41
    odorata, 41
    quinquevulnera, 41
    rosea, 41
    vandara, 41
Aeridovanda, 57
African tulip tree, see *Spathodea campanulata*
Alexander palm, see *Archontophoenix alexandrae*
Allocasuarina, 26
Anacheilum, 48, 74
    vespa, see *Encyclia vespa*

Ananas comosus, 89
Angraecum, 41, 68–69, 126
    Alabaster, 41, 69
    bicallosum, 41
    comorense, 41, 69
    compactum, 41
    didieri, 41
    eburneum, 41, 69, 126, *128*
    eburneum subsp. *xerophylum*, 69
    eichlerianum, 41
    elephantinum, 41
    humbertii, 69
    infundibulare, 41
    Lemforde White Beauty, 41, 69
    leonis, 41
    longicalcar, 69
    magdalenae, 69
    protensum, 69
    rutenbergianum, 69
    scottianum, 41
    sesquipidale, *40*, 41, 69
    sororium, *60*, 69
    Veitchii, 41, 69
    viguieri, 41
Anguloa, 143
Ansellia, 41
    africana, 41, 126
    gigantea, see *A. africana*
    nilotica, see *A. africana*
Anthurium, 33, 35
Arachnis, 14, 93, 126
    flos-aëris, 93